Green Wedge Urbanism

Green Wedge Urbanism

History, Theory and Contemporary Practice

FABIANO LEMES DE OLIVEIRA

BLOOMSBURY VISUAL ARTS

LONDON • NEW YORK • OXFORD • NEW DELHI • SYDNEY

BLOOMSBURY VISUAL ARTS
Bloomsbury Publishing Plc
50 Bedford Square, London, WC1B 3DP, UK
1385 Broadway, New York, NY 10018, USA

BLOOMSBURY, BLOOMSBURY VISUAL ARTS and the Diana logo are trademarks
of Bloomsbury Publishing Plc

First published in Great Britain 2017
Paperback edition published 2020

Cover design: Eleanor Rose
Cover image © Alice Marwick

A catalogue record for this book is available from the British Library.

A catalog record for this book is available from the Library of Congress.

ISBN: HB: 978-1-4742-2918-0
         PB: 978-1-3501-5434-6
         ePDF: 978-1-4742-2920-3
         eBook: 978-1-4742-2919-7

Typeset by Integra Software Services Pvt. Ltd.
Printed and bound in Great Britain

To find out more about our authors and books visit www.bloomsbury.com
and sign up for our newsletters.

To my parents Idê and Orlando, and grandmother Joana

Contents

List of Figures

List of Tables

Acknowledgements

The origin of this book can be traced to an intriguing research visit to a library. What I saw that day sparked a curiosity that has remained active ever since. As a researcher in planning history, I was of course familiar with the manifold manifestations of the green belt idea and their representations. I had not, however, come across the idea of green wedges until the day I saw Eberstadt's contrasting diagrams of concentric and radial growth, the former including a green belt, the latter green wedges. What surprised me the most was in fact the lack of references in planning history to this concept that, as I came to realize later, had a profound impact on planning theory. Hence, the journey started, and along this path many people have made important contributions.

Thanks first of all to my parents for their lifetime support and encouragement and to Krystyna Wieszczek for her kind support and thoughtful and meticulous comments on the manuscript during its last stages of preparation. The financial and moral support received from the Faculty of Creative and Cultural Industries and the Portsmouth School of Architecture at the University of Portsmouth have been instrumental in seeing this book come to fruition. In particular, I would like to thank Catherine Harper, Deborah Shaw and Pamela Cole.

My special thanks to Rikhard Manninen, Bette Lundh Malmros, Ulrika Egero, Tobias Grindsted, Sara Berg and Giovanni Sala for eagerly sharing their time and knowledge.

Lastly, the publisher and I gratefully acknowledge the permission granted to reproduce the copyright material in this book. Every effort has been made to trace copyright holders and to obtain their permission for the use of copyright material. The publisher apologizes for any errors or omissions and would be grateful if notified of any corrections that should be incorporated in future reprints or editions of this book.

Introduction

This book is the first major narrative of green wedges in urbanism to date. It constructs an untold history of the green wedge idea in international planning debates and evaluates its application in contemporary urbanism.

Grand narratives of Western planning history have consolidated the main branches of urban thought since the emergence of modern town planning as a discipline in the second half of the nineteenth century. The role of nature in this process of constitution has been made manifest as an essential planning tool with different functions relative to context and period. In attempts to distil key planning ideas of international relevance and their origins and development, historical scholarship has tended to concentrate on particular models of green space planning, while neglecting others. An example of this can be seen in the disproportionate attention dedicated to the green belt idea compared with alternative (or complementary) ones such as the green wedge. Green wedges have a deeper history in the twentieth century than many may expect. In uncovering their significance through time and space, this book not only aims to bring to light a fundamental side of planning debates, but also to contribute towards a more comprehensive and integrated history of urban and green space planning. The green wedge idea was at the forefront of the minds of planners debating urban growth and the provision of open spaces for modern cities and has perdured in contemporary planning.

It is unquestionable that the green belt – promoted by Ebenezer Howard in his book *To-Morrow: A Peaceful Path to Real Reform* from 1898[1] as a solution to control urban growth, secure farmland and provide a buffer zone between cities – became a prominent feature of modern western town planning. However, even in the UK the 'sacrosanct' status of green belts has been questioned, particularly due to the need for more housing, the difficulty in accessing green belt land, their often lack of attractiveness and the need for more intra-urban green space.[2] A Report on Planning Use from 2006[3] commissioned by the then Prime Minister to review the planning system in England recommended a change in the choice of planning model away from the green belt in order to allow cities to have a larger footprint and more green spaces within the urban boundary. Currently in England there is more land demarcated as green belt than urbanized. In 2014, while approximately a third of the land in England was protected and 13 per cent was designated as green belt, only 9 per cent was developed.[4] Large-scale green structures offer a frequently untapped potential for positive transformation.

Towns, cities and regions have to deal with pressure for land development, to plan for sustainability, to mitigate the potential impacts of climate change and to promote healthier and more connected communities. In this context, the importance of green spaces within urban areas has been receiving increasing attention. Despite the fact that green wedges have been planned and implemented worldwide, there is no comprehensive study evaluating their existing and potential contributions to our living environments.

This book attempts to, firstly, delineate a new transnational narrative locating the origins and development of the green wedge idea in history and, secondly, evaluate its potential to contribute to the promotion of sustainable and resilient cities and regions in balance with nature. This study converges history, theory and practice of what we are calling *Green Wedge Urbanism*, shedding light on the multiple dimensions of the green wedge idea in planning cities and regions with nature.

Green wedge: Definitions

Throughout the book, the green wedge is referred to as an idea, concept, models or a typology of green space. An 'idea' is seen here as a thought, a principle. As a concept, the book refers to green wedges in their abstract form usually associated with an assumption of implementation and the notion of a model. The idea of a 'model' in urban studies has multi-folded meanings. Weber, for instance, defined the very concept of 'city' in relation to the manifestations of socio-economic relationships in space and time, referring to city models and their sub-models. In planning terms, the concept of the model, according to Choay, derives from Thomas More's *Utopia* inasmuch as it embodies 'a critical approach to a present reality, and the modelling in space of a future' one, offering thus, 'on the level of the imaginary, a device for the *a priori* conception of built space'.[5] In other words, the model manifests itself as an 'abstract projection of built form'. The conceptualization of the 'ideal', as opposed to the faulty 'existing', makes exemplarity and reproducibility intrinsic aspirations of the model.[6] Rosenau, however, points to the fact that the model nature of certain spatial configurations may or may not have been apparent from their inception, as such may have developed over time.[7] In this book both – the emergence of a model from a localized project or a proposal with inherent aspirations of further applicability elsewhere – are considered useful definitions. In some cases, the elaboration of a model emerged from abstract representations of the idea, such as in Eberstadt's green wedge diagram; in others, specific plans – such as the *Greater London Plan 1944* or Copenhagen's *Finger Plan 1947* – would become so.

The green wedge idea became manifested as different models over time, but it generally refers to a particular articulation between open and built-up spaces in which green wedges opening out towards the countryside are interspersed between development areas.

From a landscape planning perspective, a green wedge can be presented as a typology of green space, just as an urban park or a square. This tends to happen when they are included as a non-structural element within a green space network, usually not acquiring specific hierarchical dominance. As a typology, a green wedge may also be presented as a single element not necessarily linked to a green space strategy or network.

Interdisciplinarity, locality, temporality and scale

Such a research topic presents the possibility of aligning a number of disciplines, including history, urbanism, landscape ecology and environmental planning, to mention a few. And although the book sets out to draw from, and relate to, a variety of disciplinary fields, it does so – as suggested by Lepetit[8] – from the author's core discipline around which other areas of study, in this framework, orbit. The field of urbanism is here, therefore, the springboard from which an interdisciplinary construction of the research object and the arguments of the book are articulated.

A journey through the history of the green wedge idea takes us across borders of all our continents – with the non-surprising exception of Antarctica. Examples have been drawn from the UK, the United States, Germany, Denmark, Sweden, Finland, Australia, the Netherlands, China, Japan and Brazil, among others. The dynamics of transnational exchange of ideas and their conditions of existence form a core preoccupation of the field of planning history. Ward's categorization of the forms of reception and appropriation of planning ideas by different cultures in the timeframe of the last two hundred years is precise in moving away from univocal and unidirectional flows of 'influence' to the study of complex and often reciprocal networks leading to hybrid assimilations and re-inventions of a core concept.[9] It is in this light that the dissemination, appropriation and development of the green wedge idea over time and space are here considered.

Comparison has been often employed in the task of bringing together the so far fragmented accounts and new knowledge in the development of a new historical narrative and in the analyses of contemporary case studies. As Raymond Drew stated, 'what looks like change may be continuity' and 'things seemingly unrelated may be connected', and comparison may thus help avoid inconsistencies.[10] Or, as Bloch had already suggested, comparison is a procedure that centres the focus on explaining the similarities and dissimilarities offered by series of analogue characteristics located in distinct social contexts.[11]

An associated question is the definition of scale. Green wedges came in all forms and sizes, from the transnational scale to the scale of the neighbourhood. In addition, these scales often overlap. This, in turn, has led to the need to understand multiple-scale relationships and the use of multiple focal lenses for the presentation of analyses at a variety of scales.

The structure

This book is structured in two parts. The first part constructs a history of green wedges in urbanism from their emergence in modern town planning debates until the immediate post-war period. It adopts a chronological-thematic structure comprising four chapters. The second part investigates contemporary applications of the model in urbanism following a case-study approach.

Part One starts with a background chapter delineating the historical context of designing cities and regions with nature from the seventeenth to the nineteenth century and the conditions that led to the emergence of the green wedge idea. The main argument is that the use of nature to structure urban settlements and its association with traffic infrastructure forged the definition of what the green wedge idea would become. In turn, the second chapter examines the emergence, diffusion and appropriation of the green wedge idea in different geographical and cultural contexts from the early twentieth century until the outbreak of the Second World War. It discusses how inductive analyses of the radial growth of industrial cities identified that leftover spaces between developments, often found in the form of wedges, could be positively planned into cities and regions. The chapter shows that the original green wedge model is initially defended in opposition to that of the green belt and that with the maturation of discussions on green space planning both models tended to be combined. The chapter also examines applications of the green wedge idea in the construction of the soviet city in the first two decades after the Russian Revolution in 1917. Chapter 3 argues that during the Second World War and the post-war reconstruction period, planning spacious and greener cities meant planning new healthier and prosperous futures. Green wedges were one of the main strategies used to promote such environments. The wedge form was particularly compelling as a metaphor for the opening of the city to a brighter future and the benefits of embracing nature. The chapter focuses on reconstruction plans for London and plans for selected British New Towns and other international cases. In the sequence, the book explores the roles of green wedges in regional planning and in the formation of polycentric city-regions. Chapter 4 examines the development of the polycentric corridor-wedge model through an analysis of the Copenhagen *1947 Finger Plan* and other proposals including those for Scandinavian capitals, the southeast of England, Melbourne, and cities in North and South America and Africa. The chapter also explores the roles of green wedges in the definition of the Green Heart in Randstad, in the Netherlands.

Part Two of the book analyses a number of key contemporary plans in which the green wedge idea is central. Key points of analysis include the role of green wedges as part of a cohesive network of green spaces, their uses for the provision of intra-urban recreational green space, their ecological functions and their roles in mitigating the effects of climate change and in promoting sustainable cities. This part starts with Chapter 5, which introduces the major movements and theories associated with green space planning, including sections on green infrastructures, landscape ecology and landscape urbanism. Chapter 6 explores the evolving roles that green wedges play in city-region visions for sustainable and resilient futures and the benefits and challenges involved in or derived from their implementation. It focuses on the leading international cases of Stockholm, Copenhagen, Helsinki, the Randstad, Melbourne and Freiburg. Chapter 7 focuses on green wedges from the perspective of the city, district and local scales. The case studies here are Hamburg, Milan, Songzhuang Arts and Agriculture City in China, Viikki in Helsinki, Rieselfeld and Vauban in Freiburg, Dunsfold Park in England and La Sagrera Linear Park in Barcelona.

Based on the main themes and the knowledge that has emerged in the book, the final section identifies the development of green wedge models in urbanism from its initial application for a monocentric city to contemporary networked polycentric cities and regions, and offers a theory of green wedge urbanism. The latter comprises of ten fundamental principles aimed to contribute to the planning, designing and governance of green wedges in cities and regions.

The book demonstrates that the green wedge idea has been a fundamental approach in urbanism since its inception at the beginning of the twentieth century, shows how it has developed into various models to date and indicates its potential to contribute to promoting the integration of cities and regions with nature.

Methods and sources

This book draws from a combination of primary and secondary sources. While Part One relies on archival material and existing literature in order to construct the first major narrative of green wedges in planning history to date, Part Two draws from a number of interviews, site visits and other primary and secondary sources for the analysis of the selected case studies.

Archives and libraries consulted include The National Archives in London (TNA), the London Metropolitan Archives (LMA), the RIBA British Architectural Library, the RIBA Archives at the V&A Museum and out-store, and the British National Library. As much as possible original publications and plans were used in this study. In Part Two, the selection of case studies involved the identification of plans of regional, city and local scales that presented a commitment with sustainable development and that had applied the green wedge idea. Semi-structured interviews were carried out with key government staff involved with the planning and implementation of green wedges, such as Rikhard Manninen, Head of Strategic Planning Division at City of Helsinki City Planning Department; Bette Lundh Malmros, Regional Planner and Landscape Architect, Regional Planning Division of Stockholm County Council; Ulrika Egero, City Planning Administration, Strategy and Development Department of the City of Stockholm; Tobias Grindsted, Environmental Geographer from The Danish Nature Agency, Ministry of Environment and Food of Denmark; Sara Berg, Landscape Architect from Danish Business Authority, Danish Ministry of Business and Growth; and practitioners such as Giovanni Sala from LAND Landscape Architecture Nature Development, Milan. Alongside these, research trips were undertaken to London, Harlow, Stockholm, Copenhagen, Helsinki, Milan and Hamburg.

Attempting to follow Giedion's recommendation that 'the historian must be intimately a part of his own period to know what questions concerning the past are significant to it',[12] this book's starting point is the question of how the green wedge idea could offer models for the integration of urban development and nature, capable of helping address contemporary societal challenges, such as the improvement of the quality of life of urban residents and the promotion of healthier, more sustainable and resilient places. This could not, however, be tackled without an understanding of the wealth of experience related to the origins, development and applications of the idea in history.

PART ONE

Green Wedges in History

This part presents the contextual and historical background to planning with nature, as well as the emergence and development of the green wedge idea up to the immediate post-war period. The treatment of the first four chapters embodies a chronological-thematic emphasis in a transnational perspective.

1

Urban Planning with Nature

Ever since settlements started to emerge, human relationship with nature has been marked by ambivalence. If, on the one hand, nature is a provider, it is no less a source of threat and destruction, on the other. As a consequence, the need to be close to and yet protected from nature is at the core of our tie with it. Fences, ditches or high grounds all allowed a degree of separation, which enabled human beings to escape the grasp of wild animals and floods. The very birth of architecture is considered to be linked to this dual relationship. Laugier showed that the primitive hut already contained the main elements of architecture. Later on Semper identified those as the enclosing wall, the hearth, the roof and the mound, all of which relate to the need to mediate our relationship with nature, both by separating and by taming it – as the hearth does to the fire.[1] Similarly, as settlements grew, indigenous tribes tended to adopt a circular pattern with huts disposed along the edge and a central open space. Although immersed in nature, this form of settlement provided sufficient protection.

In medieval Europe, the city walls reinforced the sharp contrast between the city and nature, being it productive countryside or wilderness. This dichotomist differentiation would become ever since ingrained in European mentality. The deterministic relationship between formal order and a virtuous society becomes a postulate in the Renaissance. The rediscovery of the works by Pythagoras, Plato and Vitruvius brings about the use of geometry as an instrument both to decipher the rules of creation and, ultimately, to plan ideal cities. This would be seen in Filarete's Sforzinda, one of the first ideal cities of the period. It was conceived as a circular city, with a pattern of two juxtaposed quadrangles and sixteen radial streets, placed on a green landscape. According to Rosenau, this was the first attempt to combine town and country planning.[2]

In *Utopia*, from 1516, More described an ideal society that defined 'virtue' as 'living in accord with nature'. By not having property rights, Utopians were able to evade the inequalities that Rousseau would see developing from it and, in that way, remain closer to the uncorrupted morals of man in the state of nature. The pursuit of the creation of settlements in harmony with nature would be the key message of *Utopia* to urbanism. As a model applicable to urbanism, *Utopia* was appropriated in manifold formats, with and without the existence of property rights.

The study of Renaissance ideal cities and their resonance in posterior city planning is well covered by the literature and it is not intended here to extend the analysis of the main concepts relating to the relationship between city and nature beyond the necessary. What needs to be noted at this point is the fact that, it can be argued, planning with nature would be pursued both by the identification of the underlying rules and ideal forms that could in turn be used to surpass nature and by responding accordingly to the conditions of the territory, whether imagined or concrete.

The Enlightenment and the pursuit of nature

As Habermas maintained, the Enlightenment held the expectation that 'the arts and sciences would further not only the control of the forces of nature, but also the understanding of self and world, moral progress, justice in social institutions, and even human happiness'.[3] The world of universal harmony and commonwealth that the Age of Reason idealized – encapsulated by the French Revolution's motto of *Liberté, égalité, fraternité* (freedom, equality and brotherhood) – was to be brought about by reason and a deep connection with nature. In this process, the overcoming of the contrasts between science and belief, reason and sentiment, man and nature, city and country would be a necessary step.

Attempts to overcome these dichotomies emerged in eighteenth-century architectural theory and city plans. Laugier held that 'we should look upon a city as a forest'.[4] Yet, this was not a call for a superficial approximation to wilderness, or primitiveness, for he maintained that nature must be seen through the lens of the rational mind. That Laugier referred to André Le Nôtre's geometrical gardens as models for city planning, and not to nature 'as it was', is symptomatic of this. Geometry, harmony, order and balance between symmetry and variety would, according to Laugier, be what would make for fine city planning.[5]

The plan for the city of Karlsruhe (Figure 1.1), founded in 1715, represents this search for balancing man and nature through the application of geometry. Karlsruhe's particular shape and penetrating green spaces would leave a great impression on nineteenth-century planners.[6] Claude-Nicolas Ledoux's *Salines de Chaux* (Royal Saltworks) (Figure 1.2), from 1773 to 1779, presented a similar

FIGURE 1.1 *Perspective view of Karlsruhe, 1721.*

FIGURE 1.2 *Perspective view of les* Salines de Chaux, *Ledoux, 1773–9.* Source: *Ledoux, 1804.*

approach.[7] Rooted in the belief of a harmonic relationship between reason and nature, the village's layout is marked by two concentric circles from which radiating streets extend into the countryside. Conversely, nature is brought into the village in a controlled and ordered manner.

According to Comte's Law of Three Stages, the French Revolution would have opened up a pathway of no return in which the pursuit of its tenets (*Liberté, égalité, fraternité*), alongside science and progress, would finally lead us to liberation and happiness. Civilization would then have moved from Theological, through Metaphysical to the Positive phase. This theory would become influential in planning thought from the second half of the nineteenth century, with varying intensities in the twentieth century, as planning would attempt to link the built environment with social evolution.

The Industrial Revolution and the disintegration of open spaces

The infiltration of job-providing factories in existing cities and the emergence of mining and factory towns, coupled with the growing mechanization of agriculture, led to extensive migrations from the countryside to towns, which were often unprepared for such a mass inflow. This was furthermore accompanied by an intense population growth. As a result, this process distorted the inner urban structures constructed historically. The compressed space of the densely built medieval fabric with its limited housing stock, the irregular and narrow streets, the primitive sewage system and water distribution mechanisms suddenly had to cater for populations often tenfold larger.

Nowhere was this more evident than in England, Germany and the United States. Between 1801 and 1851, the population of England more than doubled, from 8.3 million to 16.8 million, and by 1901 nearly doubled again to 30.5 million.[8] London's population grew from approximately 1 million in 1801 to nearly 2.4 million in 1851, and to over 6.5 million by the turn of the twentieth century. If at the beginning of the nineteenth century the majority of the German people lived in the country, by the first decade of the twentieth century 60 per cent were already living in towns or cities. The number of cities in Germany grew from eight in 1871 to forty-eight within the next forty years, with a population growth from forty to 65 million people.[9] Berlin had a population of 420,000 in 1850 and by the eve of the First World War it had grown to over 2 million. Similarly, Hamburg goes from less than 300,000 to more than a million.[10] In the same period, the population of the United States grows from 23 million inhabitants to more than 92 million people. New York City grows from nearly 700,000 to approximately 5 million inhabitants.[11]

Overcrowding, mix of incompatible land uses, poor housing, urban sprawl, pollution, unsanitary conditions, lack of green spaces and congestion were common aspects of industrial cities.[12] The effects of such inadequate towns on the public health became apparent already in the first half of the nineteenth century. Epidemics, particularly of cholera, typhoid and tuberculosis, generated an unprecedented death rate. With the starkly low life expectancy in large industrial cities, for instance twenty-six years in Liverpool in 1841 and twenty-four years in Manchester in 1843 compared to around fifty years in small market towns,[13] the social cost of living in cities was put to check. Miasma, the noxious vapours believed to emerge from an infected environment, was thought to be the agent of disease. Thus, contaminated water and stagnant foul air were deemed extremely pernicious to inner-city dwellers' health. It was also clear that in overcrowded and compressed spaces diseases could spread much more quickly. Reactions against the insalubrious urban conditions soon started to surface in manifold formats. The severe impact that miasmatic towns had on the physical, mental and moral conditions of urban dwellers led to the emergence of the Public Health Movement and calls for the creation of public parks.

Public health and social reform went hand to hand. While outdoor recreation with access to fresh air and sunlight was seen as a way to keep workers healthy and away from vices, the contact between the classes in parks was seen as a 'civilizatory' measure. The following passage from *The Report of the Select Committee on Public Walks*, from 1833, clearly encapsulates the perceived link between physical health, psychological well-being and morality:

> It cannot be necessary to point out how requisite some Public Walks and Open Space in the neighbourhood of large towns must be; to those who consider the occupations of the Working Classes who dwell there; confined as they are during the weekdays as mechanics and manufacturers, and often shut up in heated factories: it must be evident that it is of the first importance to their health on their day of rest to enjoy the fresh air (exempt from the dust and dirt of the public thoroughfares) to walk out in decent comfort with their families (...) A man walking out with his family among his neighbours of different ranks, will naturally be desirous to be properly clothed, and that his Wife and Children should be also; but this desire duly directed and controlled, is found by experience to be of the most powerful effect in promoting civilisation, and exciting Industry.[14]

This is only one of the numerous accounts about the effects of the built environment on city dwellers. In *A Morning Walk from London to Kew*, from 1817, Sir Richard Phillips wrote that the smoke of nearly 'half a million of chimneys, each vomiting a bushel of smoke per second' was found to 'destroy all vegetation' in London.[15] In *Social Problems*, from 1884, Henry George went a step further to categorically argue that 'this life of great cities is not the natural life of man. He must under such conditions deteriorate, physically, mentally, morally'.[16] In Germany, criticism of what industrialization had done to towns and cities was also strongly voiced.[17]

The processes of urban densification and sprawl increased the demand for both green spaces in the inner city and access to the countryside. As Panzini showed, while until the eighteenth century the proximity to inner urban greenery was a privilege of the noble classes,[18] by the end of the century the bourgeoisie would start making similar demands. Between 1775 to 1850, James Burton and Thomas Cubitt's Squares in Bloomsbury, London, became a new typology of green space that would directly address their demands for easy access to controlled and well-designed urban green spaces.[19] Pressure for the democratization of the access to green spaces became a priority for social reformers and public health groups. In this respect, it is worth mentioning the work of Octavia Hill, a social reformer who campaigned in favour of access to open spaces for all citizens, who proposed the preservation of existing suburban land – such as Hampstead Heath, Parliament Hill, Wimbledon and Epping – for the creation of radial green spaces in London. The first public parks destined for the masses started to appear in the 1840s: Victoria Park in East London was designed in 1844, followed by Battersea Park from 1845 and Albert Park from 1851. Manchester saw the creation of Philips Park and Queen's park in 1846, and Birmingham opened Adderley Park in 1857 and Calthorpe Park a year later. Cherry highlights the case of Liverpool and the creation of a ring of parks towards the periphery of the built-up area 'as wedges into the city itself'.[20] In Germany, Peter Lenné designed the Volksgarten in Magdeburg and the Friedrichshain in Berlin between the 1820s and the 1840s. He also redesigned the Tiergarten to transform it into Berlin's first urban park.[21]

One of the first significant proposals that aimed at defining a network of green spaces for the whole of London, as opposed to localized patches of greenery, came from the landscape architect John Claudius Loudon. His 1829 plan attempted not only to control London's sprawl but also to re-establish its lost balance with nature.[22] Loudon provided a framework for the growth of London that would keep this balance unaltered irrespective of how much the city expanded. The plan comprised concentric rings of built-up areas separated by green belts and cut through by a green wedge, which would connect all built and open spaces (Figure 1.3). This is the first time that a green wedge can be found in a large plan for the capital. Loudon's open spaces were to be zones of country and 'breathing places', not more than half a mile's (800 metres) walk away from any inhabitant.[23]

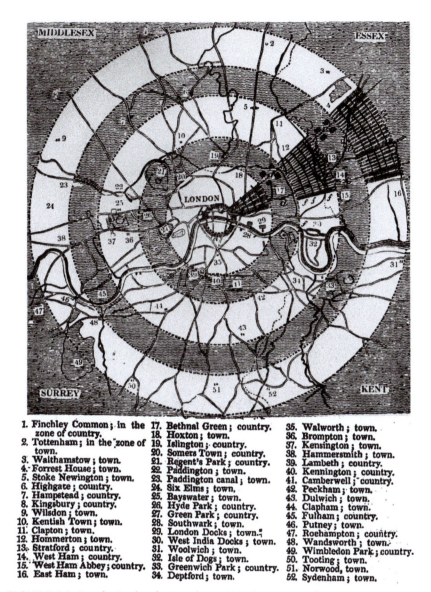

FIGURE 1.3 *Loudon's plan for London, 1829.* Source: *Loudon, 1829, 687.*

1. Finchley Common; in the zone of country.
2. Tottenham; in the zone of country.
3. Walthamstow; town.
4. Forrest House; town.
5. Stoke Newington, town.
6. Highgate; country.
7. Hampstead; country.
8. Kingsbury; country.
9. Wilsdon; town.
10. Kentish Town; town.
11. Clapton; town.
12. Hommerton; town.
13. Stratford; country.
14. West Ham; country.
15. West Ham Abbey; country.
16. East Ham; town.
17. Bethnal Green; country.
18. Hoxton; town.
19. Islington; country.
20. Somers Town; country.
21. Regent's Park; country.
22. Paddington; town.
23. Paddington canal; town.
24. Six Elms; town.
25. Bayswater; town.
26. Hyde Park; country.
27. Green Park; country.
28. Southwark; town.
29. London Docks; town.
30. West India Docks; town.
31. Woolwich; town.
32. Isle of Dogs; town.
33. Greenwich Park; country.
34. Deptford; town.
35. Walworth; town.
36. Brompton; town.
37. Kensington; town.
38. Hammersmith; town.
39. Lambeth; country.
40. Kennington; country.
41. Camberwell; country.
42. Peckham; town.
43. Dulwich; town.
44. Clapham; town.
45. Fulham; country.
46. Putney; town.
47. Roehampton; country.
48. Wandsworth; town.
49. Wimbledon Park; country.
50. Tooting; town.
51. Norwood, town.
52. Sydenham; town.

The understanding that cholera could be spread through contaminated water, which came with John Snow's study of the 1854 Broad Street outbreak in London, was a significant step towards questioning the miasma theory and realizing the importance of adequate urban sanitation. The Germ Theory would be further supported by Pasteur's experiments and Koch's discovery of the

TB bacillus. Given that pathogens were the agents of disease and that water and air were mediums for their spread, water quality control, segregated public sewage systems and the elimination of contaminated air dominated public health discussions. Furthermore, in 1877 Downes and Blunt found out that sunlight could kill bacteria. Consequently, public health officials and early modern town planners considered the provision of clean water, fresh air and exposure to sunlight of the utmost importance in interventions to modernize towns and cities.[24]

Not all proposals for urban reform concerned existing urban settlements. Believing that the Industrial Revolution was not conducing humanity to harmony and social betterment, which had been attested to by the poor life conditions in the nineteenth-century cities, the utopian socialists tried to reconnect the course of mankind in its continuous evolution with the aspirations of the Enlightenment. Drawing upon the humanist legacy of the seventeenth century, they presented significant attempts to reform society through the proposition of new communities. Social harmony was to be achieved by new modes of dwelling and social structures, as well as through contact with nature.

Robert Owen, an industrialist and social reformer, was a prominent character in the dissemination of these ideas. He introduced a series of improvements aiming to increase the quality of life of the workers at his cotton mills in New Lanark, Scotland, such as higher salaries, fewer working hours and decent housing conditions. He also attempted societal reform through education. His *Institute for the Formation of Character* from 1816 focused on the formation of the individual and on instilling a new social contract. In order to extend social reform to all, Owen intended that Villages of Unity and Mutual Cooperation be created. In line with More's *Utopia*, these villages were to enjoy communal ownership of land. They were to be dispersed in the landscape, allowing for small communities of approximately 2,000 inhabitants to live, work and recreate in direct connection with the countryside. In 1826, he was able to implement this idea in New Harmony, a village he and his supporters founded in Indiana, USA.

Similar ideas were defended in France by Charles Fourier, who proposed the reorganization of society into *Phalanstères* (Phalanges) – buildings containing each communities of 1,600 people, and by Jean-Baptiste-André Godin, who started the *Familistère* (Social Palace) of Guise in the middle of the nineteenth century. In all these cases, the new communities would be placed in the countryside, at a distance from 'civilization'. However, despite their intentions, little was materialized. Furthermore, as these models were addressed only to new centres, leaving the existing urban spaces to their own fate, their potential for large-scale transformation of society was compromised from the outset.

The rise of town planning

The impact of the Industrial Revolution upon the built environment led to the emergence of modern town planning as a reactive discipline.[25] Different national planning movements emerged to address the situation of towns and cities, such as the French *Urbanisme*, the German *Städtebau*, the British Town Planning and the American City Beautiful.

One of the first examples of large-scale urban transformations aimed at modernizing the city can be found in Georges-Eugène Haussmann's programme of public works in Paris between 1854 and 1873, launched during his time as *Préfet de la Seine*. The interventions involved opening up the medieval city through the construction of boulevards, parks and squares, the modernization of infrastructure and the construction of housing, monuments and public buildings. The plan sought to both modernize the city and transform its image into one of enlightened modernity. Almost immediately, this became an example followed by other cities across the world.

Many authors have already pointed to Germany's leading role in city planning since the unification of the country in 1871, which facilitated the growth of industrialization, the state control of land and the emergence of a great number of extension plans.[26] It is worth mentioning that their polytechnic tradition – with the first schools in Karlsruhe in 1825, Munich in 1827, Dresden in 1828 and Stuttgart in 1829 – would heavily mark the beginnings of modern planning in Germany, as can be seen in the first treatises, such as Baumeister's handbook from 1870. Zoning became a German planning priority. The Cartesian analytical method of breaking a complex object into its essential parts in order to gain a better understating of it is recuperated in the late nineteenth century. The industrial city, with its overlapping and often intertwined incompatible uses, presented a high level of complexity calling for the need to first understand the roots of its problems and then to plan accordingly. The translation of the analytical method into planning began with the survey of the different land uses and functions the city had to accommodate. This method helped not only to construct representations of the reality in its isolated facets – for instance grasping the conditions of existing green space, circulation, housing and factory areas in a city – but also to investigate how best to organize these categories in new plans. Thus, the concept of zoning developed as a way to organize the distribution of land uses, preventing perceived incompatible uses from being located near one another.[27] Baumeister, for one, promoted the use of zoning in the 1870s, which was later applied in Frankfurt in 1891, and as part of the briefs for the planning competitions for Munich, Berlin and Düsseldorf.[28]

At the same time, Camillo Sitte called for aesthetic considerations in civic design. His book *Der Städtebau nach seinen Künstlerischen Grundsätzen* (City Planning According to Artistic Principles), from 1889, was soon to become one of the most influential publications in planning theory. Theodor Fritsch's book *Die Stadt der Zukunft* (City of the Future), published a few years later, is worth noting on two levels. Firstly, in its second edition the author claimed to be the inventor of the garden city idea, as opposed to Ebenezer Howard; and, secondly, since it was greatly influenced by radio-concentric plans of the eighteenth century, such as Karlsruhe, it could be seen as one of the precedents of the green wedge idea. Drawing on the anti-urban German tradition of the nineteenth century, the book proposed new settlements in close contact with nature.[29] These would be zoned to avoid conflicting uses, each area displaying buildings of a similar character. As regards the overall arrangement, the diagrams presented in the book show an attempt to define a round settlement, similar to those presented later by Howard. However, contrary to the English Garden City model, Fritsch suggested that half of the area be given to nature, while the other half be urbanized, in a similar manner to Karlsruhe. The city could, nevertheless, develop to a full circle if needed.[30] He also proposed concentric rings, including green belts, which would be cut through by radial streets – some leading out into the countryside. Although the model is clearly based on baroque planning and presented a view of the future anchored on an imagined past, it positions itself as a way forward in facing the urban questions of the late nineteenth century, including an attempt to revisit ways of bringing development and nature together.

In Britain, the process of consolidation of this new disciplinary field can be dated to the period between the last quarter of the nineteenth century and the first two decades of the twentieth century and is often discussed by the literature in relation to the development of Ebenezer Howard's garden city idea, Unwin's approach to designing garden suburbs and the London problem.[31]

Ring vs radial growth

In European cities bound by city walls outwards growth tended to occur by the creation of concentric rings. By contrast, with the obsolescence of these fortifications or in cities not originally enclosed by them, a tentacular form of growth could be observed from the middle of the nineteenth century onwards. This was fuelled by the implementation of public transport systems, especially trains, electric trams and later motorbuses and manifested itself in sprawl stretching into the countryside along the main traffic routes and pockets of development around stations – with gaps between the 'tentacles'.[32]

Still in the 1900s, the questions of whether a town should grow indefinitely or not and how best to connect it to expansion areas were central to planning debates. Two planning models prevailed: the ring and the radial models. The first was based on the former European experience of historical growth generally involving circular development areas and a peripheral ring road, from which radial arteries would be laid out towards the expansion areas. Conversely, the radial model aimed at directing development along the axes of the main lines of traffic.

Vienna saw the emergence of a ring of development outside its walls and reinforced the model with the construction of the *Ringstrasse*. Howard's concentric model for new garden cities popularized the creation of green belts as ways of containing the expansion of towns. In Germany, the last quarter of the nineteenth century produced numerous plans that transformed former town walls into green boulevards. Following this model, by the end of the First World War many German cities built rings of deep, high-density, insalubrious tenement housing around the medieval core, while wealthy residents sprawled in suburban houses.[33]

In the light of the usual forms of growth observed in modern cities, concentric development soon proved questionable and was deemed, by planners such as Josef Stübben and Eugène Hénard, inappropriate for addressing their 'octopus-like' nature.[34] Radial planning, meanwhile, was earning increasing acclaim. The appeal of radial planning was fundamentally linked to the will to expedite circulation. Baumeister, for instance, had stated that this was one of the main tasks of city extension plans. As Ladd showed, traffic systems were also major contributors to the growth of municipal enterprise.[35] German municipalities noticed that already by the end of the nineteenth century controlling the traffic system would allow them to direct and encourage the city's growth and that its development could therefore be a profitable investment. The electrification of tramlines coincided, in a large degree, with the growing municipal control of the public transport system.[36] As Hegemann stated, the ubiquitous tram structured the city experience.[37]

This led to the mounting importance of planned traffic systems in the overall definition of extension plans in the early twentieth century. Hénard published in 1902 his thoroughly influential *Plans Comparatifs des Voies Principales de Circulation dans les Grandes Capitales* and *Plans Comparatifs des Parcs et Jardins dans les Grandes Capitales* (Comparative Plans of Traffic Arteries in Capital Cities and Comparative Plans of Parks and Gardens in Capital Cities) featuring the traffic systems and dispositions of green spaces in Moscow, Paris, London and Berlin. What is particularly significant about Hénard's work is the fact that he is one of the first to argue for the need to link radial and concentric models as well as traffic and park systems. These ideas were presented at the International Congress of Architects in London in 1906 and would have a significant impact on the debates at the 1910 Royal Institute of British Architects (RIBA) Town Planning Conference. In Britain, they would be prominent in both the plans for London and the promotion of garden cities.[38] In Berlin, Kühn would argue that the city's modern planning history was characterized by the constant competition between these two models of urban growth: the concentric ring and the radial model.[39]

While some social actors, such as rural preservationists,[40] saw the tentacular form of growth into the open country as a threat, others stood by the importance of electric trams as elements of connection with the outer urban areas and the countryside. Stübben, for instance, would argue that:

> The light railways are (…) means for the decentralization of industry, for stemming the flow of migrants from the countryside into the cities, and to some extent also for improving morality – the latter mainly because they make it unnecessary for the rural workers to lodge in the city and to come into contact with the worst manifestations of dissolute urban morality.[41]

Some years later, Patrick Geddes would consider the needs of those living not in the suburbs but in the inner city. He called for a reciprocal extension of the countryside into towns, arguing that despite progress in mass transport 'the children, the women, the workers of the town can come but rarely to the country. As hygienists, and utilitarians, we must therefore bring the country to them' (Figure 1.4). He envisioned that 'once in true development, [towns would] repeat the star-like opening of the flower with green leaves set in alternation with its golden rays'.[42]

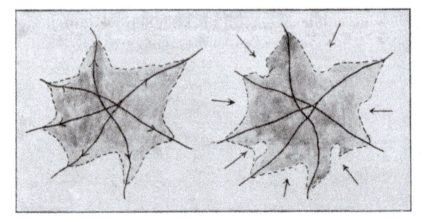

FIGURE 1.4 *Town → Country: Country → Town diagram.* Source: *Geddes, 1915, 96.*

Regardless of whether plans concentrated on existing cities or new ones, the definition of an environment with strong presence of greenery became axiomatic already in the first stages of the development of planning as a disciplinary field. With it, park systems became then ubiquitous features of overarching town plans.[43]

Park systems

The constitution of early modern planning coincided with the emergence of the urban park as a typology of green space.[44] As a reaction to the unsanitary conditions of industrial cities, lack of open spaces, increasing distance to the countryside and perceived physical, moral and spiritual decay of the urban dweller, the provision of urban parks for the masses was seen as a necessity. Yet, it was not until the last quarter of the nineteenth century that the notion of a comprehensive system of interlinked green spaces was formulated.

Then again, the definition of park systems was not intended solely to help elevate the health and morality of city dwellers but was, above all, treated as an instrument of planning.[45] Considered to be one of the first proponents of the park system idea, Frederick Law Olmsted maintained that its application was essential, 'knowing that the average length of the life of mankind in towns has been much less than in the country, and that the average amount of disease and misery and of vice and crime has been much greater in towns'.[46] He argued that to persist in such a course would only endanger mankind's 'health, virtue and happiness'.[47] The antidote had to involve the creation of parks, parkways and, ultimately, park systems – of which Olmsted and Calvert Vaux's plan for Buffalo, from 1868, is one of the first examples. Needless to say, Olmsted had a remarkable influence upon American planning practice of the following decades, including on the works of the City Beautiful and the City Planning movements.[48]

Reports on the conditions of parks in American cities and numerous park system plans emerged in that period, the case of Chicago being particularly noteworthy. After the 1871 fire, the concentration of population along the rail lines intensified and the city's tentacular growth laid out the foundations for the plans to come (Figure 1.5). Chicago's Special Park Commission took up the matter of creating a metropolitan park system and suggested in 1905 the creation of strips of parks and parkways from the wider areas on the outskirts into the city centre (Figure 1.6).[49] This study would later inform Daniel Burnham and Edward Bennett's Plan of Chicago, from 1909 (Figure 1.7).[50]

FIGURE 1.5 *Bird's-eye view of Chicago.* Source: *Burnham and Bennett, 1909, frontispiece.*

The *modus operandi* of including park systems as intrinsic elements of comprehensive plans spread rapidly not only in the United States but also in Europe. The park system implemented in Paris during Haussmann's period by Adolphe Alphand became a reference across the world. By the end of the nineteenth century, park systems were normative in the Western

FIGURE 1.6 *Special Park Commission's metropolitan park system plan for Chicago, 1905.* Source: *Special Park Commission, 1905, Map.*

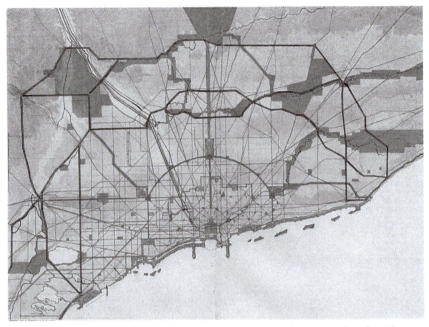

FIGURE 1.7 *Burnham and Bennett's metropolitan park system plan for Chicago, 1909.* Source: *Burnham and Bennett, 1909, between 44 and 45.*

world. In Germany, Joseph Stübben argued in his 1890 book *Handbuch der Architektur* (Handbook of Architecture) for the planning of park systems prior to the consolidation of expansion areas to ensure adequate provision and distribution of green spaces. In addition, he stressed the importance of their integration with radio-concentric traffic systems. Elements of park systems included parks, green belts, tree-lined roads and squares. A particular type of park in Stübben's treatise is the *Park-promenade* (avenue-park), which would not only link the different sorts of green spaces within the urban fabric – similarly to Olmsted's concept of the parkway – but also radially connect the city to the countryside through a pleasant route. Panzini points out that it is with Stübben that lies the origin of the notion of continuity between extra-urban routes and urban parks through linear green pathways – a notion which would become one of the main characteristics of green wedges once this idea comes into being some years later.[51] Back in France, Hénard promoted Stübben's recommendation for the integration of radial arteries and ring roads with green spaces.[52] Further systematization and development of the concept of the park system can be attributed to the work of the French landscape architect Jean-Claude Forestier who, like Stübben, saw access to the countryside as a crucial need of modern city dwellers.[53] The initial

British contribution to the development of park systems came with Howard's garden city idea, in which buildings would be laid out on a green canvas composed of a central park, large front and back gardens, tree-lined streets and a green belt.

The first decades of the twentieth century saw an intense exchange of planning ideas between Europe and the Americas and within Europe itself.[54] This happened not only through the circulation of books, but increasingly also through site visits, professional contacts, international subscriptions to newly constituted professional journals, and attendance to exhibitions and conferences. For example, Werner Hegemann visited New York and Philadelphia in 1909, just before becoming the general secretary of the first international city-planning exhibition held in Berlin in 1910, while Olmsted, Burnham and Charles McKim went on a tour of European cities in preparation for the Plan of Chicago. In 1909, around eighty British town councillors attended a field trip to Germany to study expansion plans, which was reciprocated by a group of 200 members of the German Garden City Association visiting England.[55] Park system experiences were researched and shared among planning professionals. In terms of professional journals, the launch in 1904 of *Der Städtebau,* edited by Camillo Sitte and Theodor Goecke, meant that advancements in German town extension plans could without much delay reach across continents. The foundation of the *Town Planning Review* in 1910, edited by Raymond Unwin, furthered the dissemination of foreign planning experiences in Britain and at the same time made British planning examples more available to the incipient international planning community.

With the maturation of their development, traffic and park systems became drivers of urban restructuring. Traffic routes and green spaces were used not only to connect but also – and most of all – to determine the separation of areas of incompatible uses. As such, the benefits of associating both systems in comprehensive plans became evident; but while the most important element of concentric traffic system plans, the ring road, had its green counterpart, the green belt, the radial traffic system had not yet found its prime green equivalent (see Table 1.1). Although the American experience with parkways and radial parks radiating out from inner urban areas was well known, the theoretical argumentation for the definition of a new radial planning model defined by radial arteries and green wedges was soon to become a novel formulation.

Table 1.1 Precedents of the green wedge idea

Year	Reference	Place	Author	Notes
1715	Plan of Karlsruhe	Karlsruhe, Germany	Unknown	Radial planning Balance between nature and city
1773–9	Les Salines de Chaux	Chaux, France	C. N. Ledoux	Radial planning Balance between nature and city
1829	Plan for London	London, UK	J. C. Loudon	Large green wedge and green belts as zones of open country and 'breathing places'
1868	Parks system plan for Buffalo	Buffalo, USA	F. L Olmsted and C. Vaux	The articulation of green spaces and traffic element (i.e. parkway) The idea of a park system
1890	The concept of *Park-promenade* in the *Handbuch der Architektur*	Generic	J. Stübben	The notion of continuity between extra-urban routes and urban parks through linear green pathways
1902	Plan for the District of Columbia	Washington, DC, USA	Senate Park Commission	Wedge-shaped axis defined by the Rock Creek Park and the Zoological Park
1908–9	Diagram of coastal town Park system plan	Generic London, UK	H. V. Lanchester	Radial planning and radial parks Proposal for two wedge-shaped parks in North London
1909	Plan of Chicago	Chicago, USA	D. Burnham and E. H. Bennett	Radial planning and radial parks The association of traffic system and park system

2

The Emergence and Diffusion of the Green Wedge Idea

This chapter focuses on the development of the green wedge idea from the beginning of the twentieth century to the outbreak of the Second World War.[1] Firstly, it emphasizes the role of the 1910 RIBA Town Planning Conference in its immediate reception and dissemination as a distinct model of green space planning, alternative to that of the green belt. Secondly, it discusses how the initially perceived opposition between both models was resolved, leading to hybrid proposals in the interwar period. Subsequently, the chapter considers how green wedges permeated international planning debates up to the Second World War and how soviet planning applied the idea in attempts to construct of a new socialist society.

Radial planning, radial parks and green wedges

The contrast between pre-industrial modes of urban expansion and those directly related to modern transport systems was at the core of the initial reflections about the ideal form of future cities in the first decades of the twentieth century. If concentric growth had been the norm, leading to sparsely distributed open spaces, the opening up of towns and cities along the radial lines of trains, trams and later motorbuses opened new territories for considering the relationship between city and nature.[2]

If on the one hand ribbon development, defined as development along public transport arteries stretching into the countryside and concentrating around stations, raised questions about the urbanization of the countryside and efficiency of traffic and urban form, on the other hand it prompted planners to start thinking about the open spaces left over by development as positive green spaces. In this context, the merits of the green belt came under close scrutiny. Its critics claimed it was an incongruous concept not aligned with the modern way of city building, a straightjacket denying the city the potential for expansion and a model that concentrated the green spaces away from where people lived. Instead, they propagated radial parks, as these could be articulated directly with the radiating traffic lines and thus promote a green link to other intra-urban green spaces and to the ever more distant countryside. An early theoretical attack on the green belt model can be seen in Henry Vaughan Lanchester's article from 1908 entitled 'Park Systems for Great Cities'.[3] According to him, the green belt owed its inception to the cases where a chain of open spaces took the place of obsolete fortifications, as in the *Ringstrasse* of Vienna, and although it was fact that there was a prevalent view in Britain in favour of arranging green spaces as a 'ring round the city', it was nonetheless difficult to see on what basis this view rested. Lanchester stressed that this model should be abandoned without delay and that – based on his analyses of the park system plans for Boston, Chicago, Rhode Island and Washington – the conclusion had to be that 'the parks themselves should certainly be placed radially'.[4] Lanchester developed his argument further:

[I]t is clear that a series of parks placed radially is the more reasonable method. For one thing, they do not define the city area and exercise a restrictive influence on the space within them; for another, they lead from the more densely populated areas out into the open country, thus encouraging a general exodus towards it, and they also adapt themselves to the gradual expansion of the city.[5]

If one of the main tasks of planning was to organize growth, it was also to effectively arrange the distribution of green spaces in cities. It was perceived that the radial approach would therefore present the necessary flexibility to adapt to potential urban expansion and at the same time allow for a direct connection between the city and the countryside, and that, consequently, both traffic and park systems needed to be conceived in consonance. Lanchester presented diagrams illustrating how this approach should be applied to a generic coastal town (Figure 2.1) and to London (Figure 2.2). Aware of Hénard's studies on park and traffic systems mentioned before,[6] Lanchester's analysis of London led to the conclusion that although the provision of open spaces in the capital was sufficient, they were dispersed and provided no connection to the countryside. Aiming to address these issues, his plan defined an interlinked system of existing and proposed open spaces, boulevards, parkways and significant radial parks, such as one along the River Lea and another, in the form of a wedge, in the Epping Forest.

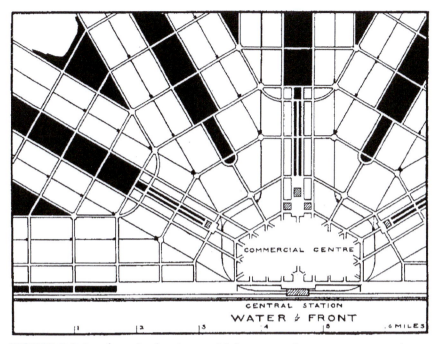

FIGURE 2.1 *Lanchester's planning model for a coastal town.* Source: *Lanchester, 1908, 343.*

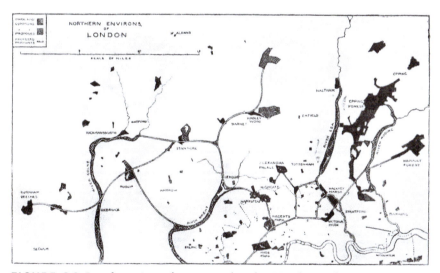

FIGURE 2.2 *Lanchester's park system plan for North London, 1908.* Source: *Lanchester, 1908, 345.*

A year later, Lanchester divulged the idea further in a lecture at the RIBA arguing that 'the country was in course of being wrecked and broken up' and that for the improvements of towns 'the first thing to be demanded was the provision of worthy routes connecting the centre with the open country'. For Lanchester, planning was instrumental in providing residents with 'all the beauties of the countryside linked up with those of the town'. His ultimate goal was that England become 'one complete Garden'. Raymond Unwin, who was present at the lecture and who would soon have the opportunity to prepare a regional plan for London, observed pragmatically that 'improvements must be designed to accompany the natural growth of towns'.[7] Once again, aligning the methods of dealing with the growth and the provision of green spaces was a question of fundamental importance to early modern planners.

Intrinsic opposition: Belts vs wedges

The process of the collective construction of the discipline of town planning was marked in 1910 by two key events: the International Town Planning Exhibition in Berlin (the *Städtebau-Ausstellung*) and the International Town Planning Conference organized by the RIBA in London. The Berlin exhibition confirmed Germany's place at the forefront of town planning. Werner Hegemann, important figure in the transatlantic and continental exchanges of the period, was appointed the Secretary-General of the Berlin Exhibition. One of the most significant sections of the exhibition were the proposals submitted for the Greater Berlin competition – which had aimed to lay the foundations for the city's expansion. The entrants had been asked to consider an area defined within a radius of 25 kilometres from the city centre and a population of 3,500,000 people. The prize-winning entries, selected from among twenty-seven entries, were representatives of the planning models under scrutiny at the time: the first-prize winner, Hermann Jansen, aligned itself with the concentric model and the provision of green belts, while the runner-up entry by Rudolf Eberstadt, Bruno Möhring and Richard Petersen was founded on the principle of radial growth and green wedges. Jansen's park system included two green belts, the first in the proximity of the existing built-up area and the second, much larger, beyond the ring of new districts. They were to be linked to each other and to the city by a number of greenways. Eberstadt, Möhring and Petersen's entry, on the other hand, utterly rejected the idea of concentric rings. For them, the modern way of city expansion was to follow the radial lines of traffic, opening up the city to the countryside that now could be brought straight into the city centres through the means of green wedges. Raymond Unwin reporting his views about the Berlin exhibition sharply stated that the winning entry had failed to address the problem of traffic, since the proposed three ring railways 'seemed of doubtful value, seeing that the greatest traffic is to the centre and from it'. Besides, in regard to the open space plan, he thought that save for the 'green girdle', the open spaces were too scattered about. In contrast, Unwin considered Eberstadt's scheme as 'one of the most interesting', since it had opted for 'radiating groups of parks', 'discarding the idea of having a complete girdle of park land around the town, as being the ideal arrangement'.[8] This new approach generated a wave of repercussions in planning circles, which would soon be magnified by the RIBA Town Planning Conference.

The RIBA conference received around 1,500 delegates from across the world,[9] including the most renowned contemporary planners, such as Stübben, Hegemann and Eberstadt from Germany; Unwin, Lanchester, Stanley Adshead, Barry Parker, Thomas Mawson, Thomas Adams and Howard from Britain; Burnham and Charles Mulford Robinson from the United States; and Hénard, Louis Bonnier and Augustin Rey from France. Similarly to the Berlin exhibition, the RIBA conference hosted diverging views over which model of town expansion was more advantageous: the concentric or the radial. Notable proposals in favour of the first strategy came from Arthur Crow, who suggested the construction of a ring of garden cities around London: the 'Ten Cities of Health' (Figure 2.3);[10] and from George L. Pepler, one of the future founders of the London Society and the Town Planning Institute, who put forward the creation of a 'great girdle' surrounding Greater London aimed

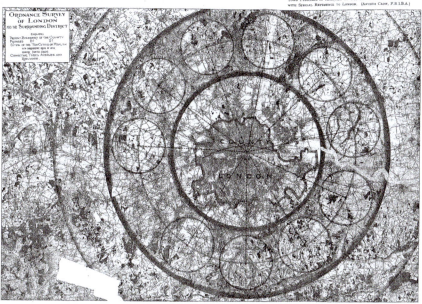

FIGURE 2.3 *Crow's proposal for Ten Cities of Health around London, 1910.* Source: *Crow, 1911, between 410 and 411.*

at facilitating traffic flow and providing a framework for the creation of a belt of garden suburbs around the capital.[11]

However, there was a clear tendency at the conference to favour the radial system. Papers by F. S. Baker, Robinson, Eberstadt and Lanchester were particularly relevant here. For Baker, representing the Royal Architectural Institute of Canada,[12] and for the American planner Robinson radiating streets running out to the suburbs were at the basis of sound town planning. Robinson even argued that the provision of long, straight and wide radial roads – which shorten the distances between the city centre and the outer zones, allowing citizens to live outside the inner city – was 'the triumph of the modern city'.[13] The understanding that planning the modern city had at its core the need to speed up circulation and reconquer the connectivity of the now dispersed urban areas led radial traffic systems to be seen as a progressive mode of structuring the urban fabric. Yet, by concentrating heavily on traffic, some of the discussions overlooked the implications of radial planning in terms of the definition of park systems. Others, however, did aim at a comprehensive radial approach that reconciled the many different systems and needs of modern cities. Among these was the work of Eberstadt, who presented his runner-up entry to the Greater Berlin competition. For him, it was time that planning broke away from the outdated repetition of concentric rings and embraced the new radial planning instead, which he advocated in unambiguous terms:

> every ring, whatever its name may be, is injurious and hurtful to town extension. (…) For the modern town (…) we must break down the ring; the pattern for modern town extension is the radial pattern. The backbone of town extension is formed by the traffic line.

In line with the new developments in park system planning, Eberstadt maintained that 'the open spaces are not green islands accidentally dispersed round the town, but systematically arranged, so as to procure open spaces and circulation of fresh air in all parts of the town'.[14] A new integrative model aligning the radial patterns in vogue with the existing leftover open spaces between strips of development was required: the green wedge. Green wedges should be created along the radial arteries as channels of greenery, sunlight and fresh air from the countryside into the city centre. Conversely, they would allow for inner-city dwellers to live in close contact with green spaces and to have a direct link out into the hinterland. If on the one hand the wedge form, widening towards the countryside, symbolized the reconnection between town and country, on the other hand it responded to the pragmatic constraints of densely built-up central areas and to the fact that land on the outskirts was more abundant, cheaper and therefore more accessible for local authorities to convert into

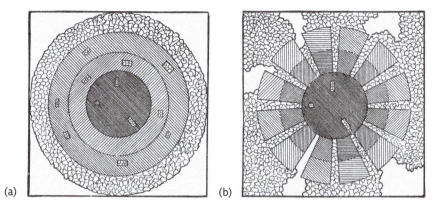

(a)   (b)

FIGURE 2.4 *Eberstadt's opposing diagrams of town extension: (a) the concentric rings and (b) the green wedge model.* Source: *Eberstadt, 1911, 328.*

parks (Figure 2.4). It is important to note that the articulation of radial traffic system, radial strips of development and green wedges would constitute a new planning model thought to be able to respond to the modern needs of circulation, growth and public health – and as an opposing alternative to the established concentric (or green belt) model.

Similarly, Lanchester read a paper illustrating an ideal arrangement for a modern city. In his study, residential districts would be cut through by wedges of parkland widening towards the countryside, and by wedges of factory areas conversely narrowing as they extended into the periphery (Figure 2.5).[15] This proposal was also further discussed in an informal evening meeting 'by the lantern', when he showed how it could be applied to North London and areas south of the Thames, drawing on his initial studies from 1908.[16]

During the discussion of Lanchester's paper, John Brodie, city engineer of Liverpool, stated that 'Mr Lanchester has hit upon, I think, the right idea'. Elucidating his point, Brodie maintained that 'the old-fashioned park areas dotted about irregularly' needed to be rethought, as it was 'very much better to carry your park-like areas out with you radially'.[17] Also present, the Secretary-General of the Berlin exhibition, Werner Hegemann drew attention to the benefits of Lanchester's approach and held up Eberstadt's plan for the German capital as an example of how the green wedge idea could be applied, reiterating that it meant

> not only bringing the traffic in a radial way to the centre, but also the parks, providing thus a broadcast fresh-air drainage to the whole city, and giving a chance to the people to get from every point of the city some park that in a radiating way reaches the broader green areas beyond.[18]

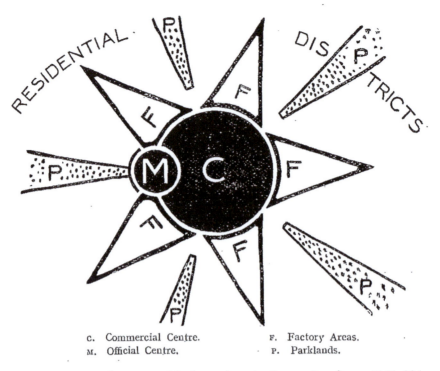

c. Commercial Centre. F. Factory Areas.
M. Official Centre. P. Parklands.

FIGURE 2.5 *Lanchester's model of a modern city.* Source: *Lanchester, 1911, 234.*

Thomas Mawson, a landscape architect and lecturer at Liverpool University, drawing on Eberstadt's diagrams, put the concentric and the radial models overtly at odds again, highlighting the perceived superiority of the latter over the former in regard to park systems:

> There are two principles on which park schemes may be developed; these are shown in diagrams prepared, I believe, by Professor Eberstadt. The first is known as the belt, the other as the radial plan. (...) All town-planners, (...) who have seriously studied the development of park schemes agreed that the radial principle is the best, as it ensures an unbroken current of fresh air into the city, takes the least land where it is most expensive, and the most on the agricultural fringe; but most important of all, it ensures an expanding proportion of park as the population increases.[19]

As discussed, the new green wedge model would directly address the pollution problem in modern cities by promoting the flow of clean air from the countryside into the urban core, while also being flexible to accommodate urban growth without compromising the inhabitants' access to green spaces.

Early ecological consciousness could also be noticed at the conference. For Colonel G. T. Plunkett, rather than urban parks, green wedges should be stretches of natural scenery, bands of countryside within the city and reserves for wild creatures. In a similar fashion to the American greenways, he proposed that they should follow geographical features such as rivers and brooks.[20]

The symbolism of the green wedge idea, in its potential to resolve the town and country dichotomy, was present in some discourses. Nowhere was it more evident than in Stasse and de Bruyne's paper. They too made a strong case against a 'few patches of verdure', arguing for the creation of 'a series of parks and avenues pleasantly leading the pedestrian (...) from the reverberating furnace of the centre to the open air, the green depths of Nature and infinite space'. At the heart of their argument was this vision of the future:

> What we want is to break up this frontal border by means of big, wedge-like plantations, penetrating far in; to transform the circular expansion of the town into a star-like-shaped figure, between the points of which would be preserved for ever bright and breezy intervals promising better things beyond.[21]

Green wedges acquired in their discourse the status of a symbol of the Enlightenment promise of a brighter and auspicious future dependant on a harmonious relationship between man and nature. To a greater or lesser extent, the metaphorical appeal of this idea will permeate visions and proposals for very different locations over the decades.

The RIBA conference played a fundamental role in the dissemination of the green wedge idea.[22] Effects of this could be seen in Britain immediately after the event. In October 1910, the journal *Town Planning Review* published a copy of Mawson's paper presented at the conference, in which he had defended the virtues of radial planning and green wedges. It was followed by a critical review of the St Louis Park System proposal rebuking its lack of green wedges: 'the map, of course, is only tentative, but it appears to us rather to neglect the provision of radial wedge park-ways, providing a series of concentric rings only connected by ordinary traffic routes'.[23]

Patrick Abercrombie would become one of the most important advocates of the green wedge idea post-RIBA conference. In the very first issue of the *Town Planning Review*, of which he was one of the founders, he pursued the topic of radial planning when analysing the Plan for Chicago. Despite admiring its sumptuousness, Abercrombie categorically stated that 'we cannot agree with Messrs. Burnham and Bennett that this rectilinear or gridiron system is the best that could be devised'. Beyond the fact that the absence of diagonal and circumferential lines was considered 'fatal' to efficient traffic circulation, 'the ideal diagram for a riparian town should be the focus type rather than the gridiron. This is to say, the radial lines should be inherent in the plan, and not an afterthought.' Moving on to comment on the park system plan, Abercrombie suggested that 'the Americans admire our Epping Forest' and were intending to achieve a similar result with the proposed 'gradually widening parkways leading into natural reserves following the lines of river valleys'.[24] Epping Forest, which had also been mentioned by Lanchester as a main radial park, would become one of the potential green wedges most referred to in the forthcoming plans for London. It is worth noting that the proposals of the Senate Park Commission for Washington (Figure 2.6) also impressed Abercrombie, in particular the

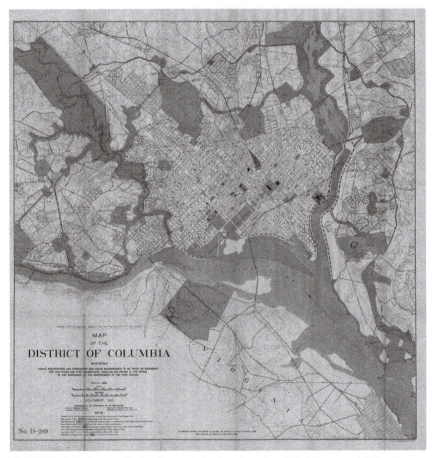

FIGURE 2.6 *Senate Park Commission's plan for Washington, 1902.* Source: *Burnham and Bennett, 1909, Plate IV.*

wedge-shaped axis defined by the Rock Creek Park and the Zoological Park: 'forming a continuous, irregular, and highly picturesque valley of more than 5 miles' (8 kilometres).[25]

In 1912, in the article 'Town Planning in Greater London: the need for co-operation', Abercrombie would argue in favour of a park system plan for Greater London that included green wedges.[26] Abercrombie pointed out that under the 1909 Town Planning Act, the areas of Finchley and Brent Garden Suburbs were being 'developed on modern lines' and that a green wedge was to be formed in the district. Octavia Hill's previous efforts to save Hampstead Heath and Parliament Hill would pay dividends, since, together with Hampstead Garden Suburb, this would insert, as Abercrombie suggested, 'a continuous wedge of green into London', providing thus a through connection to the country.[27] He considered how many other green wedges could be created and how in fact they could become elements of any park system. Indeed, Abercrombie probed the possibilities of creating green wedges in many circumstances, alerting to the fact that the opportunities would be lost should development be allowed to close in. Another example of Abercrombie's early campaign for green wedges can be seen in his judgement of a town planning competition for York. In the report he argued that the city's existing open spaces already formed 'a natural series of radiating wedges from the centre' configuring therefore 'the nucleus of a magnificent park system'; for that reason, he thought, 'it must have been one of the most congenial tasks put before the competitors to make the most of this wonderful opportunity for creating the finest park system in the country'. Not surprisingly, such opportunity had been taken in the winning proposal by Reginald Dann. Commenting on its qualities, Abercrombie stressed that the park system was 'particularly good', working strongly on the principle of green wedges rather than ring parks.[28]

In the international scenario, Eberstadt's diagrams were widely disseminated. Gustav Langen, for instance, drew on his fellow countryman's diagram to propose further fractioning of the built-up area in order to allow for the green wedges to cut across them too (Figure 2.7).[29] Langen would later, as the technical advisor of the Regional Planning Association, put forward a regional plan for Berlin in 1932, which strictly followed the green wedge model, densifying construction along the railway lines and preserving open green space between them.[30] In 1915, Martin Wagner, who would become the head of the Municipal Planning and Building Authority of Berlin from 1926 to 1933, defended his thesis on the hygienic importance of green spaces for large cities.[31] There, Wagner published Eberstadt's green wedge diagram and published one of his own showing how green wedges should assume a flexible form, widening and narrowing as appropriate (Figure 2.8).

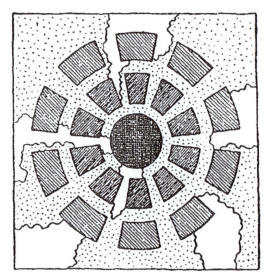

FIGURE 2.7 *Gustav Langen's diagram of green wedges, 1912. Source: Langen, 1927.*

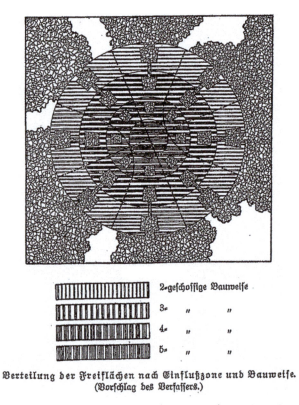

FIGURE 2.8 *Martin Wagner's diagram of green wedges, 1915. Source: Wagner, 1915, 53.*

Dissention over the radial-green wedge versus ring-green belt planning models remained evident. This is the case, for instance, in the contrasting plans for Altona and Hamburg by Fritz Schumacher, one of the founders of the *Deutscher Volksparkbund* and the Building Director of Hamburg from 1909 to 1933, and architect and planner Gustav Oelsner. It can be argued that various forms of radial planning were associated with natural processes of growth and with living organisms, particularly in Germany. Leaves and flowers were commonly used metaphors. The Geddesian understanding of the region as a holistic organism had a lasting impact in promoting such associations. The metaphor of nature appeared in Fritz Schumacher's concept of the city as a leaf (Figure 2.9) in his plans for Altona and Hamburg in 1919 and for Cologne in 1923. The leaves were transposed to the plans as radial axes of development, between which green wedges would occur, in a similar vein to Geddes's 'star-like flower'. In contrast to Schumacher's view, Oelsner concentrated on the definition of three green belts in his plan from 1925. Both ideas would be influential in future plans for Hamburg and are at the basis of the 2014 green network programme for the city, discussed later in this book.

Eberstadt's diagram of green wedges was eagerly received in the Netherlands.[32] Its impact can be seen, for instance, on the Dutch architect

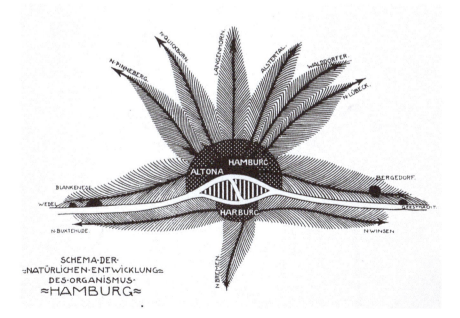

FIGURE 2.9 *Schumacher's leaf diagram for Altona and Hamburg, 1919.*

Hendrik Wijdeveld's proposal for Amsterdam entitled 'Chaos and Order' from 1920. Wijdeveld envisaged that the city centre should be kept as an urban museum, and that the expansion area should be completely remodelled along radial lines, supplemented by ring streets. Most of the territory was left to green wedges and outer green spaces, while urban concentration would happen on zigzagging lines. The title and the rigid geometrical regularity of the plan recall the Enlightenment's attempt to rebalance the relationship between urban areas and nature through reason, manifested for instance in the plan of Karlsruhe.

The green wedge idea was publicized in the United States too. For instance, in the book *Planning of the Modern City* from 1916 the American town planner Nelson Peter Lewis made reference to Brodie's and Hegemann's favourable opinions regarding green wedges published in the *Transactions*.[33] As discussed earlier, interchanges of plans, books and professionals between Europe and the Americas were intense in that period.[34] The Regional Plan of New York and its Environs, led by Thomas Adams and published in 1929, would also show references to the idea.[35] It included a regional park system consisting mostly of parkways connecting existing and new green spaces. As a typology, parkways tended to be closely related to the traffic system and geographical features, which facilitated their potential implementation in the denser areas. Although wedges would play a role in the plan in enlarging the amount of recreational areas, they were mostly considered at regional scale. In Adams' view, the Central Park was 'the point of a wedge in a north-western system of parks'.[36] One of these would comprise the area of the Harriman State Park, northwest of the river Hudson, which was to be doubled in size. He also argued that wedges should be used for the creation of agricultural zones.[37]

At the beginning of the 1910s, the green wedge idea emerged as a new radical planning model appropriate for the modern city. Initially, it was presented in opposition to the ring, or belt, model (Table 2.1). The green wedge model's main functions were to bring fresh air and greenery into the city and to provide a direct way out to the countryside. The wedge shape responded to the fact that central areas tended to be more consolidated than the periphery, reinforcing the intention of promoting a funnelling effect for the wind and allowing for an increase in the green areas as the city expanded. The green wedge model also symbolized a possible resolution of the contrasts between town and country, a connection to the beauty of nature and its beneficial psychological effects on the population.

Table 2.1 A Matrix of the opposition between the green wedge and the green belt models

Year	Reference	Place	Author	Notes
1910	Entry to the Greater Berlin Competition	Berlin, Germany	R. Eberstadt, B. Möhring and R. Petersen	Formulation of the first green wedge idea Radial planning Green wedges in association with the traffic system
1910	Diagram of the green wedge model, RIBA Town Planning Conference	Generic	R. Eberstadt	The green wedge model to replace the green belt model in the planning of modern cities Radial planning Green wedges in association with the traffic system
1910	Diagram of a modern city, RIBA Town Planning Conference	Generic	H. V. Lanchester	Residential districts would be cut through by wedges of parkland
1910	Discussion, RIBA Town Planning Conference	Generic	W. Hegemann	Highlighting the benefits of the green wedge model Reference to Eberstadt
1910	Discussion, RIBA Town Planning Conference	Generic	J. Brodie	Commendation of the green wedge model
1910	'Bruxelles Aux Champs', RIBA Town Planning Conference	Brussels, Belgium	Stasse and de Bruyne	Symbolic meaning of green wedges in reconnecting man and nature
1910	'Open Spaces and Running Waters', RIBA Town Planning Conference	Generic	G. T. Plunkett	Early ecological preoccupation Green wedges should be created along geographical features and be areas of countryside and reserves for wildlife

Year	Reference	Place	Author	Notes
1910	'Public Parks and Gardens', RIBA Town Planning Conference	Generic	T. Mawson	The green wedge model as the best for modern towns Direct opposition to the green belt model
1912	Diagram of green wedges with built-up areas broken down	Generic	G. Langen	Derived from Eberstadt's diagram Further fractioning of the built-up area
1912	'Town Planning in Greater London'	London, UK	P. Abercrombie	Green wedge to be formed in Finchley, among others
1914	Plan of Dublin	Dublin, Ireland	P. Abercrombie	Phoenix Park is seen as almost the ideal green wedge 'that one would draw on a schematic diagram'
1915	Diagram of green wedges with some enlarged green areas	Generic	M. Wagner	Derived from Eberstadt's diagram Green wedges punctuated with large green nodes
1915	*Cities in Evolution*	Generic	P. Geddes	Analogy of the city 'in full development' to the 'star-like' opening of the flower
1916	Review of the Plan of York	York, UK	P. Abercrombie	The winning entry is praised for having worked on the provision of green wedges rather than belts
1916	*Planning of the Modern City*	Generic	N. P. Lewis	Reference to Brodie's and Hegemann's defence of the green wedge idea
1919	Leaf diagram	Altona and Hamburg, Germany	F. Schumacher	Concept of the city as a leaf
1919	Diagram of green wedges	Generic/ Germany	P. Wolf	Adaptation of Eberstadt's diagram further elaborating on radial roads, transport nodes and green wedges

Year	Reference	Place	Author	Notes
1920	'Chaos and Order'	Amsterdam, the Netherlands	H. Wijdeveld	The city centre should be kept as an urban museum and development reorganized along radial roads with interspersing green wedges
1924	Diagram for an ideal city	Generic/ Germany	A. Rading	Mentioned by Purdom Model city with four green wedges, which from the hinterland to city centre would be agricultural zones and inside the core gardens and 'fields'
1930	Plan of Moscow	Moscow, Russia	G. Krasin	Workers colonies along radial lines between green wedges
1930	Plan of Moscow	Moscow, Russia	G. B. Puzis	Plan with green wedges as cultivated parks and woods
1933	Town model diagrams in *A hundred new towns for Britain*	Generic (per typology of town)	Hundred New Towns Association (A. Trystan Edwards)	A variety of typologies of cities with green wedges S. Adshead and E. Lutyens were involved
1937	Plan of London	London, UK	W. Tatton Brown	Presented at CIAM 5 Radial arteries with green wedges Radical opposition to the green belt
1939	Plan of Berlin	Berlin, Germany	Willi Schelkes	Nazi plan with multiple green wedges
1940	Park system plan for London in *Living in Cities*	London, UK	R. Tubbs	A series of eighteen green wedges and a round parkway

Year	Reference	Place	Author	Notes
1941	Model for the reconstruction of large cities	Generic	H. V. Lanchester	The diagram intercalated green wedge-housing-industry-housing-green wedge radiating from the city centre Four green wedges
1943	Plan for Greater London	London, UK	A. Trystan Edwards	Cruciform plan with four green wedges

Opposition resolved: Belts and wedges as elements of the same park system

The initial opposition between the radial and the concentric, the green wedges and green belts would soon be questioned, and planners would investigate ways to bring together the benefits of both models. This is not to say that both processes, of opposition and its resolution, did not occur in parallel. They remained present in planning discourses for decades to come.

An early attempt to articulate both models can be seen in the work of Robert Schmidt for the 'great open space commission' formed in Düsseldorf in the wake of the 1910 International Berlin Exhibition. The commission had the responsibility to propose a plan for the disposition of green spaces and a traffic system. Schmidt thought of the city as an organism. His memorandum included a diagram of an ideal distribution of green spaces in urban areas, which was marked by a green belt and four long green wedges connecting the centre to the countryside and another four shorter wedges reaching into the core of districts. The wedges would be linked by round and transversal parkways (Figure 2.10). The application of the idea to an industrial town was the object of yet another diagram, in which rings encircle the centre and irradiate radial traffic lines out into the region. The industrial zone was located to the north, while green wedges broke the mass of urbanization up, some reaching from the green belt inside the traffic rings near the centre and some stopping at the centre of the neighbourhoods.[38]

Mawson, who at the RIBA conference was adamant that the park system for modern towns should be radial and adopt the green wedge model, in a series of lectures given at Bolton in 1915 was less convinced that one model

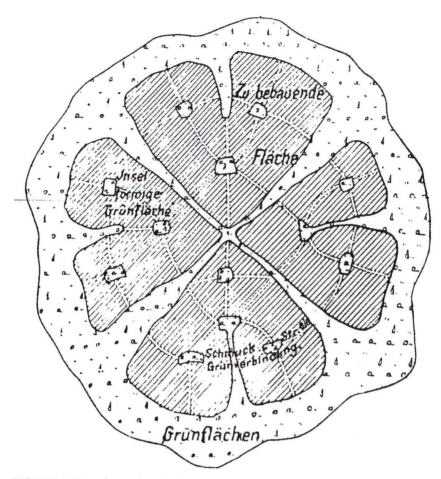

FIGURE 2.10 *Robert Schmidt's diagram.* Source: *Schmidt, 1912, 19.*

should completely exclude the other. He still highlighted that modern towns tended to grow 'in long, straggling suburbs with spaces of greenery between them', and that because of this 'the radial system of park design is the natural one', as 'these wedges of undeveloped land so often exist even in old towns ready to be turned into beautiful parks'. Mawson used Eberstadt's diagram to illustrate the green wedge model and Lanchester's study from 1908 as an example of its application. He described green wedges as

open areas stretching almost to the heart of the town from the country and so bringing in fresh air to where it is most needed, along ducts of greenery, but these wedges of greenery are naturally narrowest near the centre of the town and broadest in the suburbs, where land is cheaper and where larger parks are more called for, and more practicable. It will also readily be seen that these wedges of greenery fall very naturally into their places as a part of the park system, and the proper layout of a modern town.[39]

However, when it came down to making a proposition for Bolton, Mawson suggested combining both the ring and the radial approaches, with green wedges connected by a 'ringstrasse running through open country'.[40] The initial contradiction of the ring and radial model started to fade in British circles.

While a large number of extension plans had been developed between the end of the nineteenth century and the immediate years leading up to the First World War – such as the cases of Vienna, Paris, Chicago and Berlin – London still lacked an overall plan. Since the regional focus of Geddes's Civic Survey of Edinburgh, it had become evident that planning had to be a regional undertaking.[41] To face this task, the London Society was founded in 1912. Most of its first members had taken part in the RIBA event, including Pepler, Stanley Adshead, Thomas Adams, Unwin and Lanchester. The Society was concerned with the fact that London was 'an immense octopus and its tentacles spread further afield, north, south, east and west, with no one to guide them', the ultimate goal being 'to insist on a plan that shall govern the movements of the octopus'.[42] From 1914 to 1918, the Society prepared the Development Plan of Greater London, focusing on arterial roads and the provision of green spaces.[43] Unwin was responsible for surveying the capital's open spaces, while Lanchester was directly involved with the study of its traffic system.[44] As a result, the plan included a series of radial arteries and a park system. The proposal contained a wedge-like regional park radiating outwards in north-west London, from Stanmore to the Brent Reservoir, and another one in the Epping Forest, coinciding with Lanchester's 1908 plan and Abercrombie's recommendation from 1912.

The disquietudes caused by the distortions of modern life and their impact on the fragmentation of the being were nowhere better encapsulated than in the Expressionist movement. Reacting to the overbearing influence of the machine in all aspects of human life, the gloomy conditions of cities and the human being's state of anxiety, the symbolism of a bright, harmonious and crystalline future emerges powerfully in Bruno Taut's *Die Stadtkrone* from 1919.[45] Taut envisioned a round town of 7 kilometres of diametre, bound by a green belt, with monumental civic buildings at its core – the new cathedral of the modern age. From its centre, a green wedge would open up towards the countryside along the main wind direction to the west, bringing in fresh air, greenery and sunlight (Figure 2.11). It would be a 'people's park', with both play areas and forest grounds leading to the countryside, which could be reached from the town centre within a half an hour's walk. The representation of the green wedge shows that the background of community life was to be

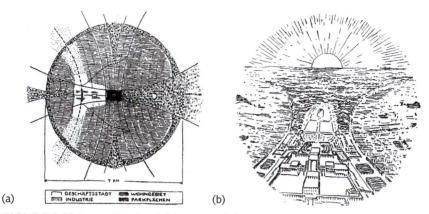

(a)   (b)

FIGURE 2.11 *Bruno Taut's (a) diagram and (b) perspective view of* Die Stadtkrone, *1919.* Source: *Taut, 1919.*

the natural environment. Taut's vision is one of hope for a harmonious future after the tragedies of urban life of the previous decades and the devastation of the First World War.

Still in 1919 Paul Wolf published a treatise entitled *Städtebau: das Formproblem der Stadt in Vergangenheit und Zukunft*, in which he builds on Eberstadt's green wedge model to further elaborate on radial roads, transport nodes and green wedges.[46] In 1922, he became the City Architect of Dresden, and in 1925 had the chance to apply it in a plan for the city. In 1930, he planned a model for a large city with M. Arlt. It presented a vision for an ideal distribution of development and greenery, combining concentric and radial traffic arteries and green spaces.[47]

In Australia, John Sulman – who at the RIBA Town Planning Conference had presented a paper on the plan for the federal capital of Australia – published in 1919 a diagram based on Eberstadt's. The diagram showed a generic city encircled by a green belt, from which green wedges would reach the core. The idea, as Freestone argued, was influential in major plans for Australia, such as the plans for Melbourne in 1929 and Perth in 1930.[48] The Plan for General Development of Melbourne addressed the common regional planning issues of the inter-war period, such as zoning, traffic congestion and urban growth. Regarding the provision of green spaces, it recognized the different models under debate at the time: the green belt, green wedges and disconnected parks and squares distributed across the city. The plan acknowledged that the city's physical configuration lent itself to the creation of an 'unequalled park system'. The proposal assumed a hybrid character, promoting the transformation of waterways into green wedges and the distribution of other green spaces in the urban fabric.[49]

During the interwar period, uncontrolled sprawl, inner city densification and congestion intensified in urban centres in Europe, the United States, and in many locations in South America and Australia. In Germany, the contrast between the unhealthy city and the healthy countryside was reinforced. Access to light and air, outdoor nature, adequate housing and the habit of exercising were preached as necessary in order to prevent city dwellers from disease, especially tuberculosis.[50] Consequently, the threat of the loss of the countryside and the shortage of green spaces within urban areas were central issues to be dealt with by any development plan at town and regional levels.[51] Furthermore, the integration of traffic and park systems remained a central tenet of planning theory.

In this context a number of proposals emerged. Among them, it is worth considering Pepler's diagram for a model city published in an article titled 'Open Spaces', from 1923.[52] He had been involved in the London Society Development Plan and had been the Chief Town Planning Inspector in the Ministry of Health since its establishment in 1919 and a member of the Unhealthy Areas Committee between 1920 and 1921. While at the RIBA conference he had been promoting the idea of a 'great girdle' around London, in 'Open Spaces' he called for a combined approach between ring and radial park system models. Pepler argued that in addition to their recreational functions, green spaces could be arranged to form ventilating axes into town centres, for which green wedges were the best choice available. The diagram illustrated a park system for a town of 45,000 inhabitants with four 'park wedges' connecting the centre to the countryside, four other parks and a parkway linking them together. The 'park wedges' were to be implemented by preserving open land between development that followed the main radial roads. Pepler proposed that the built-up area would come into direct contact with the country and that the wedges of greenery would merge with it. Here he shifted focus from the ring to a hybrid model.

In the late 1920s and early 1930s, regional planning also became popularized in Poland. Polish architectural and planning circles evidenced a direct engagement with the international debates, both in theoretical terms and in planning practice. By the end of the eighteenth century, Poland had been divided between Russia, Prussia and Austria and would regain her independence only at the end of the First World War. The end of the Napoleonic Wars, however, saw the establishment of a semi-autonomous Kingdom of Poland subject to Russian rule. In the late nineteenth century, Warsaw was object to exponential investment in infrastructure, and railways became fundamental drivers for the intensified urban growth of the following decades.[53] After the First World War, reconnecting the nation not only became a matter of physical integration but most of all a socio-cultural and economic affair. By the outbreak of the Second World War nearly half of Poland had been covered by regional planning studies.[54]

Planning for Warsaw, the capital city of this newly independent nation not only had to face the inherent difficulties of organizing a growing city but, perhaps most importantly, also embrace the symbolism of such a task. In this context, it is worth highlighting the Plan for Greater Warsaw, from 1928, by Stanisław Różański, Stanisław Filipkowski and Maria Buckiewiczówna. As was common practice, a survey of the amount of green space and their location was carried out, the conclusion being that both were inadequate, particularly in the inner areas. Similarly to many interwar schemes, this regional plan recognized the complementarity of green belts and green wedges. The central area would be reached by seven equitably distributed green wedges, which would break down the residential ring just outside the city core into a number of districts (Figure 2.12). The green wedges would be linked by a green belt, beyond which suburban areas would lie. Some of the green wedges, after reaching the green belt, would extend out into the open country, as for instance the Vistula valley.[55] Health considerations were one of the plan's main preoccupations. They manifested themselves in the attempt to isolate perceived incompatible functions, the openness of the plan and its green spaces, and the influx of fresh air into the inner parts of the city. Warsaw was to be a green, healthy city well integrated into the surrounding landscape.

Other Polish city plans followed in a similar direction. As Kozaczko showed, the green wedge model was used in several interwar plans for Poznań. This can be first seen in a proposal by Sylwester Pajderski in 1929. Subsequent to this plan a competition was organized in 1931. It is worth noting that third-prize winners Józef Reński and Władysław Günath based their entry on radial arteries and green wedges. As a result of the competition, the Urban Planning Office was established under the headship of Władysław Czarnecki, who developed yet another plan for Poznań in 1932.[56] Like the above-mentioned plan of Warsaw, Czarnecki's plan for Poznań involved a hybrid system of green belt and green wedges. A total of ten green wedges were defined.[57] Their main objectives and strategies were akin to those from international plans of the period, in particularly Germany. It is worth bearing in mind that Poznań had been under Prussian occupation between 1793 and 1871, when it became part of the German Empire. It was only in 1918, after 125 years of occupation, that it returned to Polish control. In town planning matters, Germany was still the main referential. Czarnecki prepared his plan for Poznań after a visit to Berlin to attend a town planning exhibition and to study German cities. Professional journals played an important role in the diffusion of international cases. It is known that Czarnecki subscribed to *Der Städtebau*. Furthermore, Eberstadt's opposing diagrams of ring development and radial growth with green wedges were republished in *Dom, Osiedle, Mieszkanie* (House, Housing Estate, Flat) in 1930[58] and Professor Sergei S. Shestakov's plan for Moscow – displaying

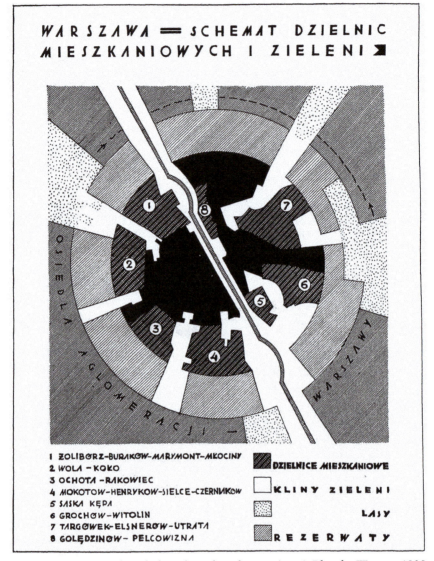

FIGURE 2.12 *Różański, Filipkowski and Buckiewiczówna's Plan for Warsaw, 1928.*
Source: *Różański, Filipkowski and Buckiewiczówna, 1928, 431.*

conspicuous green wedges – appeared as a case study in *Architektura i Budownictwo* (Architecture and Construction) in 1931.[59] It is not unreasonable to assume that Czarnecki was familiar with these references.

After the Greater Berlin Competition in 1910, it would be only in 1929 that another plan for the German capital would emerge. Put forward by Walter Koeppen and Martin Wagner, the plan was known as the 'Open spaces programme for the municipality of Berlin and the surrounding zone'. It brought together the concentric and the radial models by suggesting a large green belt surrounding Berlin from which a number of flexible green wedges would reach the innermost parts of the German capital (Figure 2.13).[60] Similarly to the cases discussed earlier, they would provide recreational spaces in proximity to residential areas, connect the inner urban areas to the countryside and improve air quality.

The opportunity to formulate a new plan for London reappeared in 1927 with the formation of the Greater London Regional Planning Committee (GLRPC) by the Ministry of Health. The task was to prepare a plan encompassing a 25-mile (40 kilometre) radius from the centre of London. In January 1929, Unwin, who had been the Chief Technical Officer for Building and Town Planning at the same Ministry, was appointed the Committee's technical adviser. Soon after his nomination, Unwin announced that the Committee had studied the provision of open spaces in the form of 'a green girdle or chain of open spaces'.[61] At the end of that year, however, in the Memorandum No. 1 of the *First Report of the Greater London Regional Planning Committee*, Unwin goes beyond that and portrayed a hybrid park system for Greater London based on the notion that the city should sit on

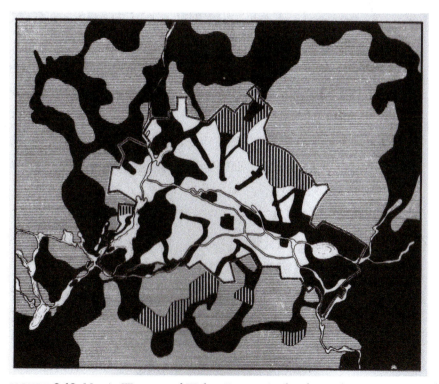

FIGURE 2.13 *Martin Wagner and Walter Koeppen's plan for Berlin, 1929.* Source: *http://www.stadtentwicklung.berlin.de/umwelt/landschaftsplanung/chronik/#n1929.*

a background of green spaces, as opposed to land waiting to be developed (Figure 2.14). As Abercrombie and many others had alerted previously, the memorandum stressed the need to reserve land to provide 'breaks and breathing spaces between the built-up zones, from which additions can be made to the parks, pleasure grounds and playing fields as required from time to time'.[62] As stated, the plan was commissioned by the Ministry of Health, for whom the adequate provision of open spaces was a priority.

In the *Second Report of the Greater London Regional Planning Committee*, from 1933, Unwin stressed that the preferred method of growth for London was by satellite development, not by continuous expansion of the existing urban fabric (Figure 2.15). This being the case, the implementation of green wedges would not be correlated to an indeterminate urban expansion, but would work alongside a girdle to create a closed park system.[63] The report proposed the creation of a green girdle as near the urbanized area as possible and a range of public open spaces within the area to be circumscribed by the girdle, including green wedges.[64] The resonance of the combined ring and radial model of the GLRPC plan for London with Wagner and Koeppen's

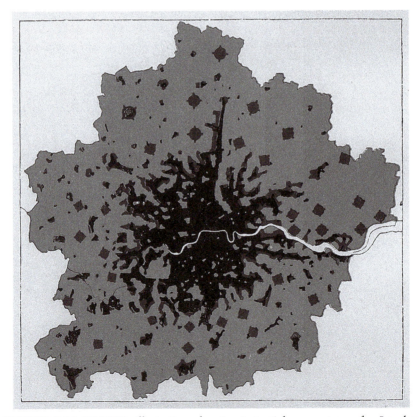

FIGURE 2.14 *GLRPC's illustration showing potential green spaces for London, 1929.* Source: *GLRPC, 1929, Ill. 16.*

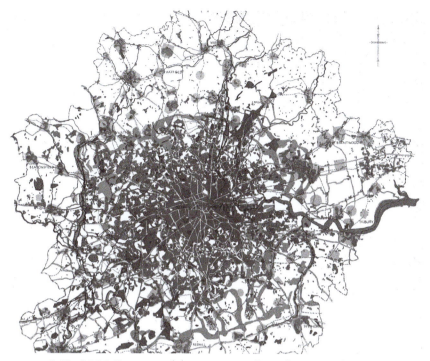

FIGURE 2.15 *GLRPC's proposal for a green girdle and green wedges for London, 1933.* Source: *GLRPC, 1933, Ill. 12.*

proposal for Berlin is noteworthy. Unwin's call for the safeguarding of existing open spaces with a view to consider them part of a park system for London was nothing short of insight: by the time of the publication of the second report, green spaces in inner London (within 18 kilometres of Charing Cross) had dwindled from 129.5 square kilometres in 1927 to only 32.4 square kilometres.[65]

In Latin America, the green wedge idea was adopted by Jean Claude Forestier in his 1923 plan for Havana, by the French architect Alfred Agache in his 1930 plan for Rio de Janeiro[66] and by the engineer Prestes Maia in his Avenue Plan for São Paulo of the same year.[67] Agache proposed the creation of a comprehensive three-tiered park system encompassing the regional, citywide and local scales. For Agache, as maintained by Eberstadt, Stübben and so many others from the period,

the city is usually represented with its tentacles stretching out into the countryside. But, it is equally indispensible that, through its open spaces, the countryside penetrates tentacles into the inner urban agglomeration, bringing to all its parts the fresh and pure air to replace the foul.[68]

The fact that the extensive circulation of planning ideas facilitated proactive planning was highlighted by Maia in São Paulo, as access to 'the recent teachings of all the town planning movement'[69] was at hand. From this and the understanding that the majority of the difficulties faced by cities were 'of universal character, originated from the peculiar conditions of the modern life',[70] the application of tested models should be considered. Maia proposed a conceptually hybrid park system for São Paulo, mixing ideas from Stübben, Hénard and Eberstadt. He argued that Eberstadt's green wedge model was formidable, but of difficult application. Despite this, Maia proposed several green wedges for the city alongside avenues in valleys, such as the Vale da Aclimação and Anhangabaú Avenue.

Back in Europe, arguably one of the main planning occurrences of the interwar period was Cornelis van Eesteren's General Extension Plan (AUP) for Amsterdam, from 1934. Van Eesteren joined Amsterdam's town planning department in 1929, where he worked for thirty years. Given that he was the chairman of the *Congrès internationaux d'architecture moderne* (International Congresses of Modern Architecture – CIAM) between 1930 and 1947, it is not surprising that the modernist fascination for the definition of principles for the 'functional city' – such as zoning and increased access to sunlight, greenery and fresh air – transpired in his work. The network of green spaces proposed in the AUP includes green fingers and wedges reaching deep into the city between districts. As Zonnefeld states, this solution was by no means unique in the country, as 'the city of green wedges and urban lobes became the doctrine behind many of the plans for Dutch cities in the 1930s, 1940s and 1950s'.[71]

As a final addition to this section, it bears acknowledging Abercrombie's description of an ideal park system in his book *Town and Country Planning* from 1933. Similar to Mawson's explanation, Abercrombie discussed the two approaches in park system planning: the concentric belts and the 'radial park wedges'. He used a version of Pepler's diagram from 1923, including the same features, in which both ideas were merged. Abercrombie highlighted that 'the diagram shows a combined scheme for the town surrounded by an inviolable Green Belt of open country. (...) These major radials called by the Germans "Ausfall Strassen" have the exhilarating effect of pointing from the centre of the largest city direct at the open country'.[72]

Abercrombie's book summarizes how the interwar period consolidated the green wedge idea's place in Western modern town planning and resolved their initial opposition to the green belt, since both systems tended to be combined (Table 2.2). The direct connection to the countryside that green wedges could provide and their sanitary role were some of their most explored functions. In the post-war context, green wedges would be used as instruments of hope for a better future both in reconstruction plans and in those for new towns.

Table 2.2 The green wedge and the green belt models combined

Year	Reference	Place	Author	Notes
1912	Diagram of city model	Dusseldorf, Germany	R. Schmidt	Biological reference Green belt and four long green wedges connecting the centre to the countryside and another four shorter wedges reaching into the core of districts
1915	Lectures in Bolton	Bolton, UK	T. Mawson	Recognize the green wedge as the best model, but the proposal for Bolton combines the green belt and green wedge models
1918	London Society Development Plan	London, UK	London Society	The proposal contained a green girdle and a wedge-like 2,000-acre regional park from Stanmore to the Brent Reservoir, and another one in the Lea Valley.
1919	Die Stadtkrone	Generic/Germany	B. Taut	Round town with a green belt and central green wedge
1919	Diagram of city model	Generic/Australia	J. Sulman	Diagram based on Eberstadt's showing a green belt and green wedges
1923	Park system diagram	Generic	G. L. Pepler	Four green wedges connected by a parkway
1925	Plan of Moscow	Moscow, Russia	S. Shestakov	Cruciform plan with four large green wedges and a green belt
1928	Plan of Warsaw	Warsaw, Poland	S. Różański, S. Filipkowski and M. Buckiewiczówna	Seven green wedges linked by a green belt

Year	Reference	Place	Author	Notes
1929	Plan of Berlin	Berlin, Germany	M. Wagner and W. Koeppen's	Hybrid plan with a green belt and various green wedges
1929	Plan of a Green City	Near Moscow, Russia	K. Melnikov	It included a wedge-like green space leading to the central hotel in the city, a 'Laboratory of Sleep'.
1930	Plan of Moscow	Moscow, Russia	S. Strumilin	Green belt surrounding the centre beyond which production centres would be located and green wedges
1930	Park system plan for São Paulo	São Paulo, Brazil	P. Maia	River valleys to become green wedges and accommodate radial roads
1930	Park system plan for Rio de Janeiro	Rio de Janeiro, Brazil	A. Agache	The countryside was to penetrate tentacles into the inner urban agglomeration
1931	Plan of Magnitogorsk	Magnitogorsk, Russia	E. May	Districts were separated by green wedges, which linked the city centre to a green belt
1932	Plan of Poznań	Poznań, Poland	W. Czarnecki	Included ten green wedges and a green belt
1933	GLRPC's plan London	London, UK	GLRPC (Unwin)	Greenbelt and green wedges
1933	Diagram in *Town and Country Planning*	Generic	P. Abercrombie	A version of Pepler's 1923 diagram
1934	AUP	Amsterdam, the Netherlands	C. van Eesteren	Hybrid green space plan with fingers and wedges

Year	Reference	Place	Author	Notes
1937	Diagram of an ideal park system	Generic	R. Mattocks	Version of Pepler's 1923 diagram
1939	Parks and Open Space Plan of Tokyo	Tokyo, Japan	–	Green belt with wedges along river valleys flowing into the city as recreational spaces
1940	Pabst Plan for Warsaw	Warsaw, Poland	H. Gross and O. Nurnberger	Nazi plan to replace Warsaw with a new city Large green wedge south of the Vistula River
1942	Scott Report	England, UK	Scott Committee	Mention to '"wedges" of green penetrating towards the heart of the town itself' from the green belt
1944	Plan of Melbourne in *We must go on*	Melbourne, Australia	F. Heath and F. O. Barnett	Green wedges and other radial parks leading to an agricultural belt

The socialist city

The quest for the creation of the socialist city was foremost in Russia after the 1917 Revolution. The transformation of all aspects of life, a break with the past and the construction of a new and better man and woman were the essential tasks ahead. Liberated from alienating work, class struggle, economic oppression and cultural inequality, the modern socialist individual would be in a better position to join the march of progress towards happiness already enunciated by the Enlightenment. In this light, the reinvention of the Soviet territory according to the principles of socialism became one of the main tasks of planners. How should new cities be designed in order to promote the values of socialism? How should existing cities be transformed? How should the regions and the whole of the national territory be reconfigured?

Although the answers to these questions were multiple, as Kopp showed, a common theme was the negation of the 'traditional' capitalist city.[73] The stereotypical historic growth of cities in concentric rings around a market square was seen as a consequence of the capitalist mode of production and its social implications. Furthermore, this model of city expansion would have caused intrinsic social segregation as the working class tended to live in crammed and unsanitary housing surrounding the city centre, while wealthier residents benefited from inhabiting the salubrious green suburbs. In this pattern of land use, the distinction between town and country, centre and periphery persevered. The inequalities of access to modern housing, sanitation, light, air and greenery – represented in the distribution of classes within the city – were to be abolished. Engels had argued that 'it is not utopian to declare that the complete emancipation of humanity from the chains which its historic past has forged will only be complete when the antithesis between the town and country has been abolished'.[74] The achievement of this goal presupposed town and country planning at national scale. Engels' views found fertile ground in the minds of those involved in the construction of the environments suitable for promoting the new socialist conditions of life and the 'new individual'. As El Lissitsky stated, dissolving this contrast was paramount:

Social evolution leads to the elimination of the old dichotomy between city and country. The city endeavors to draw nature right into its center and by means of industrialization to introduce a higher level of culture into the country.[75]

Marx had criticized the isolation and lack of access to culture by the countrymen,[76] while Engels had raged against the excessive urban densities of large cities and their impact on workers, stating that 'life in large cities is, in itself, injurious to health'.[77] If the country, on the one hand, was a place looked at with condescension due to the lack of higher cognitive endeavours, 'idiocy' and abandonment, on the other hand, it allowed for direct contact with nature, providing a healthy and beautiful environment. In turn, if the city was characterized by ugliness, disease, oppression and submission to the machine, it was too a place of industrial employment, cultural and artistic drive and 'social condensers'.[78]

Therefore, a new form of town and country planning was needed, and the new conditions of existence for 'free' planning were at hand: the dissolution of property ownership without compensation, which happened early in 1918, the state control of land and economy and the inexistence of significant local regulations. These were in fact some of the main problems that Western planners faced on endeavouring to implement bold plans with large-scale green spaces, such as green belts and green wedges. Having had the ambition to suppress the opposition between country and city and the unequalled prospect to execute it, a key question here is whether and what role green wedges played in the construction of the expected new conditions of life in the socialist city. Did the socialist quest for the dissolution of the opposition between town and country, centre and periphery, man and nature find a valid model in the green wedge idea? If so, how did green wedges come to existence in the Soviet context?

A preliminary response to these questions emerged in 1925 – prepared amidst the turmoil of the first years following the Revolution – in the Greater Moscow Plan led by the engineer Sergei Shestakov.[79] The Moscow question had been tackled since the beginning of the 1920s. In 1921, a Commission for the 'Unburdening of Moscow' was appointed, which was followed by the setting up of a 'Special Learned Commission' for 'New Moscow' and a Commission for the Creation of Greater Moscow. The first had the task to lessen the strain on housing and infrastructure by evicting redundant enterprises and consequently freeing up space. The second came up with the New Moscow Plan, which was, however, found to be marked by romantic revivalism and intensely criticized. The third, the Greater Moscow commission, relied on the technical expertise of municipal engineers and suggested a radical transformation of the capital city.[80]

This regional plan presupposed that Moscow would become one of the 'world's greatest cities', with a population of 6 million by 1960. The plan considered an area eight times larger than that occupied by the city in 1925 and proposed the construction of twenty-six garden cities.[81] Moscow had grown concentrically around the Kremlin, with radial arteries stretching out towards the countryside. The French planner Hénard had used it as a case study in his comparative studies of traffic systems, which included Western capital cities such as Paris, London and Berlin, to justify the importance of a conjoined use of ring and radial roads.[82] Shestakov would follow the existing radio-concentric structure for the restructuring of the Soviet capital, combining both traffic planning models with their green space equivalents: the green belt and green wedges. The plan resembled a cross, whose centre would be the preserved historic built-up area and the main axes the green wedges (Figure 2.16). They would split the urban fabric into four new residential areas, each with direct access to the industrial zones adjacent to the centre. The wedges would be linked by an outer green belt, which would be bound by a further traffic ring lined with an industrial belt. The traffic arteries would connect Moscow to satellite towns beyond. Shestakov presented, thus, a model that combines green wedges and a green belt at the scale of the city, but that also embraces the region – with the proposition of associated satellite towns.

Although the plan was not implemented, it did impact the zoning laws in the Russian capital in the subsequent years.[83] Key criticisms of the

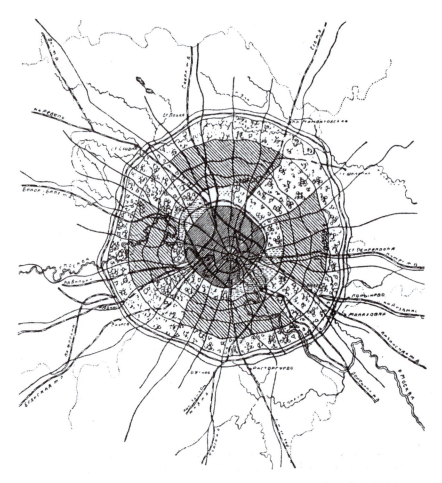

FIGURE 2.16 *Shestakov's plan for Moscow, 1925.* Source: *Shestakov, 1925, cover.*

plan were that most of Moscow's factories would have to be squeezed in the second ring, while suburban housing would be too far away from the central area. Even though property right considerations did not constrict it as much as they would do in the West, the 'incalculable' cost of such an enterprise was clearly an issue. In the end, the work of the commission was discontinued.[84]

The exchange of ideas during the interwar period was by no means solely happening in the West. During Lenin's New Economic Policy (1921–8), numerous subscriptions to Western architectural periodicals came from the USSR, and international visits by Soviet delegations and exhibitions were organized to overcome the perceived state of Soviet backwardness. Bliznakov showed that technical journals received in Russia included the German

Städtebau, the British *Architecture Review* and the US *American Architect*. During this period, foreign exhibitions showcased the works of Walter Gropius, Bruno Taut, Ludwig Hilberseimer and Hugo Haring.[85] By 1931, around forty cities were being planned or constructed in the USSR[86] and due to lack of local expertise at this scale, foreign experts were imported to accelerate the process of industrialization of the country.[87] In the 1930s approximately a thousand foreign architects, half of whom were Germans, went to the USSR to work.[88] As discussed previously, the German experience with the radial model of town expansion and the associated use of green wedges was considerable by that period; an experience that would be carried over to the USSR with the large migration of German professionals.

The planning debates intensified with the publication of the first Five-Year plan in 1928. Fighting for ideological dominance, 'Urbanists' and 'Disurbanists' interpreted socialist principles differently. For Urbanists, guided by the theories of Leonid Sabsovich, the city was the 'social condenser' that would brew the new socialist men and women able to share their time among productive work, cultural development and physical training. For Disurbanists, following Mikhail Okhitovich's theories, the complete integration between man and nature was the ultimate goal and for that to happen all cities should be dissolved and the population dispersed in the territory.[89]

In 1929, the Green City competition for a leisure city for 100,000 people near Moscow attracted the attention of Urbanists and Disurbanists alike. A number of entries took the opportunity as an experimental vehicle for the definition of criteria for the construction of the model Soviet city. If according to Le Corbusier himself, he was the 'first to advocate that the city should be a huge park',[90] he was clearly not alone in this line of thought. Konstantin Melnikov's entry would follow the same principle. His ideal vision embraced the physical and psychological regenerative effects of close contact with nature. It included large tracks of green space comprised of farms, gardens, a forest, a zoo and a wedge-like green space leading to the central hotel in the city, a 'Laboratory of Sleep' (Figure 2.17) – with sleep chambers playing sleep-inducing sounds, diffusing smoothing aromas and containing rocking beds. Amidst the calming influence of nature and the technological apparatus of this retreat, the exhausted workers from Moscow would be able to rest and get cured through sleep.[91] Although the theme of rest has permeated the debates about urban green spaces since the eighteenth century, Melnikov's visionary proposal makes it central to the planning of socialist life.

Differently to Melnikov's idea, some proposals pointed to a blurring of former recognized types of traffic system and green space as attempts to emancipate the socialist city from established forms of the past, and indeed the present. An example of that is Mikhail Barsch and Moisei Ginzburg's plan

FIGURE 2.17 *Melnikov's plan for a Green City, 1929.*

suggesting the dispersion of Moscow's residents along arterial roads, linking the city to the countryside.

The CIAM's increasing preoccupation with the urban scale, visible in the shift from the design of modern housing to the problem of the rational city represented in the discussions of the CIAM 4 and by Le Corbusier's Athens Charter, found in the Green City competition a springboard for explorations leading to the increasing importance of greenery in city plans. Le Corbusier was asked to comment on the entries to the Green City competition and was subsequently invited to provide advice on housing and town planning for Moscow, which he did in the document *Résponse à Moscou* from June 1930, which included plans for its reconstruction. This work was then developed into the *Ville Radieuse*, published in 1936.

In 1930, architects and planners from the various theoretical factions presented model plans for Moscow. Arguably related to the Disurbanists' view, the engineer German Krasin adopted the radio-concentric model and proposed the coordination of ribbon development along radial lines as 'workers colonies', between green wedges, while G. B. Puzis, associated with the League of Contemporary Architects (OSA) led by Ginzburg, would drive green wedges as cultivated parks and woods right into Moscow's core. On the side of the Urbanists standpoint, Stanislav Strumilin, for example, developed a diagram for the decentralization of Moscow in which the city centre retains political, administrative and cultural significance, but production would occur only beyond a green belt that would encircle it. The six production centres would gravitate in a concentric manner beyond the green belt in proximity of residential areas located on strips of development. Green wedges would be interspersed between the built-up fabric, accommodating agricultural and wooded areas.[92]

Planning new cities, rather than transforming the existing ones, was in principle easier to undertake. The Five-Year Plan aimed to found two-hundred industrial and a thousand agrarian cities, for which plans were needed. Urban settlements no larger than 200,000 were preferred in order to find a balance between excessive concentration and dispersal. Ernst May, one of the most important European planners of the interwar period, was invited to move to Russia with his team in 1930 to contribute to this task. His experience in the *Neues Frankfurt* programme and Russian connections qualified him to lead the Soviet city planning efforts. While most of the world was facing the effects of the Great Depression, the prospect of planning entire new cities could not have been more tempting. Up to the end of the first Five Year plan in 1933, the group – usually referred to as 'the May brigade' – planned more than twenty cities, including the steel-producing city of Magnitogorsk.[93] The plan for Magnitogorsk articulated the idea of the provision of *Existenzminimum* (minimum housing), derived from the *Neues Frankfurt* presented at CIAM 2, in 1929, with the contemporary discussions of the most rational way of lot development of CIAM 3. The original plan presented a grid composed by neighbourhood units[94] and was permeated by green spaces. The units were demarcated by horizontal linear green spaces, while the districts were separated by green wedges, which linked the city centre to the proposed green belt (Figure 2.18). One of the main preoccupations of the May brigade was to combat air pollution by dispersing the noxious fumes. The wedges in this case attempted not only to do that but also to enhance connectivity to the countryside and access to green recreational space. The plan was later simplified and the number of wedges reduced. In the end, the overall planning for the city was taken over by a group of Russian architects who made an academic plan in 1934. This step

FIGURE 2.18 *May's brigade plan for Magnitogorsk, 1931.*

away from the inventiveness and experimentation that was found in Russian architecture and planning of the 1920s is accompanied by a tendency towards Socialist Realism, which had been signalled by the winning entry of the Palace of the Soviets competition in 1932. May's plan shrunk further to only one neighbourhood unit.[95] Ironically, today Magnitogorsk is one of the most polluted cities in the world.

According to Mumford, the concept of the 'Functional City', the main theme of CIAM 4 held in 1933, 'was the most significant theoretical approach of CIAM'.[96] CIAM 4 was originally planned to take place in Moscow and provide guidelines for the planning of new cities in the USSR. However, its setting up coincided with the Soviet turn away from modernist principles and the congress was held aboard a cruise ship to Athens. The Athens Charter's, as Le Corbusier's account of the congress became known, presented the four city functions of: dwelling, work, transport and leisure. Under Leisure, very typically for the planning debates of the period, the Charter raised the problem of lack of sufficient green spaces and their distribution away from dense central areas. The demolition of central areas was the proposed solution to bring green spaces into the inner urban fabric. Although specific typologies of green spaces are not articulated in the text, the problem of quantity, distribution and, consequently, access to greenery was a central topic. This was no new recognition of the state of greenery in major Western cities, but it set the scene for future applications of the green wedge idea under the banner of functionalism.

Regardless of affiliation, if on the one hand there was an initial rejection among Soviet planners of forms and city-building processes recognizably Western, on the other hand, however, clearly evident is a struggle to come up with innovative yet feasible urban and anti-urban ideas for building the new socialist settlements, and consequently the new individual. Although there is no question about the creative energy of this period, this internal contradiction contributed to most of the avant-garde proposals being deemed utopian and out-of-touch with the real needs of the industrialization of the country. In those endeavours, the green wedge idea was used both as a pragmatic and as an ideological tool. It provided for a possible organization of the territory in which the whole society would have equal access to greenery, open space, light and fresh air and in which the symbolic boundaries between country and town could be broken, as El Lissitsky sought, pushing civilization into the rural areas as well as bringing nature into the urban realm.

Another question that can be posed is how much of the Soviet experience was a testing ground for the planning activities that were to come in the West in the post-war period, when Europe would get the closest to the *tabula rasa* condition. It will be discussed later how Abercrombie's plans for London started off exactly with the aspiration of coming up with ideal solutions free from the chains of property rights, tight legislation and preoccupation with funding. The British planners' appeal for the nationalization of town and country planning and the decentralization of population and industry may have drawn from the Soviet experience more than commonly acknowledged.

While the question of balancing the relationship between town and country was at the core of attempts to promote the green wedge idea, it can also be argued that its appropriation occurred from different particular standpoints. In British circles, the garden city ideals and the resolution of the metropolitan question were central. Resolving the dichotomy between belts and wedges became a pursuit of many authors. In Germany, the *Stadtlandschaft* concept played a fundamental role in how the search for harmony between nature and built environment were manifested. A variety of proposals tended to fluctuate between these two referential positions. As for the Soviet planning, the green wedge idea appeared fundamentally as a possible means of resolving the opposition between town and country.

This chapter has shown that green wedges had four main functions in the interwar period. First, they had a sanitary role in bringing sunlight, fresh air and greenery to the inner parts of the city. Second, and perhaps most importantly, in a period when the countryside was increasingly distant from the city core, these wedges allowed a direct link from the centre to the open country through pleasant green routes. Third, they were to provide easy access to open space, mainly recreational grounds, to every citizen. And lastly, they were instruments of planning, inasmuch as they could be used as zoning tools to connect or separate areas.

3

Towards a Bright Future: Green Wedge Visions for the Post-war Period

While the inter-war period saw the growth of regional plans, the post-war period in Europe unsurprisingly prioritized the reconstruction of war-damaged cities and the construction of new settlements. A central question was whether cities should be rebuilt as they were or replanned along visionary lines.[1] Moreover, the planning of new towns offered testing grounds for the most up-to-date planning theory. This chapter focuses on the identification of how green wedges were conceptualized in order to help the reconstruction efforts, both in their physical dimension and as symbols of the aspiration for the construction of a more harmonious society in the wake of the war.

London: The green wedge metropolis

The most intensive period of bombing in Britain occurred between September 1940 and May 1941. Planners soon came to the conclusion that cities should not be reconstructed as they were. The widespread war destruction was an opportunity to turn a page in history and devise new visionary plans.[2] The first problem at stake was how replanning would operate. Nationalization of planning, the coordination between town and country planning and decentralization of industry away from congested areas became central for British planners. State-led reconstruction policy was to create the backdrop for the physical and social transformation of the country. One of the first legislative instruments in this direction was the Barlow Report, published in 1940, which recommended the reduction of population from central areas and the decentralization of industry. It presented an opportunity to promote national planning and to consider more efficiently how to control land use. In 1941, the Expert Committee on Compensation and Betterment, the Uthwatt Committee, was established to formulate a legal framework to support the compulsory purchase of areas needed for reconstruction, which indicated that the matter of compensation would not necessarily be an impediment to executing the new plan. A Consultative Panel on Physical Reconstruction followed shortly. In 1942, the Report of the Committee of Land Utilisation in Rural Areas, known as the Scott Report, defended a better coordination of town and country planning and stressed the need to preserve agricultural land.

Property ownership was a clear obstacle to large-scale planning, since compensation due to compulsory purchase could make any visionary planning unviable. Some professionals, such as Donald E. Gibson, Coventry's City Architect and Planning Officer, would argue for 'some form of nationalization of the land' as the 'only solution for Britain'.[3] Similarly, the Director of the Institute for Research in Agricultural Economics at Oxford University, C. S. Orwin, argued that 'whatever way the problem is regarded, it seems impossible to be fair to the community so long as private property in land persists' and that 'acquisition of the freehold of the land by the State … must be accepted as a pre-requisite of planning control'.[4] In fact, nowhere else in Britain was the problem of acquisition of land from private owners and compensation more paramount than in London.

Only a month into the Blitz and the London County Council (LCC) was already discussing alternatives for the future of the capital. These did not exclude such bold solution as, for example, acquiring the entire London. It was indeed suggested that the area to be obtained should not be limited to just the county, but extend to Greater London.[5] Such a step would greatly facilitate the implementation of an ideal plan by overcoming the problem of separate ownerships of property. The council only wondered how long the process could take if they were given 'a free hand and a large staff'.[6] It is not surprising that policy makers and planners in Britain saw the Soviet interwar planning experience as enviable examples of what public ownership of land, centralized power and funding and lack of strict regulations could do to favour idealistic plans in a short period of time.[7]

London's inherited problems were perceived to derive from unplanned growth. Overcrowding, lack of green spaces and their ill-distribution, an obsolete road system, unsanitary conditions, inadequacy of housing supply and a haphazard mixture of incompatible land uses needed to be tackled.[8] On top of this, the war destruction framed the discussions on reconstruction in a manner that polarized visionary planning and reconstruction 'as it was', as two irresolvable options with no gradient between them. Indeed, it was with the focus on bold planning interventions brought up by the war and the promise of government and a legal system support to give planning effective transformative power that many plans for bombed cities would start, including those for London.

Diagraming the future

A number of unsolicited visionary plans for London were published in the early 1940s, some having been in preparation since the late 1930s. This is the case, for instance, of the MARS Group[9] who presented their first plan for London at the CIAM 5 in 1937, led mainly by William Tatton Brown. Its purpose was to 'convert the dynamic that caused unplanned ribbon development into the precursors of a new urban form'. Radial arteries would drive the location and direction of development beyond the urban fringe and the land between them would become green strips. As Gold showed, this could also be applied to the inner areas, where green wedges of countryside could be driven into the heart of the capital, as opposed to implementing a green belt.[10] This was followed by the exhibition *New Architecture* organized in 1938, which included a section on town planning.[11] The group finalized their plan for London by 1939, although it was published only in 1942.

In 1940, Ralph Tubbs, who was the Secretary to the MARS Group and later became a member of the RIBA Reconstruction Committee, prepared another exhibition, this time about the future of living in cities after the Second World War. This led to a publication in 1942 in which he severely criticized the propagation of garden suburbs and urged for the focus to be put on reconstructing the existing cities. Tubbs centred his attention on the case of London, proposing a diagrammatic park system plan. He was adamant about the need to clear space for green areas, irrespectively of whether areas had been bombed or not: 'new green spaces and new parks must be created. Trees can replace the devastation of bombed areas. We must pull down more if necessary'.[12] The term 're-destruction' is used to indicate the need to actively forge the ground upon which to build the new London. Embedded in his proposal is the modernist belief in creating the appropriate environment for the emergence of a new man, healthy and lucid. For that to happen it was paramount to tackle the lack of adequate provision of greenery, sunshine and fresh air into dense urban spaces.

The park system plan contained a series of eighteen green wedges arriving directly at London's core and a round 6-mile-radius (nearly 10 kilometres) parkway connecting them (Figure 3.1). Tubbs's green wedges included the axes of Wimbledon–Battersea, Greenwich–London Bridge, Hampstead Heath–Regents Park (considered by Abercrombie in 1912), and Victoria Park–Lea Valley. Some of them would re-appear in subsequent plans for the

FIGURE 3.1 *Ralph Tubbs' park system plan for London, 1942.* Source: *Tubbs, 1942, 31. Copyright © Ralph Tubbs, 1942. All rights reserved.*

capital, including the RIBA plan and Abercrombie's plans. Tubbs attempted to reconnect the city and the countryside. In a rhetorical tone, he argued: 'Let us regain the thrill of passing from town to country'.[13] Notwithstanding Tubbs' unrestrained wish to carve green spaces out of London's urban fabric, he was aware that, at that time, a local authority could barely afford to buy land and not put it to a profitable use. Tubbs awaited with anticipation a new policy on compensation, which the Uthwatt report was to some extent expected to bring about, as the only way to push forward such a plan.

The MARS plan published in the *Architectural Review* in June 1942 gave green wedges a new dimension. Instead of considering the existing somewhat round urban boundary, it employed the axis of the Thames as the backbone from which sixteenth perpendicular strips of development – intercalated with green wedges – would be placed (Figure 3.2). These green

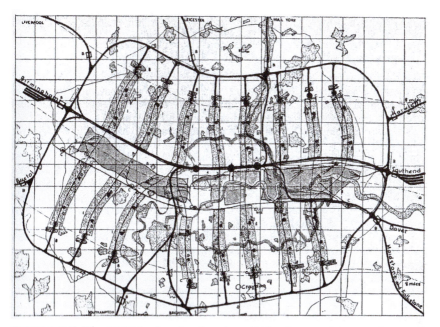

FIGURE 3.2 *The MARS plan for London, 1942.* Source: *Korn and Samuely, 1942, 150.*

spaces would be 'ribbons of open country' penetrating into the heart of the city. A green belt, according to Arthur Korn and Felix Samuely, would be inappropriate to bring open spaces within reach of all residents of London, and would be, therefore, 'of little significance'.[14]

While Tatton Brown and Tubbs alike opted for the most prevalent implementation of green wedges on a predominantly radial plan, the final MARS plan opted for a linear structure. Yet, in terms of the role that green wedges were to play, all three plans assigned them with the same ambitions: to provide continuous green links to the countryside from the inner city, furnish every inhabitant with easy access to urban open space and inundate London with fresh air. None of them allowed leeway to a green belt.

Another proposal in the wave of visionary ideas for London can be found in Lanchester's diagram from 1941. He published a series of articles in *The Builder* in which he offered his views on reconstruction, including a model for large cities.[15] The diagram contained the city core, four green wedges – similarly to Pepler's 1923 diagram – and four built-up areas (Figure 3.3). It intercalated green wedge-housing-industry-housing-green wedge radiating from the city centre, which would allow, according to the author, a reasonable proximity of houses to places of work and open spaces. This diagram was not much different from the one from 1910, but only more explicit about placing

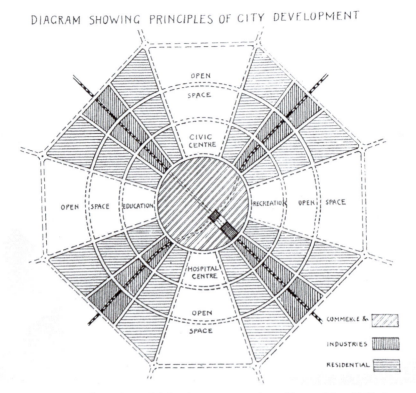

FIGURE 3.3 *Lanchester's model for the reconstruction of large cities, 1941.* Source: *Lanchester, 1941, 569.*

industries along lines of traffic and about the location of key facilities. Perhaps its most striking characteristic was its similarity to the city models put forward by the Hundred New Towns Association.

Its founders included Arthur Trystan Edwards. He joined the department of Civic Design in Liverpool in 1911 and the Ministry of Health after the end of the First World War where he stayed for six years.[16] In 1934, the association published a report advocating the redistribution of the industrial population and the creation of a hundred new towns of 50,000 inhabitants each. It showcased a variety of town model diagrams featuring green wedges.[17] A decade after his seminal work on the creation of new towns, Trystan Edwards would apply the green wedge idea to the reconstruction of London. He studied the implications of the forecasted depopulation and war destruction in the capital and put forward a radical plan for Greater London published in an article in February 1943. The diagram follows very similar principles to Shestakov's 1925 Greater Moscow plan. Like the Russian example, Trystan Edwards proposed a radical reorganization of London into a central area plus four axes of development, with four vast green wedges between them (Figure 3.4). But unlike Shestakov's amalgamation of belts and wedges, for Trystan Edwards, the wedge was still seen as an 'alternative to the Green Belt', an altogether 'new element in urban planning'. According to him, the plan's main idea rested upon two main characteristics: the 'conservative' and the 'radical'. The author argued that most of London's historic structures were located within an area of approximately 8 miles (13 kilometres) extending from east to west and 5.5 miles (9 kilometres) from north to south. Outside it, with few exceptions, he proposed a radical and 'large program of demolition and replacement' to take place. In a special section called 'The Green Wedges', he described the idea as follows:

> To the periphery of the central Metropolitan area it is proposed to introduce four Green Wedges of open country or park. The built-up areas in between the Green Wedges would thus form separate townships associated with the central Metropolitan area, with the result that the pattern of Greater London would be cruciform. The advantage of this arrangement is that no part of the central metropolitan area will be more than four miles [6.4 kilometres] from open country. It might take 50 years or more to clear the Green Wedges of the vast majority of buildings in them, leaving only

FIGURE 3.4 *Trystan Edwards's proposal for the reconstruction of London, 1943.* Source: *Trystan Edwards, 1943, 128.*

certain historic villages and a number of new buildings which might be used for recreational purposes.[18]

According to this proposal, the metropolitan area would end up with 1 million inhabitants and the other wings about one and a half million each. Every township bounded by the green wedges would be replanned as a self-contained entity. The green wedges between the associated townships were not to be used for agricultural purposes, but only as parks and playing fields, with some allocation for aerodromes. The author admitted that it could take '50 or even 100 years to carry out' the plan, but once completed it would provide a 'healthy, convenient and dignified urban life'.[19] This proposal, however speculative, was based on a firm belief that the opportunity had to be taken for a radical change embedding the optimism that was being encouraged on the political stage.

The task of replanning London was also pursued by institutions, such as the RIBA. In May 1941, the RIBA formed a Reconstruction Committee, which included Lanchester, Tubbs, Maxwell Fry, Abercrombie and John Henry Forshaw;[20] and in July, the London Regional Reconstruction Committee (LRRC) was constituted. Its membership comprised nominations from the RIBA and the Architectural Association, and included Arthur Kenyon, Stanley Hamp and Lanchester.[21] In the Second Interim Report from May 1943, the LRRC published a reconstruction plan. The report reiterated many planning tenets from that time, such as the relocation of industry, decentralization, the need for legislation and a national planning authority. The plan suggested the reorganization of London into a series of self-contained communities which would be bound by four ring roads, a number of radial arteries, open space and natural features. The report emphasized that much greater open space should be provided in and around the defined communities and that, with proper planning, the area of open spaces could be nearly doubled. To achieve this, the acquisition of undeveloped land for conversion into public open spaces and a coordinated approach between the different local governments were seen as paramount. The LRRC argued for the establishment of an interconnected system of open spaces, which, among other things, would define the boundaries of communities, allow for the passage of air and uninterrupted routes to the open country:

Open spaces in isolated patches do not provide uninterrupted passage of air which is essential for great populations; it is important that internal open spaces be connected to the open country on the perimeter. Land has, therefore, been cleared along major traffic routes to ensure continuity of open space; it is on this type of development that the LRRC have based much of their planning.[22]

The Lea Valley-Epping Forest axis is mentioned as an example of a continuous green space linking London and the countryside. It is worth noting that this location is selected by the LRRC as a 'test area' for the implementation of their open space strategy. This axis would form a wedge from Finchley through to Hampstead (Figure 3.5). The funnelling of fresh air into the city, the link to

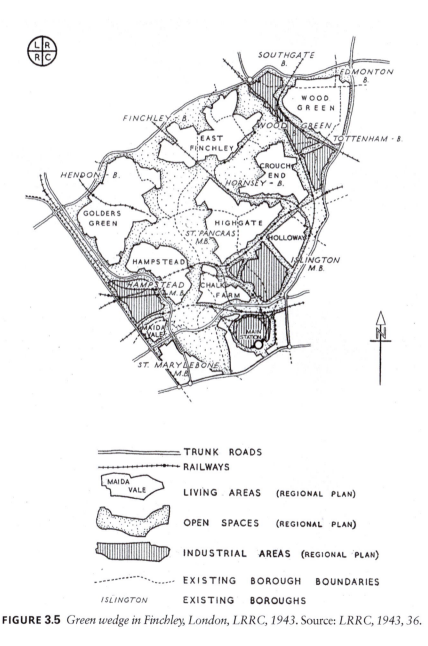

TRUNK ROADS

RAILWAYS

LIVING AREAS (REGIONAL PLAN)

OPEN SPACES (REGIONAL PLAN)

INDUSTRIAL AREAS (REGIONAL PLAN)

EXISTING BOROUGH BOUNDARIES

EXISTING BOROUGHS

FIGURE 3.5 *Green wedge in Finchley, London, LRRC, 1943.* Source: *LRRC, 1943, 36.*

radial arteries and the provision of green connections to the open country were principles to be achieved. The LRRC report expands on the subject:

> It is considered that open spaces radiating from the centre to the perimeter are essential to form tracks to and from the heart of the metropolis ... it would be possible, starting from the centre of London, to walk, through green ways free from close contact with buildings, into the open country. Thus the country could be brought into closer relationship with the town. There should be no necessity ever again to admit that there are children in London who had never seen a wild flower or a grazing animal until they were evacuated into the country.

The LRRC's work was disseminated mostly through the publication of the report and an exhibition. As Larkham showed, the exhibition panel 'The London of the Future' detailed the plan's subdivision of urban areas into self-contained communities by the traffic arteries, the River Thames and green spaces.[23] It is noticeable that a number of potential green wedges mentioned in the previous decades reappeared here, such as the axes Hampstead-Finchley and the Lea Valley-Epping Forest. The Thames became a vast green wedge in East London, leading out into its estuary.

It is noteworthy to point out that the link between green spaces and traffic arteries, envisioned as edges of reconstructed autonomous communities, present in the LRRC plan would later find resonance in the County of London Plan and the Greater London Plan.[24] The most substantial contribution of the LRRC plan to the debates about green wedges is in fact the focus on the original principle of association with traffic arteries. At the same time, green wedges still served as linking elements between city and countryside and as channels for injecting greenery, fresh air and sunlight into the inner core of London. This is done at large scale with the east-west green wedge along the Thames.

The County of London Plan 1943

Alongside these unsolicited proposals, commissioned plans for the capital were being developed. The London County Council (LCC) started considering the future of London as early as 1940. Two alternatives were at issue: to rebuild London as it was or to 'redevelop the whole of London on an ideal scheme'. Lewis Silkin, who was then an MP and would later become the Minister of Town and Country Planning, urged the council to be visionary, stating that 'London must not be rebuilt as it was before the war. We have a great opportunity and we must take it'.[25] The LCC's first draft of the 'Memorandum on Replanning and Reconstruction of London' affirmed that the war damage provided not only the opportunity but also 'the excuse (if such [was] needed) for combining replanning with reconstruction'.[26] It is worth mentioning that Silkin had been on a town planning tour in the Soviet Union in 1937, while he was the Chairman of the Housing Committee of the LCC and a member of its Town Planning Committee, which may have enthused him to push for an unrestrained plan for London. The LCC Architect, Frederick Robert Hiorns was also in favour of a major replanning, as there was a 'case for comprehensive improvement on bold lines'.[27] Later Lord Latham, the Leader of the LCC, corroborated this view stating that London should not incur the same 'mistake' twice:

> Wren's great plan for the City, after the Fire, was never put into execution. Clashes between irreconcilable interests supervened. Neither this nor any other condition must be allowed to prevent the carrying out of the twentieth-century plan of London.[28]

At the end of 1940, there was a feeling at the LCC that 'financial difficulties must not stand in the way' of the creation of a new London.[29] The process for the definition of a plan was swiftly set in motion. In March 1941, the Ministry of Works asked the LCC and the City of London to draw up reconstruction plans 'without paying much attention to existing town planning law'[30] as a new legal framework was being formulated. In 1940, the Barlow Report signalled that the redistribution of population and industries away from London would be pursued. Furthermore, the establishment of the Uthwatt Committee in 1941 further suggested that a radical new plan could indeed come to be implemented. This meant, respectively, that London could be replanned much more 'spaciously' – as it would accommodate fewer people – and that large-scale moves, which would be convenient, for instance, for the update of the traffic system and the creation of large green spaces, would no longer be irresolvable matters due to litigation over compulsory purchase of land. The development of this legal framework forged the initial conditions for the application of the green wedge idea in London.

Abercrombie, who was professor of Town Planning at University College London and the most prominent name in British planning at the time, was appointed in April to draw up the plan with the LCC Architect J. H. Forshaw.[31] The main aspirations of the LCC plan were to reorganize London into a series of self-sufficient communities, to separate conflicting land uses, update the housing stock, improve the traffic system and to create a comprehensive park system.

The need for more green spaces and their coordination into a linked system was presented as a response to a number of considerations. Firstly, more green spaces would allow for a more spacious, and therefore healthier and more modern, environment. This would guarantee an adequate influx of fresh air and access to sunlight and provide recreational spaces throughout the entire county. Secondly, they would create, predominantly through the use of green wedges, a direct connection to the countryside. Thirdly, wedges of greenery would help form the proposed community boundaries and establish buffer zones along lines of traffic.

Bearing in mind that the tuberculosis death-rate and the infant mortality rate in London were 50 per cent higher than the average of, for instance, the boroughs and urban districts in Hertfordshire,[32] planning 'spaciously' – with generous provision of green spaces and their adequate distribution – was seen as the key to achieving a healthy environment. At a lecture given at the Royal Sanitary Institute in November 1943, Forshaw expressed the view that the main aim of town planning was 'to secure the health and welfare of the people in their homes, at work and in their leisure' and that 'a more generous spacing of buildings' would allow 'the unpolluted air and sunlight to exert their beneficial effects'.[33] At the beginning of the war, the average open space provision for some of the largest cities in England was less than 3 acres (12,140 square metres) per 1,000 people.[34] The plan set out to provide the more generous ratio of 4 acres (16,187 square metres) of open space per 1,000 inhabitants in the inner areas and three more in the outer zones, reaching a standard of 7 acres (28,328 square metres). This would have, at least, doubled the amount of green spaces in the capital.[35]

The issue of open space referred to not only their quantity but also their appropriate distribution and organization into a system. One of the plan's objectives was thus to 'provide a properly coordinated system of parks throughout the whole County with continuous green wedges or parkways leading out to the Green Belt and linked at the centre by an inner "Green Ring"'(Figure 3.6).[36] The intention was to finally make green wedges the driving force of the new park system for London. According to Abercrombie and Forshaw, 'the existing open spaces within the County and beyond [were] already loosely grouped in the form of wedges ... happily to be found between the radiating sprawl of outer London' and any development in these spaces would be 'strategically disastrous'. As a result, the park system plan for the county was indeed to be 'a practical application of the theory of the green wedges'.[37]

The plan argued that 'the Green Belt and surrounding countryside need bringing more into the centre through green wedges formed by the existing undeveloped public land',[38] while parkways along the ring roads would give access from one wedge to another. The park system was to be organized on different scales (Figure 3.7) and create a framework starting from the smallest and most local open spaces and expanding all the way to the

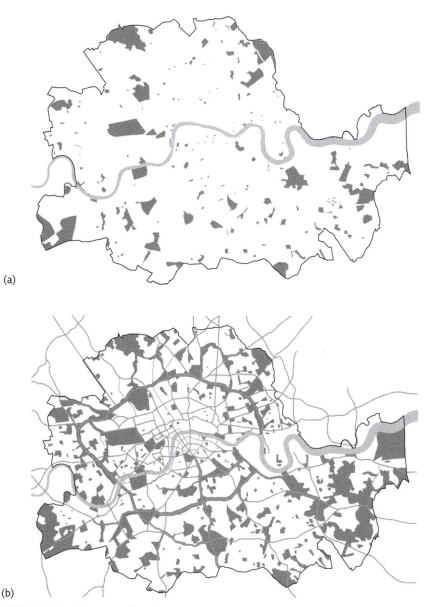

(a)

(b)

FIGURE 3.6 *Diagram of (a) the existing open space and (b) the park system plan of the LCC plan. Based on Abercrombie and Forshaw, 1943, Plate XI – Existing Open Spaces (between 40 and 41) and open space plan (between 46 and 47).*

countryside. In essence, the plan's ambition was that the dweller could get from doorstep to open country through an easy flow of open space: 'from garden to park, from park to parkway, from parkway to green wedge and from green wedge to Green Belt'.[39]

The plan described thirteen areas to be transformed into green wedges leading towards the green belt, including the axes St. James's Park–Greenford, Regent's Park–Hampstead Heath, Victoria Park–Lea Valley, Wanstead Flats–Epping Forest; Ruskin Park–Crystal Palace and a couple radiating out of Greenwich Park, among others.[40]

As in the RIBA LRRC plan, linking green spaces with the traffic system was adopted in the County of London Plan. For Forshaw, 'an essential protection the community needs is against the danger and noise of through traffic – a protection to be secured by a precinctual arrangement of roads or the presence of open spaces and green wedges as buffers between built-up areas'.[41] Greenery would be buffer zones between the communities, encouraging their identity and breaking up the urban form. Most importantly, green wedges would help separate residential areas from the main lines of traffic as well as from areas of unwanted proximity such as factories.

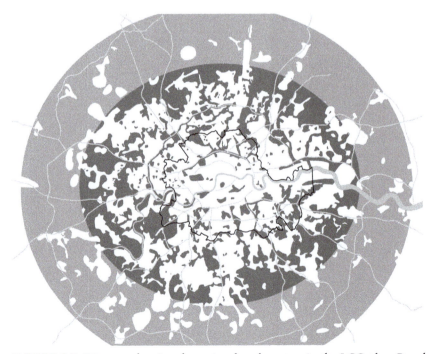

FIGURE 3.7 *Diagram showing the regional park system in the LCC plan. Based on Abercrombie and Forshaw, 1943, Plate XII – Regional Park system (between 40 and 41).*

It was anticipated that allotments would become a 'war necessity' and that the demand would eventually decline with peacetime. The plan is rather dismissive of them, suggesting that they be dispersed within the residential areas, as their concentration had 'negligible, if any, amenity value'.[42]

The idealism of the park system plan resonated positively with the local authorities and other bodies who had been requested to send their comments about the plan back to the LCC by the end of 1943.[43] Some prominent individuals and social actors also supported the scheme, such as the Chief Officer of the Parks Department; the RIBA, which noted that the allocation of 4 acres of open space per 1,000 inhabitants was reasonable providing that additional 3 acres were allocated in the outer zone; the Minister of Town and Country Planning, who welcomed the proposal and suggested that the amount of green space should even be increased to more than 4 acres wherever possible; the Minister for Agriculture and Fisheries, asking for allotments to be considered in addition to the four-acre standard. Some others, such as the Town and Country Planning Association, thought that this standard was in fact far too low.[44]

However, if in 1940 there was an overall feeling of idealism in the political spheres as well as in the architects' visions, by 1943 questions over the plan's feasibility and the financial implications of its realization tinted the debates. There were those more directly involved with financial matters in the LCC who cried for restraint. For instance, A. R. Wood, the Comptroller of the Council, argued in a report from May 1943 that the realization of the plan would be an 'impossible achievement' without much enlarged financial resources made available. Wood was concerned that much rateable value had been lost with the bombing and more still would be lost if a substantially larger area was reserved for open spaces. In addition, national economic support was elusive and viewed with suspicion. If the provision of 4 acres per 1,000 people was to be achieved, then one-fifth of the whole area of the county would need to be public open space and this 'would involve capital expenditure nearly as large as the Council had spent on the whole of its housing operations during the fifty years up to 1939'.[45] Herbert Westwood, the Valuer, was no less dismayed by the proposed green space provision and urged the Council not to commit to 'carry out any of the proposals in the plan', as the cost was 'incalculable'.[46] Westwood went on to warn that even if assuming that these proposals were only tentative and diagrammatic, 'the publication of the Plan may be a cause of embarrassment to the Council'.[47] Against this advice, the plan was in fact published in July 1943 and exhibited to the public for two months. To break the impasse, Forshaw suggested in 1944 that an interim target standard of 2.5 acres (10,117 square metres) would be a good compromise and highlighted that Abercrombie was in 'full agreement' with this measure.[48] This was accepted as a phase towards the seven-acre target for 'ultimate achievement'.[49]

Although disputed and not implemented, the green wedge-based park system in the LCC plan acted as a precursor to the Greater London Plan 1944. The LCC plan set forward the principle of articulating a park system from neighbourhood to regional scale. It converted the wedge-like gaps between development along traffic lines and river valleys into the basis upon which to build a comprehensive system of greenery for London.

The Greater London Plan 1944

Soon after the LCC started working on its plan, discussions about the need to plan regionally emerged. In September 1941, in a meeting that included Abercrombie, Pepler and Forshaw, it was noted that the 'outside authorities were highly suspicious' of the LCC plan and to avoid a lack of coordination that an avalanche of local plans could generate, Abercrombie should be asked to carry out a plan over the Greater London area on behalf of the Standing Conference on London Regional Planning.[50] Given the fact that the scope of the LCC plan was restricted to the arbitrarily created borders of the county and excluding also the jurisdiction of the City Corporation, the Greater London Plan provided the opportunity to resolve the regional question already posed in the 1920s.[51]

The ideas of population relocation beyond the outer green belt, control of London's growth and the improvement of inner city standards were developed and embraced more fully in the Greater London Plan. It assumed that Greater London's population would not increase above the 1938 figure of about 10 million people and that decentralization should occur by relocating a million people from the inner ring to expanded towns and eight new satellite towns, which were to be built 50 miles (80 kilometres) away from London's core. Abercrombie proposed establishing four rings to structure the general master plan, the first encompassing the inner central area, the second circling London at around 12 miles (20 kilometres) from Charing Cross, the third being the 'Green Belt Ring' with a mix of playing fields and farms, and the fourth the 'Outer Country Ring'. Moreover, he proposed that the transformation of the existing city should happen mainly by improvements made to the traffic system, the formation of self-sufficient communities and the provision of a comprehensive park system.

The Greater London Plan presented a considerably more elaborate park system than the London County Council plan. It prescribed a standard of 10 acres (40,469 square metres) per 1,000 people, as opposed to 7 acres in the LCC plan. It also presented a more developed description of the system's main ambitions, functions and components, while pursuing similar overarching principles of using green spaces to control sprawl, provide salubrious spaces for recreation, create continuous connections to the countryside and define self-sufficient communities.

Abercrombie determined that London should not grow beyond its 1939 fringe and that a green belt should be established as a way of guaranteeing this. However, the green belt would not stand in isolation in regard to the rest of London's open spaces, but be linked to them as part of a park system. It must be remembered that one of Abercrombie's reoccurring core preoccupations regarding the provision of a park system for London's region was the lack of connectivity between the built-up centre and the verge of the urbanized area. Making use of Howard's term, he assumed that the country was the real 'magnet' attracting Londoners and that it would generate a 'centrifugal urge to fly from bricks and mortar and get into the country'.[52] Arguably London's lack of green spaces had reached a point that required 'taking children out in buses to Outer London to see its green fields'. This would be a 'further indication of the necessity of keeping Outer London's open spaces free of building'.[53]

Ultimately, the park system merged belts and wedges. It would consist of typologies covering a range of scales. The idea of allowing residents to go from their house in the inner city to the open countryside through green spaces – formerly put forward in the LCC plan – was pursued. Abercrombie alerted the reader that many green wedges – or 'interpenetrating wedges of varied open land'[54] – could have been created in the past, but little had been done in this respect. He warned that the clock was ticking and it was time to act. Hence, any land leading from the heart of London to the open country considered essential for the creation of green wedges was to be bought, kept free from building and be open to the public.

Twenty-four green wedges connecting the first and the third rings were proposed (Figure 3.8). They were described in Appendix 20. It is worth noting that the plan had only two appendices that referred to green spaces: 'Open Spaces Survey and Proposals' (Appendix 19) and 'Green Wedges-Proposals' (Appendix 20), with no appendix for green belts. This suggests the comparative importance that Abercrombie attached to the wedges and their implementation. The green wedges ranged from long to short, continuous to broken and were, as much as possible, to be converted into public recreation zones and playing fields. The plan incorporated all the green wedges delimited in the LCC plan, to which it added eleven more. Similarly to the RIBA LRRC plan, it considered the River Thames one of the green wedges; in Abercrombie's words: 'the finest natural wedge into London'.[55] Indeed, river valleys, considered 'very valuable as green wedges of lungs to towns in their vicinity', were to function as green wedges throughout Greater London (Figure 3.9). In addition, they were also of 'great value in maintaining

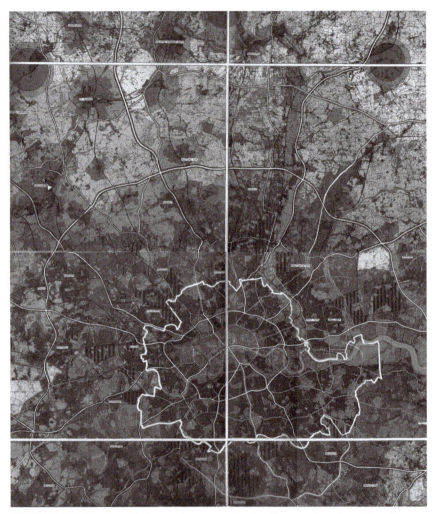

FIGURE 3.8 *Section of the park system in the Greater London Plan.* Source: *Abercrombie, 1945.*

the physical separation between expanding communities, and thereby helping to maintain and emphasize their independent community life'.[56]

By this time, large open spaces were seen as worthy allies in times of war. Abercrombie, in his plan for Plymouth published in 1943, stated that 'parks and town gardens could withstand bombing and fire better than our solid buildings' and that war had brought forward the advantage of more spacious planning, which would lessen the effect of aerial attack and provide emergency land that could be converted into allotments to reinforce food supplies.[57] Green wedges here would help break up the mass of buildings, minimize the proliferation of fire, increase the dissipation of smoke, provide escape routes and congregation points in the event of attack and be available for temporary conversion into allotments.

It appeared that this plan might be the one to get implemented after the war. In December 1944, the Minister of Town and Country Planning forwarded copies of the plan to the local authorities and the county councils for consideration. Their views were then submitted to the Advisory Committee for London Regional Planning, formed to coordinate Abercrombie's plan.[58] A series of sub-committees was set up, including one focusing on open spaces. This sub-committee delved into the range of scales of the open spaces provision in Abercrombie's plan and ultimately supported the whole scheme.[59] The Advisory Committee then reported to Silkin, the Minister of Town and Country Planning, who subsequently circulated a memorandum setting out his views on the Committee's report back to the local authorities and county councils to help them develop detailed schemes for their particular areas.

Silkin himself thought that the plan seemed feasible, if still 'modest relative to need'.[60] The Minister was in agreement with the standard for open space prescribed in the Greater London Plan and expressed his intention to 'prepare a plan to show the land around London, which, as green belt or green wedges, must be preserved from development'. He also expressed his contentment over the fact that the Open Spaces Sub-Committee fully supported the proposals for green wedges within the region. For Silkin, the preservation of the green wedges was essential. They were seen as particularly vulnerable owing to the pressure for housing and for the expansion of existing industries after the end of the conflict. Therefore, he emphasized 'the necessity for the same strong action as will be required in safeguarding the green belt'. Silkin made clear his adherence to the idea of green wedges and committed to their implementation:

> [P]lanning authorities should not permit any development on land shown for retention as greenbelt or green wedges, unless they have proved to the satisfaction of the Minister that there is an unanswerable case for reconsideration of the boundaries.[61]

Despite Abercrombie's and Silkin's efforts to call attention to the green wedges and to keep them building-free, the idealism behind the possibility of radically transforming London was eventually shaken by legal constraints and lack of funding. Although the formation of the Ministry of Town and Country Planning in 1943 meant a move towards the coordination of planning also at national level, the 1943 and 1944 Town and Country Planning Acts, which gave new powers to local authorities for the acquisition of land, were perceived as unsatisfactory.[62] Lord Latham, leader of the LCC, considered the 1944 Act as a 'great betrayal' and a 'triumph of the rights of property'.[63]

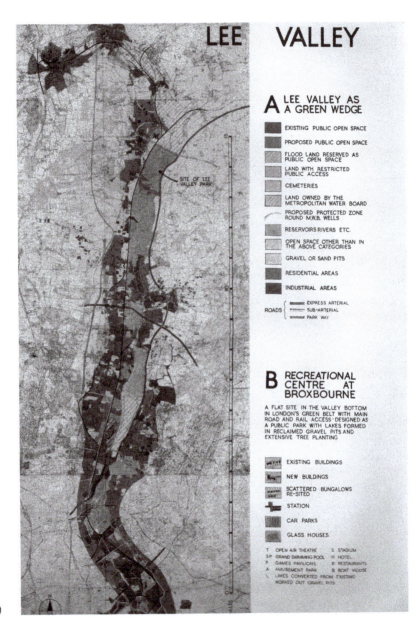

(a)

(b)

FIGURE 3.9 *(a) Plan and (b) view of the Lea Valley Green Wedge.* Source: *Abercrombie, 1945, Plate Lee Valley and Plate: The Lee Valley Green Wedge, Looking south towards London (before 171).*

With the end of the war, the economic crisis and the consequent limitation in funding, the focus was on the overwhelming need for housing and other aspects of reconstruction, rather than on radical replanning.

The war had brought with it the feeling that the time had come to end the negative effects of London's unplanned growth. Visionary plans relied on the conviction that in the long term the benefits of radical reconstruction would greatly outweigh its enormous costs. Green wedges were very much part of those radical reconstruction ideas. They became symbols of hope for a better and brighter future. At the same time as they offered opening up a physical path to the remote countryside, they were also allegories of the search for a balanced society in harmonious contact with nature. Another specific contribution of the war-time planning reflections to the post-war context was the growing importance of open space in times of conflict. Spacious planning was seen as a pre-emptive move against air raids and the demise of large populations. Here again green wedges would help avoid the proliferation of fire in the city and serve as congregation points and escape routes. In this context, they could also become temporary allotments to support food supply. With the national preoccupation with agricultural land and the need to consider town and country planning jointly in the 1940s, discourses about considering the wedges as tracts of nature or agricultural land arriving from beyond the urban fringe became stronger, and were particularly evident in the Greater London Plan. An elaboration on a previous function can be seen in the growing importance of wedges in zoning, particularly in their use as buffer zones between traffic arteries and residential areas, as well as boundaries of communities.

Although green wedges had been discussed by British planners for decades, few examples of their implementation could be seen. If green wedges were to go from the open country to the inner core, they needed to cut through numerous privately owned properties and administrative boundaries. These, coupled with difficulty in controlling intra-urban development, problematized their planning and most of all any attempt at their potential execution. In some other countries where public ownership of land at large scale was customary, the implementation of green wedges tended to be facilitated. In Britain, however, the lack of a legal apparatus and the economic crisis that came with the end of the war only added to the problems that needed to be overcome to implement green wedges in London. Notwithstanding that the idea did not materialize in the capital as planned, green wedges gained a boost of popularity in the new towns. Being able to plan from scratch, with the support of the New Towns Committee, and to count on the economic and legal powers bestowed upon the new towns' corporations undoubtedly helped make green wedges a reality.

Trying to understand the reconstruction debates without considering the significance that contemporary planners ascribed to green wedges is to see only a partial picture of the multifaceted nature of what planning a 'new London' meant at that time.

Other British cities

As Larkham and Lilley showed, replanning was undertaken not only by bombed towns but also by those where little or no damage had occurred.[64] In 1941, Lord Reith, the Minister of Works and Planning between 1940 and 1942, lectured in many bombed cities, such as Manchester, Coventry, Southampton, Plymouth and Portsmouth, encouraging local governments to 'plan boldly' and 'comprehensively'.[65] For example, Manchester started its replanning process in 1943, publishing a plan in 1945. A section entitled 'Green Wedges' in chapter 10 on 'Public Spaces' in that plan presented the idea almost as a tenet:

It is generally agreed that in order to obtain the greatest possible value from new open spaces any attempt should be made to bring the countryside into the city by extending wedges of greenery from a green belt on the boundary towards the central area.[66]

R. Nicholas, the author of the plan, pointed out that although the wedges should continue into the city centre, in the case of Manchester that would prove too costly, and so he suggests that from the 'Intermediate Ring Road' these green spaces should continue inwards in the form of 'major and minor parkways, linked up with existing and proposed parks to form a continuous system'. For the model to work in the densely built-up areas, the wedges needed to be malleable.

Under the 1947 Town and Country Planning Act, development plans were to be drawn up by cities and counties and updated not less often than every five years, and submitted to the Minister for approval. Permission became required for development, as the local authorities controlled land use. In the wake of this, development plans were created across the country. An example can be found in William Holford's study for the County of Cambridgeshire. A former architect graduate from the University of Liverpool, Holford succeeded Abercrombie as Professor of Civic Design there in 1937 and from 1948 at University College London. Holford's plan, from 1950, stated the case for limiting Cambridge's growth, but allowing for a band of development land for the University in the west. Green wedges were to penetrate into the heart of Cambridge. As Healey showed, the plan shaped the city's pattern of development in the following forty years and the green wedges became the basis of the formation of the Cambridge green belt.[67]

New towns and green spaces

Having been on the planning debates for decades, the campaign for the construction of new towns is well documented, but an overview is needed if only to highlight the conditions that allowed new towns to be central to planning theory and practice during the war and in the post-war years. With the end of the Second World War, some of the responses to the fundamental question of what cities should be like could now be put into practice. The English experience soon became a worldwide reference. One cannot ignore that creating new towns as a solution to the problems of the industrial city had a significant precedent with the publication of Howard's garden city idea in 1898, and the subsequent construction of Letchworth and Welwyn Garden City. New towns were also an expectation following the First World War, as Osborn corroborated with the publication in 1918 of *New Towns after the War*, which envisaged the construction of a hundred new towns.[68] The claim was pursued in the 1930s as exemplified by Trystan Edwards's work in the Hundred New Towns Association. It is worth remembering that in the summer of 1937 the Town and Country Planning Association organized a major exhibition, 'The Satellite Towns Exhibition',[69] aiming to influence the course of post-war reconstruction policy. By 1940, the distribution of industry and population away from large cities had become an official recommendation. This was made manifest in Abercrombie's Greater London Plan, which suggested the creation of eight towns around the capital to take overspill population and in the development of other policies such as the New Towns Act 1946.

In October 1945, the New Towns Committee was appointed with Lord Reith as the chairman, and soon produced two interim reports and a final report, published in July 1946.[70] The New Towns Act followed the same year, allowing the Minister of Town and Country Planning to designate sites for new towns. The Ministry was also in charge of appointing and funding a development corporation for each new town and of approving all the master plans. With political support and appropriate legislation in place, work could commence. There were three phases of new town designation. In the first, between 1946 and 1950, fourteen new towns were designated: eight around London to serve the capital's overspill, two in north-east England, one in south Wales, two in central Scotland and one attached to a pre-war steel works.[71] The second phase presented a rather meagre counting with only Cumbernauld in Scotland being designated between 1950 and 1961, but the third phase, encompassing the period from 1961 to 1970, saw the designation of further fourteen new towns.

A committee of officials under Pepler worked out the basic principles for planning new towns and the various ways of getting them built,[72] which were then laid out in the *Final Report of the New Towns Committee*. Some of the new towns' expected characteristics, at which the committee arrived, included small-to-medium size, low-density and copious open spaces. The guidelines for the provision of open space took into account the recommendation of the *National Playing Fields Association,* which was the norm at the time, of 7 acres per 1,000 people, with a minimum of 10 acres.[73] A 1966 survey of open spaces in ten of the first new towns showed that in fact all of the studied towns had a total amount of open space well above that ratio, ranging from 11 acres (44,515 square metres) per 1,000 to 28 acres (113,312 square metres) per 1,000 inhabitants. Moreover, in many new towns open space was the second-largest land use after residential land.[74]

The idea of transforming the landscape into a positive element of planning, which had been so thoroughly defended by individual actors such as Unwin and Eberstadt, is elaborated further in plans for the post-war new towns. Frederick Gibberd went as far to proclaim that 'the idea of landscape as land not built on, mere open spaces, a negative element, is dying; in the new towns it is buried'.[75] There was a strong intention in the *Final Report of the New Towns Committee* that the green spaces should be linked together and considered holistically within park systems, with surrounding open areas to be used mainly for agricultural purposes. With regard to the traffic system, it was recommended that radial roads formed the boundaries of neighbourhoods. The report further recommended that whenever green wedges were planned, they should be linked to the traffic system:

> If the conception of the plan included a wedge or wedges of open space connecting with the green belt, or a parkway in a valley, it would be advantageous, if practicable, to site a radial road or part of the outer ring road therein. Such a road may also run through or alongside a park or woodland reserve.[76]

Although the issue of connectivity between town and country did not acquire the same level of significance for new towns as it did for London, since their medium size naturally facilitated contact with the country, green wedges were still used for this purpose. Total separation between town and countryside was not an absolute directive. The report suggested that the landscape treatment could be varied, according to the situation, recommending either that the boundaries of new towns blended with the surrounding open country, by the use of green wedges, or that they stood in sharp contrast with it:

> In one case it may be desirable to merge the town quietly into the surrounding landscape, by planting ecologically related to what exists already, with green wedges penetrating from outside into the town area. In another it may be better that the town should stand out sharply from its rural setting, a clearly defined boundary accentuating the distinction between country and town.[77]

As mentioned before, all the plans for new towns had to be approved by the Ministry. This meant that general post-war planning principles supported by the New Towns Committee's report – such as the idea of neighbourhood units, green belts and green wedges – were largely followed. As a matter of fact, it has been suggested that the first-phase plans observed the recommendations of the New Towns Committee[78] too strictly and that the later plans were able to have more freedom in their design choices. Green wedges can be seen across the timeframe of the new towns, as for instance in the cases of Harlow, Stevenage, Crawley, Hemel Hempstead, Basildon, Runcorn and Corby.[79]

Harlow was one of the original satellite towns proposed by Abercrombie's Greater London Plan. Upon designation in 1947, Gibberd was appointed by the Ministry of Town and Country Planning to prepare a master plan for Harlow considering a population of 60,000 people.[80] In an article on his vision, Gibberd summarized the 'accepted canons of planning', arguing that 'the technical solutions' to the problems of designing such a town consisted of the separation of zones, their connection to an effective road system and the definition of a green belt. With regard to the latter, however, Gibberd saw Howard's green belt as an original state of what became known as green wedges:

> Ebenezer Howard's agricultural ring is now a partial solution only. The agricultural land requires to be extended into the town itself in the form of tongues or wedges separating areas of building. The size and shape of these wedges is largely a matter of aesthetic selection once the space-needs of farm units and the connecting links to the agricultural hinterland have been determined.[81]

Gibberd explored further the notion of connecting urban areas to the countryside making a case for linking up the 'footpath system with the green wedges' in order to enable the inhabitants 'to walk out of the town from their own neighbourhood without traversing any other area of bricks and mortar'.[82]

In his plan for Harlow (Figure 3.10), Gibberd located the city centre on a hill to the north of the site, defined neighbourhood units of 6,000 to 15,000 inhabitants clustered into districts, which in turn were bordered by

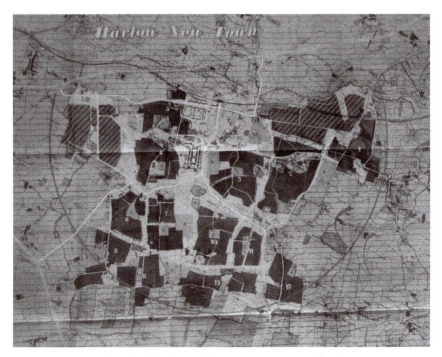

FIGURE 3.10 *Gibberd's plan for Harlow, 1947.* Source: *Gibberd, 1947.*

green wedges leading out to the countryside. The east and west 'agricultural wedges' were linked together by a natural valley with the town centre as their focus.[83] The wedges were instrumental features to break up the mass of buildings, separating zones and, particularly, giving shape to the districts. Gibberd rendered them the backbone of Harlow's open space system.

The approach of using natural features such as river valleys to transform them into green wedges was also adopted in plans for other new towns, as for example in Hemel Hempstead. The Development Corporation set up in 1947 had the task to increase the town population from 20,000 to 60,000. The landscape architect G. A Jellicoe was appointed to develop a plan, which was exhibited already the same year. Taking advantage of the valley of the River Gade, Jellicoe defined a green wedge connecting the countryside directly into the town centre. In Stevenage, first new town to be designated, the Fairlands Valley Park acts in a similar manner. Even in the smallest new town-to-be, Hatfield, planned for a population of 25,000, green wedges made a mark. Lionel Brett Esher, the author of the plan, in a later interview reflected upon the dichotomy between belts and wedges, stating that:

> I have since come to think that it would have been better to have abandoned the idea of the green belt and let London grow in certain tentacles, which is what cities always wanted to do, keeping wedges of greenery in-between them; and that would have been closer to what people want, whilst you are bringing wedges of the countryside as close to the heart as you could.[84]

Another notable instance of transforming natural features for green wedges is the new town of Runcorn, planned by Arthur Ling. Ling was a communist architect and planner who held important roles within planning departments in London. He had visited the Soviet Union in 1939, was secretary of the MARS' group Town Planning Committee and joined the LCC to work with Forshaw in 1941. Subsequently, he played an important role in the preparation of the LCC plan and became the leader of the Town Planning Division of the Architect's Department in 1945.[85] In his plan for Runcorn, a large green wedge was located in a valley extending to Manchester Ship Canal.

The British experience in the replanning of London and the planning of new towns influenced many planning experiments across the world. After Abercrombie retired from his Professorship at University College London in 1946, he worked in a regional plan for Colombo in 1948 and undertook planning consultancies in Malta, Hong Kong, Cyprus and Ethiopia.[86] As Home showed, the new town idea was applied in many colonies, including Hong Kong, Singapore, Malaysia and India.[87] In Israel, forty new towns were established in the years up to 1964 (ten of which were built between 1949 and 1950) and, as Aran-Glikson points out, in these new towns 'the green belts separating the neighbourhoods from each other are often developed to green wedges, creating a natural connection between the town centre and the surrounding landscape'.[88]

New towns and the green wedge idea were spreading closer to Britain too. Tapiola, in Finland, for instance, built in the early 1950s, was laid out with a centre and residential areas grouped along neighbourhood-unit principles to the east, west and north divided by large green wedges, similarly to Harlow. As Hall showed, in Finland the evocative term 'Forest Town' was intentionally used to describe the search for an organic integration of new suburbs and satellite towns built around 1960.[89] Attempts to greatly increasing the provision of greenery in cities fast became widespread internationally. For the German architect and urban planner Hans Bernard Reichow – who in 1948 developed the concept of *Stadtlandschaft* in his book *Organische Stadtbaukunst: Von der Großstadt zur Stadtlandschaft* (The Organic Art of Building Towns: From the Big City to the City Landscape) – living in close relationship with nature was a necessity for the betterment of people. Reichow advocated that such connection between man and nature should happen at different scales, from the residential cells, through neighbourhoods, to districts, similar to Abercrombie's adaptation in the Greater London Plan of Perry's neighbourhood unit concept into communities and districts.[90] The presence of green wedges in his concept is multi-layered. They defined the central spine in neighbourhoods, from which the residential cells branch off. And as organisms grow, so would the city. Laid out as compound leaves, the radial built up areas could extend if necessary. Between them, green wedges would be formed. The green spaces would be mostly forested and destined for food production.

In 1954, he received the commission for a new town of approximately 2,000 dwellings: Sennestadt, which would become one of the most significant new town plans of the post-war period in Germany to be based on the concept of *Stadtlandschaft*.[91] In this plan, Reichow proposed the creation of two green wedges: one running east-west and the other running north-south along the axis of the Bullerbach River valley, which together divided the town into four districts. These wedges were designed mostly as parks, containing various sports, leisure and educational facilities, but some allotments were also planned. At the centre of the north-south wedge, as in Taut's *Die Stadtkrone*, Reichow located the 'crown of the city': a civic centre. It is evident that in Reichow's vision blending nature and city involved the proposition of green wedges. They were not only a way of zoning and ensuring the residents' proximity to nature, but a principle aimed at overcoming the dichotomies man-nature, city-countryside, leading to higher standards of living and human development.[92]

Planning new beginnings

In Germany, planning discussions in the 1940s were also shaped by the needs of reconstruction. Similarly to the British case, questions over rebuilding cities as they were versus reconstructing them along ideal lines predominated. Visionary plans were spacious, allowing residents to benefit more plentifully from access to sunlight, greenery and fresh air. Not only did this approach in German reconstruction draw from Abercrombie's plans and the British new towns, but it also pointed to the pursuit of the *Stadtlandschaft*, the city-landscape. Within this framework, the biological reference of the city as a living organism reappeared as a conceptual field. This was influenced by the garden city movement and the work of pre-war individual actors such as Robert Schmidt, Patrick Geddes and Fritz Schumacher.

It is worth pointing out, however, that such references also impacted upon Nazi planning. Speer, who had been appointed General Building Inspector for the Reich Capital in 1937, nominated the landscape architect Willi Schelkes to prepare a park system plan for Berlin that took account of his monumental architectural plans. The green plan was intended to strengthen the health and working power of the German people. Schelkes took the view that a radial plan would be best suited, as it would not contradict Speer's monumental east-west and north-south expansion axes that would lead to central Berlin. Presented in 1939, Schelkes' plan laid a very large number of green wedges evenly across Berlin.[93]

A year later, the Nazis prepared a plan to replace Warsaw, which they intend to obliterate, with 'a new German City' whose population would be reduced from 1,300,000 to 130,000 people. The plan prepared by Hubert Gross and Otto Nurnberger organized new areas on both sides of the Vistula. On its southern side, between the river and the main development area to the west, a large green wedge was located (Figure 3.11). It engulfed the inner area and also surrounded the city as a green belt. Another plan along similar lines was produced in 1942. Both plans tend to be referred to as the Pabst Plan.[94]

With the end of the war and the devastation of Berlin, the task of replanning was immense. In 1945, Hans Scharoun was appointed the director of the Department of Building and Municipal Housing for Greater Berlin and in 1946 exhibited the *Kollektiveplan*. His vision was to replan Berlin as a modern metropolis in accordance with the contemporary dictates of planning theory. The plan was based on the criticism of the concentric-ring form of city expansion, which had been the historic pattern of Berlin's development, and favoured the strengthening of the development of strips along the river Spree.[95] Housing would be located away from industry, in park-like districts. The core of the city would contain the administrative and cultural buildings around the Tiergarten, acting very much like a *Stadtkrone*. Scharoun's plan

FIGURE 3.11 *Pabst Plan for Warsaw, 1940.*

capitalizes on the idea of re-approximation of cities with nature as a principle to be applied to the post-war metropolises.

Scharoun's plan articulated not only the *Stadtlandschaft* but also what Gibberd called the 'accepted canons of planning' – as exemplified in contemporary British plans such as the deconcentration of population, the restructuring of the city based on the neighbourhood unit concept and the large increase in urban greenery. Another noteworthy manifestation of these ideas can be seen in Konstanty Gutschow's plan for Hamburg from 1944. His plan defined neighbourhood units along lines of transport – again using large green wedges between the development areas.[96]

The impact of European planning theory and post-war reconstruction activity can be extended well beyond Europe. Plans for Tokyo, for instance, included both green belts and green wedges, as can be seen in the Green Space Plan of 1939 and in the 1946 plan.[97] The first defined a green belt at a 15-kilometre radius from the core to control sprawl, with wedges along river valleys flowing into the city as recreational spaces. The latter came into being following concerns about the spread of fires during bombings. The open spaces would also provide refuge and escape routes through the green corridors and wedges.[98]

Another interesting example to examine is the case of Melbourne. It is worth highlighting here the work of Frank Heath and Frederick O. Barnett published in the book *We Must Go On*, from 1944, in its depiction of a park system proposal for Melbourne presenting six green wedges and other radial parks, similar to British radical proposals for London from that period.[99] In addition, in 1951, Alfred J. Brown and Howard M. Sherrard published the book *An Introduction to Town and Country Planning*. It drew heavily on British planning experience to that date, becoming highly influential in Australian planning circles. A revised edition, published in collaboration with John H. Shaw in 1969, included a foreword by Abercrombie and was dedicated to the memory of John Sulman, one of the precursors of Australian planning and of the green wedge idea in Australia. When discussing the establishment of a park system, they referred to Robert Mattocks' article published in the *Town Planning Review* in 1937 as the best definition of 'the modern viewpoint on park systems'.[100] Mattocks had argued for a hybrid system based on Pepler's diagram from 1923. Brown, Sherrard and Shaw studied closely both the 'Ring or Belt System' and the 'Radial or Wedge System' and stressed that in relation to the latter there was 'much to be said for this arrangement, which enables fresh air from the country to reach the heart of the city', upon which they argued that Melbourne furnished 'a good case for the application of this arrangement'. They referred to the Town Planning Commission Report of 1929 that recommended the treatment of waterways as parkland as a first step in the application of the model. Heath's plan was also highlighted in a similar vein.[101] All in all, they proposed a combination of both belt and wedges, owing to the fact that 'the belt system by itself has obvious limitations' and advised that the linking up of the major parkland, green wedges and green belt should be aimed for and, if possible, be considered in conjunction with the planning of an arterial road system.[102] The park system plan in the Melbourne Metropolitan Planning Scheme Report from 1954 indeed provided a series of large peripheral and radial parks, running mostly through valleys. The intention was similar to the 1929 plan regarding the use of geographical features in the creation of parks near residential areas, which would provide a direct link to the open country.

In the United States, references to the green wedge idea both on the scale of the city and of the region can be found since the immediate post-war years. In 1946, Sanders and Rabuck published the book *New City Patterns: The Analysis of and a Technique for Urban Reintegration*, which proposed ways to resolve the dichotomy of working in the city and living in the suburbs

typical of American cities. The book included a wheel-shaped diagram entitled
'urban planning objectives', which presented six radiating axes each containing
residential developments of varying densities, business areas, shopping
centres and industry. Between them six green wedges penetrate into the
business district and the high and medium-density residential areas. A radio-
concentric pattern of roads and railways connected all areas (Figure 3.12).[103]
The authors applied the idea to Baltimore, suggesting that the city's extension
areas be divided into large planned districts with intervening green wedges.
The book's addendum gives out an indication of the authors' possible sources
of inspiration, as it displayed – what they considered to be – 'outstanding'
examples of master plans from abroad. These included plans for Stalingrad,
Frankfurt, Amsterdam and the RIBA LRRC plan for London (in particular the
LRRC proposed green wedge in Finchley). It was noted that 'at the time of
going to press the Greater London Plan by Professor Abercrombie was not
available to the authors'.[104] In a review of Sanders and Rabuck's book, this
city model was highly praised. It was remarked that 'there is great force in
a sound idea' and that 'such a city would have unobstructed country air and
sunlight penetrating to its core, and it would be a healthful and convenient
place in which to reside'.[105]

Transatlantic exchanges of planning ideas acquired strength with the rise of
Nazism, as a number of German architects and planners would seek refuge in
the United States. For instance, Walter Gropius, after a short stay in England,
moved to the United States in 1937 to head the Architecture department at
Harvard, and later invited Martin Wagner, who had been dismissed as Berlin's
Chief City Planner in 1933, to join him; Mies van der Rohe arrived in Chicago
in 1938 to work at the Illinois Institute of Technology, followed soon by Ludwig
Hilberseimer.

During their collaboration, Gropius and Wagner published a number of
essays and city plans. In *The New City Pattern for the People and by the
People*,[106] they advocated that the overcoming of the distinctions between
city and country was the task of town planning and that the reconnection
between architecture, planning and landscape needed to be done through
design. Gropius and Wagner sought to implement this in a number of
proposals developed by their urban design studio in Harvard, as for instance
in their radio-concentric plan for the redesign of Boston, from 1947. In this
study, two large green wedges connect a green belt with a central park.[107]
Gropius and Wagner did not only simply apply their planning baggage into the
American context but, as Mumford showed, assimilated the influence of the
American context, in particular their experience in the planning of suburban
sites, such as Radburn and the Greenbelt towns. Their new communities
were intended to provide healthier accommodation for urban workers amidst
nature.[108]

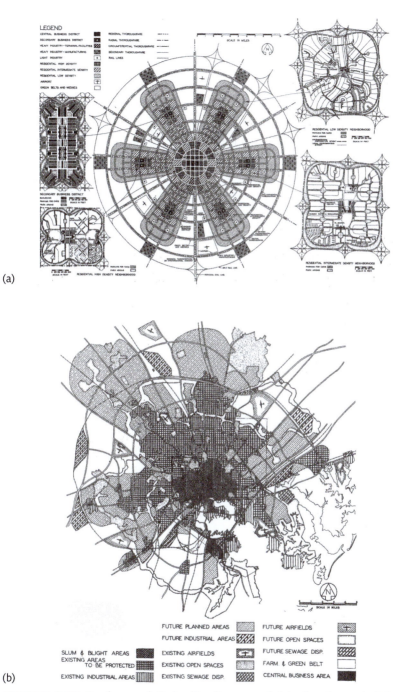

(a)

(b)

FIGURE 3.12 *Sanders and Rabuck's diagram of (a) planning principles and (b) application to Baltimore.* Source: *Sanders and Rabuck, 1946, diagram 23 (between 60 and 61) and diagram 110, 151.*

The work of the modernist émigré Ludwig Hilberseimer in Chicago is also of relevance to the understanding of the relationships between health, town planning and contact with nature in the period. Born in Karlsruhe in 1885, Hilberseimer was from an early age familiar with the fan-like disposition of its green spaces. In 1927, he published *Großstadt Architektur* (Architecture of the Metropolis), his vision for the mechanized metropolis of the future. The stark abstraction and representation of life exemplified there assumed a complete separation of natural and artificial worlds, which stands in contrast to his work of the post-war period. He lectured from 1929 to 1933 at the Bauhaus and in 1938 attended Mies Van der Rohe's invitation to move to Chicago to take up a professorship of urban and regional planning at the Illinois Institute of Technology. Since his arrival, he worked on developing a settlement model for the post-war period. In 1955, he published the *Nature of Cities*, a treatise that articulated the development of civilizations in history to specific urban forms, akin to Geddes approach.[109] Although Hilberseimer stated that it was 'strange to think that the extraordinary advancement of our technology has all but destroyed the city',[110] the realization of the Enlightenment's promise of a better future led by the transformative power of the human mind, technology and the integration of man and nature was for him still a task for planners. However, the quest for the alignment of the *zeitgeist* with the shape and functioning of cities would require a new settlement model.

As we would see in the first writings of fellow countryman Eberstadt, Hilberseimer suggested a framework permitting 'free and unhindered urban growth'. The premise was that proper zoning and skilful planning would well articulate the different functions of the city, eliminating thus any potential adverse influence of one upon another and leading to a 'healthy community life'.[111]

Hilberseimer's book is anchored in the planning debates of that time. The decentralization of industry and population, the merging of city and country, the promotion of spacious planning as a way of improving access to sunlight, greenery, fresh air and of mitigating the impacts of air strikes, as well as a focus on the creation of self-sustaining regions – which had been at the core of many planning activities in the international scenario – were seen as necessary for the emergence of a new society in harmony with the territory.

His settlement model resonated with aspects of a number of planning ideas, ranging from the linear city proposals of Soria y Mata, Miliutin and the MARS group to the British new towns. The settlement unit he proposed would locate the industrial area on one side of a traffic artery, while commercial and administrative buildings would be placed on the other side along a green buffer. The residential areas would sit beyond, accommodating also green spaces, schools, recreational areas and other facilities. There would be a complete separation of pedestrian and vehicular movement. The settlement units could be combined into communities, leading on to the formation of cities.

According to Hilberseimer, one of the main problems faced by urban society was air pollution. For him, planning would be 'the only truly efficient remedy'[112] to combat the dire effects of industrial pollution upon residential areas. The preferable shape of the settlement unit was the rectangle; however, fan-shaped settlements could be formed dependent on wind patterns, geographical features and the site topography (Figure 3.13).[113] In no circumstance industrial air pollution was to reach residential areas. The green wedges appear here as consequences of decisions taken at regional level. They were buffer zones, acting as boundaries between units and safe passages for pedestrians to reach the countryside, public buildings and the recreation areas. Although there is a clear attempt to break down the built up form, as Hilberseimer believed that 'the space concept of our age tends towards openness and breadth',[114] the green wedges remained clearly marked even when reaching the urban fringe. Hilberseimer's settlement unit

FIGURE 3.13 *Hilberseimer's large 'fan-shaped' community, 1955.* Source: *Hilberseimer, 1955, 217.*

and aggregate cities prioritized the integration between city and nature at regional scale. Green wedges were to be laid out as air pollution buffers, functioning also as recreational and productive landscapes.

Hans Blumenfeld was another German planner who had an important role in promoting the idea of green wedges in the United States. He had worked in German, Austria and the Soviet Union before moved to New York in 1938, when he took up a position of member of the city planning commission of Philadelphia. In 1949, Blumenfeld described in his paper *Theory of City Form: Past and Present* numerous city models, highlighting the 'star-shaped city', which was marked by radial strips of development intercalated with green wedges. He argued that this may be regarded as a 'rationalization of the pattern of settlement', which was 'evolving throughout the modern world'. For Blumenfeld it went beyond that, as the star-shaped city transcended the notion of city form into a 'new concept of the urban landscape'.[115] Considering its application to New York region, he tentatively stated that he was 'personally inclined to visualize such strips of development as radiating from the city centre, interlocking with green wedges extending from the open country into the heart of the city'.[116] His description of the 'star-shaped city' would be later on recuperated in urban design theory by authors such as Kevin Lynch and Cliff Moughtin.

As seen in this chapter, reduction in densities, redistribution of population into newly planned settlements and the implementation of neighbourhood units were fundamental planning tenets. Zoning remained a powerful tool to avoid the proximity of conflicting land uses. The integration between built-up areas and nature, or the countryside, was high on the planning agenda. Not only did this represent the result of combined town and country planning, but also a search for a more balanced environment, in which social values would flourish. Plans for new settlements or damaged cities tended to integrate the functionalist discourse asserting the importance of sunlight, fresh air and greenery, and adaptations of Howard's garden city idea and of Perry's neighbourhood unit concept. Mumford's cultural and historical approach to the study of cities became highly influential in planning culture, as did the pursuit of more harmonious relationships among men and between built and un-built areas. In Germany, the latter became theorized as the *Stadlandschaft* (the city-landscape). The comparison between the city and a living organism reinforced the feeling that cities should then offer an integrated experience blending the urban and the natural. Planners often tended to see the war destruction as an opportunity to replan on bold lines, following the most up-to-date planning principles.[117] Green wedges and belts tended to be linked in one single model. It was also seen how the provision of these large green structures was in cases associated with the construction of satellite towns (Table 3.1).

Table 3.1 Green wedges and the socio-spatial reorganization of the city-region into neighbourhoods, districts and satellite towns

Year	Reference	Place	Author	Notes
1943	RIBA LRRC Reconstruction plan of London	London, UK	RIBA LRRC	Green wedge in the axis Lea Valley-Epping Forest, in Finchley and along the axis of the Thames
1943	*County of London Plan 1943*	London, UK	P. Abercrombie	Green wedges to be the basis of the park system plan 'from garden to park, from park to parkway, from parkway to green wedge and from green wedge to Green Belt'
1944	*Greater London Plan 1944*	London, UK	P. Abercrombie	Detailed park system plan based on green wedges 'Green Wedges-Proposals' (Appendix 20) Proposed the construction of New Towns around London
1944	Plan of Hamburg	Hamburg, Germany	K. Gutschow	Neighbourhood units defined along lines of transport with green wedges between the development areas
1945	Plan for Kingston upon Hull	Kingston Upon Hull, UK	P. Abercrombie and E. Lutyens	Green wedges and green belt
1945	Plan of Manchester	Manchester, UK	R. Nicholas	'any attempt should be made to bring the countryside into the city by extending wedges of greenery from a green belt on the boundary towards the central area'. Section titled 'Green Wedges', under chapter 10 – public open space

Year	Reference	Place	Author	Notes
1946	*Final Report of the New Towns Committee*	UK	New Towns Committee	New towns to either blend with the surrounding countryside by the use of green wedges or to stand in sharp contrast to it
1946	Diagram of planning principles Plan of Baltimore	Generic-Baltimore, USA	S. E. Sanders and A. J. Rabuck	Diagram of a radio-concentric model presenting six radiating development axes and six green wedges Application to Baltimore
1946	Review of the Merseyside plan – TPR 19, no. 2, 104	Merseyside	Anonymous	'the fatuous "Green Belt", which used to be such a popular concept, is replaced by the "Green Wedge" whereby the open country is brought from several directions near the centre of the built-up area'
1946	Plan of Tokyo	Tokyo, Japan	–	Green wedges would facilitate escape and provide refuge in case of fire and bombing
1947	Plan for Harlow	Harlow, UK	F. Gibberd	Agricultural wedges defining the boundaries of residential districts
1947	Plan of Hemel Hempstead	Hemel Hempstead, UK	G. A. Jellicoe	Green wedge along the valley of the River Gade
1947	Plan for Boston	Boston, USA	W. Gropius and M. Wagner	Radio-concentric plan with two large green wedges connecting the green belt to a central park
1949	Plan of Hatfield	Hatfield, UK	L. Brett	A central green wedge and two minor ones

Year	Reference	Place	Author	Notes
1949–64	Plans of New Towns	Various, Israel	Various	Green belt and wedges often employed in plans for new towns
1950	Plan for the County of Cambridgeshire	Cambridgeshire, UK	W. Holford	Green wedges were to penetrate into the heart of Cambridge.
1950	General Plan of Oslo	Oslo, Norway	City of Oslo	Restructuring of the city into neighbourhoods and districts delimited by green spaces Green wedges linking the city to a ring of natural areas in the outskirts
1953	Plan of São Paulo	São Paulo, Brazil	H. Lefevre	Green belt and green wedges
1954	Plan of Sennestadt	Sennestadt, Germany	H. B. Reichow	Two green wedges splitting the town into four districts
1955	Plan for fan-shaped communities in *The Nature of Cities*	Various, USA	L. Hilberseimer	Key preoccupation is to avoid air pollution in residential areas Green wedges appear as buffer zones and green links to the countryside
1956	Plan of Tapiola	Tapiola, Finland	A. Ervi	Green wedges delimiting districts
1960	*Urban Prospect*	Generic	L. Mumford	'ribbons of green must run through every quarter, forming a continuous web of garden and mall, widening at the edge of the city into protective greenbelts'
1967	Plan of Runcorn	Runcorn, UK	Arthur Ling	Large green wedge located along a valley extending to Manchester Ship Canal

4

Polycentrism and Regional Planning

By the 1940s, emphasis on spacious planning, reduction of urban population density and the introduction of greenery on a large scale to the interior of cities was axiomatic in Western planning theory. In the post-war period, special attention was paid to the association of some of the inter-war functionalist principles – such as strict separation of functions, the provision of sunlight, greenery and fresh air – with the reinvigorated preoccupation with social cohesion and community building of the immediate post-war. Abercrombie's Greater London Plan and the British new towns aroused particular interest. In addition, Lewis Mumford's *The Culture of Cities*, from 1938, and *The City in History*, from 1961, would also frame visions of replanning and reconstruction in the light of the importance of historical and cultural discourses. This chapter examines how planning at the scale of the territory led to the emergence of new approaches, in particular the corridor-wedge model.

Organizing the territory

If, as suggested by Hall, Germany had been the main reference for the Nordic countries in terms of both technological advancements and cultural endeavours since the mid-nineteenth century, the rise of Nazism and the German occupation of Norway and Denmark prompted an ideological reorientation towards Britain and the United States. The construction of new national identities went hand in hand with physical reconstruction. Abercrombie's plans for London and Mumford's *The Culture of Cities* soon generated considerable interest in that region.[1]

Unlike London, however, the Nordic capital cities did not have to face the full extent of the problems associated with multiple private land ownership when devising their post-war master plans, as most land was in public ownership. Free planning, thus, became a possibility almost detached from considerations regarding compensation and lawsuits.

The geography of Nordic capital cities played a fundamental role in the historical pattern of land occupation, influenced mostly by major natural features, such as rock formations, and the proximity to water and forested areas. Besides, the implementation of radial traffic arteries since the 1920s created the backbone for future visions for these regions. In this context, it is hardly a surprise that the green wedge idea would become key in planning debates in the North.

The 1947 Finger Plan

Copenhagen reached half a million dwellers at the turn of the twentieth century.[2] In line with the international discussions about regional planning of the 1920s, a regional traffic plan was put forward in 1926, setting the framework for Copenhagen's radial pattern of urban expansion ever since. It marked the departure from the previous pattern of growth in concentric rings towards a focus on development along the newly established radial arteries. The conundrum of sprawl and consequent lack of access to open spaces had been a concern throughout the first decades of the twentieth century and in 1936 the Planning Board of Copenhagen tried to address it through a regional green space plan. The plan designated areas to be safeguarded from development and connected the inner urban areas to the attractive forests, lakes and coastal zones to the north and northwest. It consisted mostly of ring and radial parkways – possibly influenced by the American park systems plans of the period.[3] Yet, Copenhagen did not take this as an opportunity to relate traffic and park system plans given that the 1936 green space plan was elaborated almost as a separate entity from the 1926 traffic plan. In 1938, the Danish government passed a Town Planning Act that transferred planning control to individual municipalities. In 1945, now informed also by the debates on post-war reconstruction, it decided that another plan was needed.

Recognizing the difficulties that Copenhagen's historic pattern of concentric growth was posing to contemporary life – in regard to the increased distance to the countryside, lack of urban open spaces and the common problems associated with lack of zoning and poor housing conditions – Steen Eiler Rasmussen and Peter Bredsdorff, the authors of the plan, considered what key planning models for growth would be most appropriate for the case of Copenhagen. Should a Disurbanist approach, as debated in the USSR in the 1930s or as suggested by Saarinen in his book *The City: Its Growth, Its Decay, Its Future* (and cited by Rasmussen and Bredsdorff), be adopted? Should the linear city model championed by Soria y Mata and the MARS plan for London be followed? Or else should Copenhagen adopt the idea of satellite towns or the green wedge model of Abercrombie's plans?[4] Rasmussen and Bredsdorff categorically stated that although 'the growth of the city in layers ought now to be stopped', they did 'not want to create satellite towns', to utterly disperse the population nor to form a linear city. Instead, the plan was to be based on the green wedge model, building on the radial traffic infrastructure planned in 1926 and constructed in the 1930s, particularly the S-trains. Known as the 1947 Finger Plan, it resolved to direct growth along main radial arteries, the 'fingers', while preserving green wedges between them (Figure 4.1). Housing

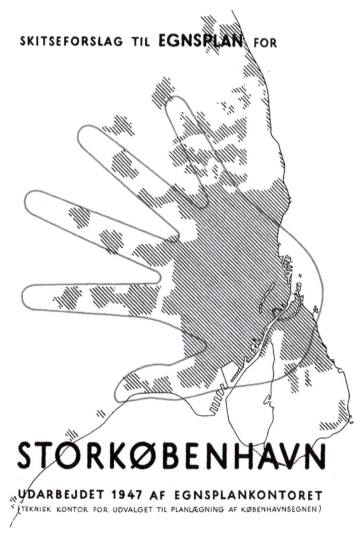

FIGURE 4.1 *The 1947 Finger Plan. Based on Egnsplankontoret, 1948, cover.*

areas would be at most 1 kilometre away from the railway stations and green wedges would 'extend right up to the built-up areas served by trams'.[5] A supplemental plan of motorways was also envisaged with radial roads built along the edges of the fingers.

The central area and its surrounding ring would form the 'palm'. New industrial centres were to be situated at the intersections of the ring with the radial electric railways, at the base of the five fingers. This was intended to facilitate access of workers to their places of work and the industries' access to the proposed new harbour. In addition, the railway stations would be the cores of suburban centres around which residential areas of approximately 10,000 people would be grouped. The interlocking nature of the fingers and wedges meant that the balance between built-up areas and open space would be maintained. What is more, green wedges provided a range of benefits. Firstly, they addressed the need for recreational open space in close proximity to the urban fabric and allowed direct access to the hinterland. Secondly, in times of food scarcity, they offered the possibility of growing food near the city, or indeed within it. Thirdly, they would control sprawl between the fingers, in the areas not served by the S-lines.

Despite the fact that the plan had no legal basis for its implementation, as since the Town Planning Act of 1938 planning had become a task of individual municipalities, it did formulate a shared framework upon which regional planning could occur. With the passing of the 1949 Regulation of Built-up Areas Act, it was possible, to some extent, to control urbanization according to its guidelines.[6] In the subsequent decades, Copenhagen experienced intense population growth. In 1962, a revised plan was published and focused on the development of the two southernmost areas: the Kobe and Roskilde fingers.[7] The urbanization of the fingers intensified in the 1960s, which made them successively 'thicker' than stipulated. The use of cars also grew substantially in the period, stimulating further urbanization of the fingers and overall suburban development, which placed extra pressure upon the green wedges. This was followed by the Regional Plan from 1973, marked by the definition of a main development corridor with four regional centres at its intersections with the fingers. In the 1970s, initiatives at local, regional and national levels protected the green wedges, creating the legal basis for their safeguarding to date.[8]

The answer to the initial question of 'what type of city would be most expedient'[9] not only empirically capitalized on the existing conditions of Copenhagen but also redefined a model of urban development that was deemed to provide an optimum solution to internationally recognized problems of industrialized cities: the green wedge model. And although its application was not without hindrance, the Finger Plan set out the guidelines for the future development of Copenhagen up to this day.

Other Scandinavian capitals

Other Nordic capital cities were also objects of regional plans since the end of the Second World War. Abercrombie's plans for London, the New towns and Copenhagen's Finger Plan offered fundamental references for the application of the most updated planning theory. In this context, it is worth noting that in 1950 a plan for Oslo emerged after the city incorporated the municipality of Aker and saw its population grow to 425,000. The plan adopted the principles of restructuring the city into neighbourhoods and districts, defined by green spaces. Its park system focused on providing green pedestrian routes, such as green strips and green wedges, out into a ring of natural areas (Figure 4.2). The total amount of green spaces in the plan represented two-thirds of the area of Oslo.[10]

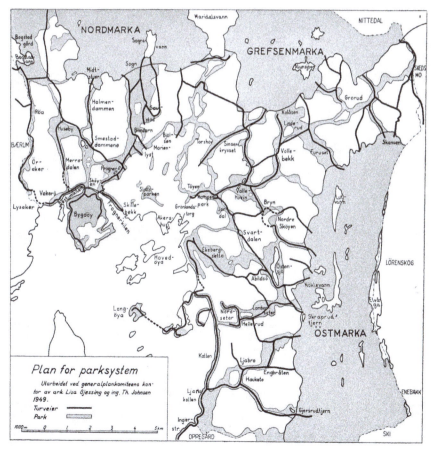

FIGURE 4.2 *Park system plan for Oslo, 1950.*

In a similar vein, the master plan for Stockholm from 1952 focused on the reorganization of the city based on neighbourhood units and districts, increased housing provision, improvement of the traffic system (including the introduction of the subway) and the structuring of a regional recreational system. Led by Sven Markelius, Stockholm's City Planning Director between 1944 and 1954, it assumed that Greater Stockholm would have not exceeded 1.3 million inhabitants by 1970, that a good proportion of the population would remain in the central areas and that suburbs and nearby towns would accommodate the overspill from the capital. It dedicated a great deal of attention to planning neighbourhoods, which were to become the basis of the future structure of Stockholm. The plan directly referred to Abercrombie's view for London as well as to some of the new towns, such as Harlow. Regarding recreational green areas within Greater Stockholm, as it was the case in these British examples, the plan stated that it seemed more appropriate to base its system on green wedges rather than on a green belt, as both the topography and the traffic system invited such a solution.[11] These wedges were described to some extent and included green and blue spaces, as for instance: the axis between the islands and water areas of Lake Mälaren, and the open areas of Djurgården and zoo Brunnsviken; the axis of the military training grounds in Solna, Spånga, Sollentuna and Järfälla; and axis of Järvafältet, Haga Park and Brunnsviken. Other green wedges were also to be created, including: one in the Södertörn countryside, another in Tyresta, the axis of Nacka-Erstavik-Tyresö, between Farsta and Ågesta, and between Vårby and Mälarhöjden. Stockholm, due to its geographical location and unlike many Western cities, was able to expand in a landscape that was mostly forested, making the limits between planned green spaces and undeveloped land blurred (Figure 4.3).[12] But in any case, the plan recommended that large and small green spaces should be interconnected given that this would not only increase the amount of green spaces and help balance their distribution but also facilitate access to them.

Within the urban fabric, very much like in Abercrombie's plans, the wedges were to split the neighbourhoods, functioning also as zoning tools. The theoretical model (Figure 4.4) to be applied at local scale placed the metro station with public facilities in the middle, a dense residential area surrounding it, and work places and smaller neighbourhood units defined by green wedges around the main expanded core.[13]

Between 1953 and 1960, Helsinki also developed a plan for growth. The redistribution of industry along the coast and the main arterial lines coupled with the definition of neighbourhoods and districts were key strategies to reorganize the city. The proposed park system played an important role in breaking down the built-up area (Figure 4.5), and in so doing substantially increased the provision of green space across the region.[14] The central park of Helsinki, derived from Bertel Jung and Eliel Saarinen's plan of 1918, acted here as a green wedge extending out into the territory.

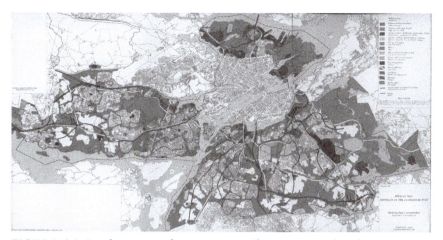

FIGURE 4.3 *Land use map showing proposed green space distribution.* Source: *Stockholm Stadt, 1952. Courtesy of the City of Stockholm.*

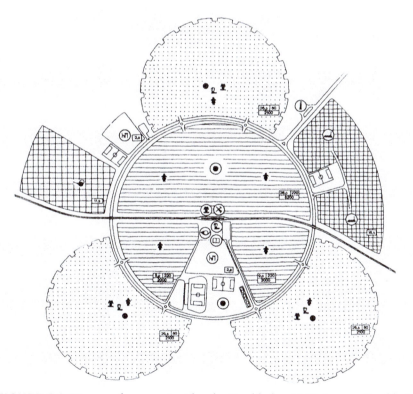

FIGURE 4.4 *Diagram from master plan for Stockholm, 1952.* Source: *Stockholm Stadt, 1952. Courtesy of the City of Stockholm.*

FIGURE 4.5 *Master plan for Helsinki, 1953–60.* Source: *Halsingin Kaupungin, 1960, Kartta VI.* © *Helsiki City Planning Department.*

These examples show the articulation of the preoccupation to restructure the existing city into neighbourhoods and districts, so conspicuously developed in the Greater London Plan, with the traffic system, as championed by the 1947 Finger Plan. The radial public transport arteries became vectors of growth, with urban and suburban centres developed around the stations. Green wedges were structural elements in these plans, both in terms of the delimitation of neighbourhoods and districts and as recreational and agricultural zones between axes of development.

The corridor-wedge model

The Nordic experience soon became referential in regional planning internationally. The large-scale plans of the Nordic capitals and their subsequent implementation, particularly in the case of Copenhagen, facilitated theoretical explorations of planning ideas, but most of all generated a testing ground from which other countries could draw. Their influence was felt in the Americas, Europe, Australia and Africa.

Planning the metropolis: The case of São Paulo

Perhaps in few cities the need to organize growth was more prominent than in São Paulo in the 1950s. Its population in the 1940s was already double that of the 1920s and saw a further increase by 70 per cent between 1940 and 1950, reaching more than 2,200,000 inhabitants. By 1954, it was commonly reported that a building was erected every 7 minutes. This was a result of the city's industrialization process, and although the lay-press labelled it as a symbol of progress as the city was reaching its fourth centenary of foundation, local planners such as Anhaia Mello, Carlos Lodi, Cardim Filho and Henrique Lefrevre were concerned that if the city carried on along this path, it would turn into a Mumfordian 'necropolis'. This was not, however, a unanimous assumption. Robert Moses, the individual actor behind the public works in New York since the 1920s, for example, prepared a plan for the city in 1950 indeed in support of the metropolitan ideal.

Criticism of the metropolis soon became manifested in writings and plans, mainly from the Department of Urbanism founded by Anhaia Mello in 1947. These constantly referred to Geddes, Abercrombie, Purdom and Mumford and put forward the axioms of polycentrism, deconcentration of population and the definition of neighbourhood units and large networks of green space as strategies to save São Paulo from the aforementioned dooming forecast. The most current theoretical models were considered for their suitability for a plan for São Paulo, including the new towns idea and the corridor-wedge model. The first was put forward by Henrique Lefevre, the first Director of the Department of Architecture and Urbanism of the municipality of São Paulo, in 1953 as the solution for the city, whereas the latter was defended by Carlos Lodi, the Director of the city planning division, in 1957.[15]

According to Lefevre, the 'monstrous, inhumane, dark and nauseating' megalopolis had to be resisted. This involved the relocation of industry and population to new towns located beyond a green belt, in a similar manner to Abercrombie's proposal for London.[16] Accordingly, as part of a multi-scale open space system, Lefevre recommended green wedges penetrating into the city.

Lodi, on the other hand, aimed to structure the city's growth within bands of development along radial arterial routes. Districts would be largely independent and ultimately composed of neighbourhood units. Concentric rings would complement the transport system and an agricultural green belt would delimit the city's growth and be the starting point of numerous green wedges.[17] Despite these recommendations, the growth of the city remained out of control, frustrating any attempt at a cohesive green space plan in the years to come.

Corridor wedge in the United States

The polycentric city concept was prominent in planning debates in the United States in the 1960s. Strongly influenced by the development of the British new towns and the structuralist approach found in Scandinavian capitals, some American planners would turn their attention to the corridor development-green wedge model as an efficient way of dealing with metropolitan growth.

A foundational reference in this regard is the Year 2000 Plan for Washington, DC, published by the National Capital Regional Planning Commission in 1961. By 1960, Washington region had reached a population of 2 million and the plan aimed to define an urban model capable of accommodating a population of 5 million inhabitants, which was forecasted for the year 2000. Before making its recommendation, the Planning Commission considered a number of growth forms, including satellite towns and linear developments, but eventually proposed intense corridors of development around regional centres along rail lines and expressways intercalated with green wedges (Figure 4.6). The corridors would be developed with a gradient from high-density housing around the regional centres to low-density areas near the fringes to the green wedges. The definition of green wedges would secure nearly 1,214 square kilometres of open space. It has been reported that the Year 2000 Plan won the endorsement of President Kennedy and 'made a powerful impression' on a number of planning commissions in the United States,[18] only to be superseded later by other plans.

The *Metrotowns for the Baltimore Region*, published in 1962, argued for a similar approach. The report described the work developed in the Metrotowns and Regional Cities Research Project, which aimed at formulating techniques for the general application of the European new town and development corridor experiences to the problems of metropolitan growth in America. The term 'metrotown' was coined by the Baltimore Regional Planning Council to mean a new planned growth area in a regional plan for the decentralization of population and employment from the large metropolitan centres. They would house between 50,000 and 200,000 inhabitants and contain a centre with a wide range of activities, services and employment. Metrotowns would have a degree of autonomy, but would still be significantly interdependent on the rest of the metropolis. Physical separation of one metrotown from another would happen by green buffer zones.[19] Applied to Baltimore, the metrotowns were organized in corridors of development separated by green wedges, with a spider-web network of traffic arteries linking the centres. Adopted in 1967, this plan was influential in the development of similar studies elsewhere.[20]

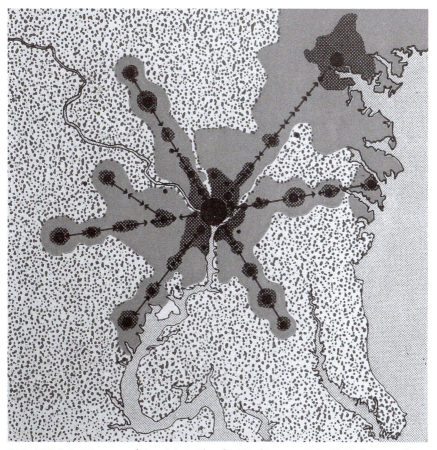

FIGURE 4.6 *Diagram of Year 2000 Plan for Washington, DC, 1961.* Source: *Great Britain, 1963, 187.*

Further evidence of the dissemination of the corridor-wedge model in the American planning milieu is the plan for Chicago from 1967. Again, after considering different growth models, the authors opted for a 'Finger Plan'. A clear allusion to Copenhagen's plan from 1948, the Chicago plan suggested growth in corridors along the commuter rail lines radiating outwards from the city.[21] The plan was described in the popular media as 'a complex of corridors with wedges of farmland'.[22]

Visions for South East England

If the green wedge concept infiltrated Nordic planning discussions arguably through the diffusion of Abercrombie's plans for post-war London, conversely the appropriation and development of green wedges in association with radial corridors typical of post-war Nordic planning had in turn a direct influence upon the debates about regional planning in England in the 1960s and 1970s. Curiously enough, despite the fact that green wedges had been promoted consistently by British planners in the first half of the twentieth century, it would be the Nordic influence that would reignite discussions about this model back in England. Copenhagen and Stockholm regional plans, for instance, became references on how to holistically deal with transport, densification and promotion of access to greenery.

Although the Green Belt Act had been passed in 1938, it was not until the 1950s that the London green belt received ministerial approval. By 1955, local authorities had been encouraged to designate green belt areas around their own towns too. The fact that the main function of the green belt was one of restriction – to 'prevent development' – as stated in 'The Green Belts' published by the Ministry of Housing and Local Government in 1962, generated questions over its applicability to other parts of the country already in the early 1960s.

The quest to halt the gravitational pull of London and rebalance the distribution of population and employment remained at the forefront of planning debates in England in the 1960s. In this context, visions for the South East are of particular interest for several reasons. Firstly, they attempted to shift the paradigm from 'distribution' of population, dealt with by Abercrombie's Greater London Plan, to the question of how to plan for growth;[23] secondly, this preoccupation led to questions being raised over the functions of London's green belt and the suitability of the green belt model for the region; and finally due to the consideration given to the green wedge model at a regional scale, following the examples from Scandinavia.

The South East Study, published in 1964, projected that there would be an increase of 3.5 million people in the South East by 1981. Planning debates in the country concentrated on defining the best ways to accommodate growth away from London, the central questions asked being: what pattern of development would be suitable? Was the green belt at all a valid model for the South East given that the region's main need was to accommodate growth while the green belt was in actual fact designed to avoid it permanently? Regarding the latter, for the authors of the South East Study there was 'a real conflict here'.[24]

By then, criticism of low-density small- to medium-sized new towns was increasing not only for their perceived lack of 'urbanity' but also due to their apparent inability to provide an adequate range of employment, educational opportunities and social and cultural activities required if they were to be counterpoints to the capital. The South East Study considered that to compete with London the region needed to be treated as a whole since, it was observed, large schemes tended to offer improved services and attractions, which would entice large employers and thus stimulate further growth. Hence, the plan proposed the development of 'large and strong' centres of growth: three new cities and a number of large to medium-sized expansions.[25]

At the same time as the study aimed to enhance the South East's contribution to the country's economy offering a counterpoint to London, it was also responding to the acute land problem around the capital, as converging population pressures reached the green belt. Views about the future of the green belt tended to be polarized. Criticism of this model focused on its functions and boundaries, arguing that the understanding of the green belt as 'a playground for Londoners' was 'belied by facts' and that much of it consisted of areas often unavailable to the public and of poor quality. Its negative nature, freezing land as it was regardless of its quality, relinquished the possibility of change.[26] As potential alternatives, the study raised that there were two 'new approaches': one to push the boundaries of the green belt back to release land close to London and the other, 'more radical', to implement the model adopted in the Nordic countries of corridors of development with interlocking green wedges. It stated that the latter proposal involved

> abandoning the green belt in its present form, and constructing an entirely new one. This would not take the form of a constricting girdle. Instead, development would be allowed to radiate from London along the main lines of communication in roughly star-shaped fashion; in between, wedges of green would be carried right into the built-up area.[27]

The study maintained that this pattern would offer two advantages: keeping town and country separate, but at a close distance, and providing the flexibility for radial development needed to meet the demands of the growing population, without destroying the green wedges. Curiously enough, the study considered that 'the main difficulty about this idea is that it [had] come too late' and that 'if the green belt had first been defined at a time when the facts of population and employment growth in London were fully known, this [the corridor-wedge model] might have been the chosen pattern'. In so doing, the plan evidenced a failure to recognize that the green wedge idea not only was a foremost feature in Abercrombie's plans for London but also had a history of proposals for the capital spanning at that time more than fifty years.[28] It is hardly credible that the green wedge idea could still seem 'radical' and appear as coming 'too late', as if it had no history in the country and was indeed completely novel. Perhaps it was the articulation of corridor development with green wedges at regional scale, featuring so conspicuously in the planning of Scandinavian capitals, that was seen as so innovative. In any case, the study recommended that London's green belt be kept, but that more emphasis should be placed on 'positive' planning as a way to enhance the quality and functions of its open spaces, as well as their accessibility to the urban population, beyond its initial aim of halting indiscriminate urban sprawl.

The matter of planning models and their applicability to the region was pushed further in the South Hampshire Plan from 1966, led by Colin Buchanan. The plan observed that 'there seemed to be only three patterns': the centripetal, the linear, and the grid; and that 'any structure that we could devise would, it seemed, have to be a variant or development of one of these three'. Representations of these models were used to investigate their supposed performance in conditions of growth and change. The criteria of analysis involved: maximum freedom of choice, communication and association for people throughout the area, that each phase should function efficiently and independently as the structure grew, that the structure should be changeable and versatile, and lastly that it should be able to grow without risking 'deformation of distortion'.[29] In this light, Buchanan's team opted for what was called a 'directional grid'.[30] This structure was to be based on a transport network consisting of a hierarchical grid of routes (red and green) and nodes. 'Red' routes would serve the main development areas, while 'green' routes would be through routes across the green areas.

Applied to the area, the directional grid followed the axis between Southampton and Portsmouth and was broken down by river valleys, including wedge-like spaces along the valleys of the River Itchen and the River Meon (Figure 4.7). These would link the countryside and natural areas of the South Downs to the sea, serve as recreational zones, provide reserves to cater for future recreational needs and act as buffer zones separating one urban area from another. These green wedges, combined with the woodlands and the coast, would form the open space system at regional level within the study area. Existing villages, which lay within the proposed grid, were not to be 'surrounded by miniature belts', but integrated into the regional system proposed, while maintaining their identities.[31] At district level, green routes and other localized green spaces would complement the system. They would house education and recreation facilities, as well as provide green links to other parts of the grid and the wedges.

Similarly to the South East Study, the seminal role of the proposed traffic system within a comprehensive planning framework was key. If in the case of Greater London the existing transport infrastructure already radiated out, for South Hampshire a linear corridor structure seemed the most natural solution instead, as a chalk ridge and the sea pressed the area from each side in. Because of this particular condition, the interspersed green spaces would occur across the proposed axis of development, not between axes as suggested in the South East Study.

The Strategy for the South East, from 1967, pursued the idea of redistribution of population by creating a 'counter-magnet' to London: new growth areas

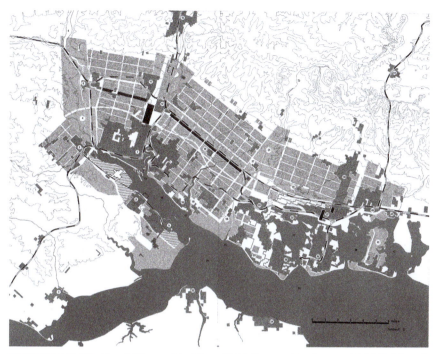

FIGURE 4.7 *The South Hampshire Plan, 1966.* Source: *Buchanan, 1966, Foldout 5.*

beyond London's commuting range.[32] It was forecasted that the South East would need to accommodate an added 4 million people before the end of the century. The development of the South Hampshire city-region was to be the first priority, followed by Milton Keynes and Ipswich city-regions.

Building on previous studies about the different models of regional development, the strategy once again argued for an axial pattern of development. According to the authors of the Strategy, recent plans for major metropolitan areas had shown 'remarkable unanimity in advocating development in the form of corridors or axes, following major lines of transportation'.[33] Although it seemed to them that this pattern of development had to be implemented, it was to be adapted in the form of 'sectors' and 'country zones'. Sectors would be axes of development along interconnected parallel radial transport lines, as opposed to single ones, allowing thus more flexibility for growth in width. As this proposed pattern would both direct and control development, the plan considered it to hold out 'the best possible chance of maintaining wide continuous areas of unspoilt land' between the sectors, which would act as regional green wedges. In addition, the strips of development would not be continuous, but interrupted by country zones cutting across. Apart from avoiding uninterrupted urban development, they were intended to provide for 'the necessary recreational and amenity needs of the growing population' and to continue to make land available for agricultural use.[34] If the green belt was still seen as an important way of controlling London's expansion, the Strategy for the South East was reluctant to recommend it for the region for two reasons: firstly, because it would be ill-fitted for a radial pattern of the proposed dimensions and, secondly, because of the 'frequent failure to make full use of land protected from development by green belt status'. Positive planning was again brought up as a way to improve the quality of open land and its access to the population.[35]

The case of Melbourne

The need to find the 'best' model for urban growth was also keenly felt in Australia in the 1960s and 1970s. The options under discussion were corridor development, satellite towns, traditional ring growth or a hybrid of these. As McLoughlin pointed out, the model of corridor development with associated green wedges was commonly advocated by both the Town and Country Planning Board – a professional body of planners created to advise on planning matters and help coordinate local authorities' plans – and the Melbourne and Metropolitan Board of Works (MMBW).[36] As discussed previously, the green wedge idea was hardly new in Australia by that time. John Sulman had, already in 1919, published a diagram based on Eberstadt's one to illustrate the idea, arguably influencing Melbourne's plan from 1929 and Heath and Barnett's plan from 1944. Despite the fact that the green wedge idea had been part of the planning vocabulary in Australia for decades, it is likely that the recognition given to the association of green wedges with corridors of development and transport arteries in recent international debates led to further exploration of the concept.

The corridor-wedge model became consolidated as the chosen option for Melbourne from the early 1960s. Similarly to the examples seen before, development was to be concentrated around centres along main lines of communication, which would be separated from each other by green wedges. The preoccupation with directing urban growth was associated with the need to balance it against the preservation of the countryside. In 1971, the MMBW published *Planning Policies for the Melbourne Metropolitan Region*, which reiterated the model. The document proposed an urban structure based on seven development corridors interspersed with 'substantial' and 'permanent wedges of open country' to accommodate a predicted growth of 5 million inhabitants by the year 2000 (Figure 4.8).[37]

The corridors would be between approximately 6.5 and 9.5 kilometres wide and contain all future outward urban expansion. However, they were not to be necessarily fully developed. Melbourne's green wedges were conceived as instruments to control sprawl and mainly as agricultural and recreation

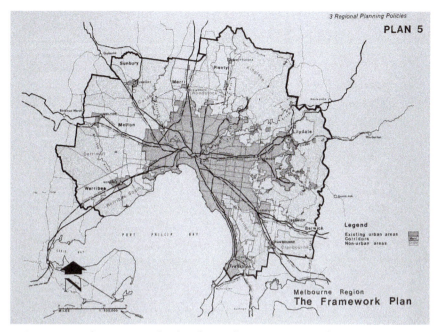

FIGURE 4.8 *The Framework Plan for Melbourne Region, Plan 5, 1971.* Source: *Planning Policies for Metropolitan Melbourne, 1971, 53. Courtesy of A/Executive Director, Planning Implementation.*

areas. Besides, the plan showed an early concern with environmental protection. In particular, this can be seen in the definition of green wedges along waterways in order to avoid flooding and to protect water quality and as buffer zones between sources of air pollution and noise and residential areas. As Buxton and Goodman showed, from this period until 1990 the green wedges were rigorously protected.[38] The corridor-wedge model remains to date at the core of spatial planning in Melbourne.

Other cases

Many other concurrent regional plans opted for the corridor-wedge model in order to direct growth and preserve access to large-scale green spaces near the urbanized areas. In 1965, Paris published a plan for its metropolitan region, the *Schema Directeur d'Aménagement et d'Urbanisme de la Région de Paris* (SDAURP), based on that model. It considered that the region would reach a population of 14 million people by the year 2000. The plan's main aim was to balance the expected population growth in axes of development, which included the construction of eight new towns. Green wedges would be formed between these corridors.[39] The plan was revised in 1969, but it still maintained the main principles. Further examples of the model's application in Europe include Plan of Geneva of 1965, the Regional Development Plan of Ruhr of 1966 and the plan of Hamburg of 1969.[40]

The model also reached Africa in the mid-1970s. Recent studies have shown how planning was part of Nordic aid to East Africa in the period, which started in the 1960s at the same time that countries such as Tanzania, Zambia and Kenya were becoming independent. With sovereignty, the newly formed countries searched for a new identity and forms to promote prosperity. The efforts to transform tribal societies into modern welfare states found in the Nordic countries worthy examples to emulate. The case of Tanzania is of particular interest. Funded by Nordic aid, Finish architects and planners developed a number of regional plans for Tanzanian towns, such as Tanga Town. The publication of the Arusha Declaration in 1967, known as Tanzania's most prominent political statement for social equality, defined the ideological framework for the plan. A requisite was that the town should be developed in balance with the countryside, in order to prevent it from draining resources from the traditional rural villages in the surrounding area.[41]

The master plan was led by the architect Rainer Nordberg with team members being Bo Mallander, Antti Hankkio, Mårten Bondestam, Jaakko Kaikkonen and Paavo Mänttäri. Located by a bay facing the Indian Ocean, the town had to expand southwards. The plan, spanning a period of 20 years from 1975, was based on three radial transport arteries radiating out onto the countryside from the town centre, with development concentrated around centres along these routes and two concentric ring routes complementing the major traffic system. Two large green wedges were to be formed between the radial lines and additional green buffer zones would cut across the districts. It is worth highlighting the idealist aspect of the proposal in aiming to achieve rapid social change through the implementation of an internationally recognized urban model. Even in conditions so greatly different physically, socially and culturally to those where it had been originally developed, the corridor-wedge model was seen as equally able to balance growth and open spaces and used to promote social equality.

The Green Heart and green wedges of Randstad in the Netherlands

The Netherlands entered the modern era without a single dominating metropolis, differing in this aspect from other European countries such as Germany, France, Austria or the UK. Although industrialization proved to be a magnet attracting workers to Dutch cities in the nineteenth century too, the influx of people was absorbed regionally.[42] This happened predominantly in the west of the country, in the cities of Amsterdam, Rotterdam, The Hague and Utrecht, and their surrounding areas. This agglomeration became known as the Randstad (peripheral-city). The post-war debate about the redistribution of industry and population, championed in England, coupled with Lewis Mumford's campaign against the megalopolis, expounded in his book *The City in History*,[43] resonated with the dilemmas that the Netherlands was facing at that time: should these cities be allowed to grow one into the other? Should some of the industrial activity be relocated to other parts of the country? In 1958, the report *The Development of the Western Netherlands* suggested the general structure for the Randstad and what would become known as the 'Green Heart'. The approach taken aimed to strengthen the value of large-scale regional industrialization and the interdependence of the cities, villages and green spaces. The settlements would surround the Green Heart, which would have been approximately the size of Greater London, and would have their physical forms preserved by green wedges. These were to be at least 4 kilometres wide and act as buffer zones. If van Eesteren's AUP from 1934 could be seen as the most important occurrence in Dutch planning in the interwar period, after the Second World War the encountering of the peripheral polycentric urban structure of the Randstad with the associated Green Heart takes precedence. Burke described it as the 'Greenheart metropolis'. For it to remain thus, as he concluded in the mid-60s, three conditions had to be observed: there must be no expansion of any of its constituent cities beyond the limits set by the green wedges along the ring, no expansion inwards towards the Green Heart and no large-scale use of developable land in the Randstad for buildings that could be located in other parts of the country.[44]

It is worth noting that the green heart model inverted the logic of the application of the green belt into the planning of cities and regions. While in the green belt model the large green space is surrounding the city, with the green heart the major green space is encircled by urbanization (Figure 4.9). Furthermore, previously green wedges would necessarily connect the city core – with its associated urban characteristics such as density, traffic and pollution – to a green belt or the surrounding countryside located on the outskirts. In the green heart model, as the urbanized area is the surrounding element, the green wedges make inward links to a large green (not 'grey') core. Other planning ideas had already placed a central green space at the urban core before, such as Howard's garden city or Olmsted's New York City's central park, but the Green Heart assumed, it could be argued, an unprecedented large scale in order to accommodate the needs of the polycentric urban structure of the Randstad.

In the 1960s, in line with the debates about the nature of the green belt in London or the green wedges of Copenhagen, the Green Heart was considered mainly as rural land to be protected for agriculture. This can

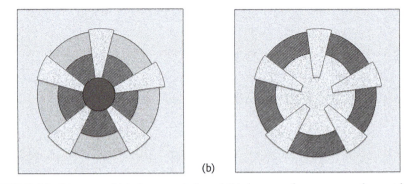

(a)   (b)

FIGURE 4.9 *Diagram of (a) the green belt and (b) the green heart approaches, with green wedges.*

be easily understood in the context of the food shortages during the war still vivid in the collective memory. However, offering access to outdoors recreation amidst nature but near to where people live also formed part of the conceptualization of the Green Heart.

This chapter has shown that the perception that planning needed to have a regional – and in cases national – dimension, developed since the 1920s, not only meant that planning had to include the countryside in its remit but also that it needed to consider other nearby urban and rural settlements. At a time when many Western cities were envisioning their futures in a much greener environment, the consolidation of the regional dimension brought to light that the scope of open space plans could now not only embrace intra-urban spaces and an eventual green belt but indeed expand much further afield. In addition, in the 1950s and 1960s, the consolidation of polycentric city-regions, expanded along comprehensive public transport routes, potentialized a renewed form of relationship between the urban and the territory (Table 4.1).

Table 4.1 The corridor-wedge model

Year	Reference	Place	Author	Notes
1942	MARS Plan of London	London, UK	MARS Group	Green belt considered 'of little significance' to London Linear plan with sixteen strips of development intercalated with green wedges
1948	1947 Finger Plan	Copenhagen, Denmark	E. Rasmussen and P. Bredsdorff	The plan directed growth along main radial public transport lines, the 'fingers', while preserving green wedges between them
1949	*Theory of City Form*	Generic / Philadelphia, USA	H. Blumenfeld	The 'star-shaped city' is considered a 'rationalization of the pattern of settlement', which was 'evolving throughout the modern world'
1952	Plan of Stockholm	Stockholm, Sweden	S Markelius, City of Stockholm	Reorganization of the city into neighbourhoods and districts Articulation of traffic system, park system and development Green wedges to be the basis of the region's park system
1957	Plan of São Paulo	São Paulo, Brazil	C. Lodi	Restructuring of the city into districts along transportation arteries separated by green wedges

Year	Reference	Place	Author	Notes
1962	The Year 2000 Plan for Washington, DC	Washington, DC, USA	National Capital Regional Planning Commission	Corridors of development around regional centres along rail lines and expressways intercalated with green wedges
1962	The Metrotowns for the Baltimore Region	Baltimore, USA	Metrotowns and Regional Cities Research Project	Metrotowns organized in corridors of development separated by green wedges, with a spider-web network of traffic arteries linking the centres
1964	The South East Study	South East, UK	Ministry of Housing and Local Government	Criticism of the green belt Application of the corridor-wedge model
1965 and 1969 (revised)	*Schema Directeur d'Aménagement et d'Urbanisme de la Région de Paris*	Paris, France	SDAURP	Corridor wedge applied to Paris region
1965 and 1975 (revised)	Plan of Geneva	Geneva, Switzerland	Geneva	Corridor-wedge model
1966	*Greenheart Metropolis*	Randstad, the Netherlands	G. Burke	Randstad surrounding a green heart Green wedges would be buffer zones between the cities
1966	The South Hampshire Plan	South Hampshire, UK	C. Buchanan	Linear regional plan with green wedges connecting the sea and the South Downs
1966	Regional Development Plan of Ruhr	Ruhr, Germany	SVR	Corridor-wedge model applied to the Ruhr region

Year	Reference	Place	Author	Notes
1967	The Strategy for the South East	South East, UK	South East Economic Planning Council	Corridors in the form of sectors, with green wedges
1967	Finger Plan for Chicago	Chicago, USA	Northeastern Illinois Planning Commission	'a complex of corridors with wedges of farmland'
1969	Plan of Hamburg	Hamburg, Germany	Baubehorde-Landesplanungsamt	Eight corridors of development with green wedges
1971	*Planning Policies for the Melbourne Metropolitan Region*	Melbourne, Australia	MMBW	Seven development corridors interspersed with 'substantial' and 'permanent wedges of open country'
1975	Plan of Tanga	Tanga, Tanzania	R. Nordberg	Three radial corridors of development with two green wedges
1977	*A Pattern Language*	Generic	C. Alexander	'interlocking fingers of farmland and urban land, even at the centre of the metropolis'

PART TWO

Green Wedges Today

This part of the book attempts to examine the roles that green wedges have been playing in helping cities and regions shape sustainable and resilient futures. Initially, it presents the major benefits derived from the integration of nature in urban environments. This is followed by the analyses of the planning, implementation and transformation of green wedges in key international case studies from the scale of the region to the neighbourhood.

5

Green Spaces, Networks and Contemporary Challenges

This chapter identifies the benefits of planning with nature and presents brief analyses of how the green wedge idea found fertile grounds in some of the main theories related to urban design, green infrastructures, landscape ecology and landscape urbanism. The chapter evidences that the combination of the green wedge's large size, proximity to residential areas and ease of access to it can play an important role in improving health and the quality of life in cities. The main argument is that the application of the green wedge idea to both existing and new urban settings has the potential to significantly improve the lives of people across the globe. With the prospect of global population growth and climate change, planning sustainable and resilient futures necessarily involves the integration of urban and ecological systems.

The benefits of green spaces

It has been argued that contact with nature is a human need.[1] Kaplan and Kaplan's seminal work shows that green spaces can have significant positive effects on people's well-being. Accessing a green space can generate a resting effect and restorative power, replenishing a person's capacity to undertake directed attention.[2] Indeed, it has been reported that the main reasons why people choose to go to green spaces is to relax and to be 'in nature'.[3] Research found statistically significant relationships between the use of urban green spaces and self-reported experiences of stress, suggesting that the more often a person visits green spaces, the less stressed he or she will be.[4] However, even short visits have positive effects on perceived stress relief and mood improvement. The impact of green spaces in reducing stress levels is particularly beneficial in large cities, where reported stress levels are higher.

There is evidence that higher degrees of naturalness lead to higher restorative potential.[5] This is corroborated by some studies in the Nordic countries, which reported that forest is the preferred environment for mental rest, providing ideal grounds for 'recharging our batteries'.[6]

The psychological benefits of passive or active social interactions that can happen in green spaces cannot be disregarded. The social functions of these spaces contribute to helping meet people's need to be gregarious, influencing directly their well-being. Community participation in, for instance, communal gardens and allotments offers opportunities for interaction across ages and social groups leading often to an enhanced sense of belonging, social cohesion and satisfaction with the local area. These activities can also ameliorate the life of residents with mental health problems. A recent survey of mental health patients reported that 90 per cent of the people who took part in green exercise activities said that the combination of nature and exercise was most important in determining how they felt. Contact with green spaces may also reduce the need for medication and services for mental health patients.[7]

The recreational function of green spaces is pervasive. Probably because it directly addresses the human need for contact with nature, presenting both psychological and physical benefits. Recreation is a core function of green spaces in nearly all plans analysed in this book and in a large proportion of research studies involving urban greenery. It encompasses a range of activities, from passive, such as sitting and enjoying views, to more active such as walking, playing games, hiking, running and so on.

In terms of physical health, green spaces can help in a number of ways. First of all, it has been shown that views of or access to green spaces can facilitate recovery from illness.[8] Secondly, as green spaces encourage physical activities in all age groups, a number of direct health benefits derive from their use, including reduction or maintenance of adequate body weight, higher levels of fitness and cardio-vascular health. It is also known that an active lifestyle helps avoiding strokes and type-2 diabetes. Obesity is of particular concern as it is associated with a range of health problems including cardiovascular disease and cancer. Alarmingly, by 2050 obesity is predicted to affect 60 per cent of adult men, 50 per cent of adult women and 25 per cent of children in England.[9] As obesity tends to be conditioned to physical activity and food intake, green spaces can help address the problem by encouraging a more active lifestyle and supporting mechanisms to engage citizens in healthier eating. This can include, for example, involving residents in urban agriculture and community gardens, providing increased access to food producers in the countryside, supporting healthy food markets and increasing the availability of healthy food in green spaces and surrounding areas.

Quantity and size of green spaces in people's living environment also appear to be associated with residents' health and mortality. Adults who live in greener environments tend to report better general health and tend to have a lower risk of premature death.[10] A European-level study found that the likelihood of residents' being physically active in residential areas with high levels of greenery was more than three times higher than of those in similar areas with low levels of greenery.[11] There is evidence supporting the fact that the larger the size of the green space, the more likely people are to use it. This is hardly surprising, since large green spaces can potentially offer a wider range of functions, experiences and activities for people of different age groups, socio-economic status and interests when compared to small green spaces.[12]

It is well documented that the use of green spaces is also directly impacted by the proximity and accessibility of residents to them. A survey on the use of green areas in Denmark showed that there was a steep decline in use frequency with increasing distance, especially over the first 100–300 metres and that the effect of distance gradually levels off as distance to green areas increases. The relationship was so direct that the distance to green areas was considered to be a far better predictor of stress levels than the actual use of green areas.[13] In a study of Swedish cities, it was found that residents who live 50 metres or less from the nearest green area generally visit urban open green spaces three to four times a week, while those whose distance was 300 metres, visited green spaces only 2.7 times a week on average. If the distance was 1,000 metres, such spaces were visited only once a week.[14] A similar relationship between the use of greenways and proximity to them was found.[15] These green routes can be particularly important to allow children and older residents direct access to green spaces undisturbed by vehicular traffic. As seen before, access to green spaces is vital to well-being, but can be problematic particularly to elderly residents. By 2050, the proportion of the world's older adults is estimated to double from about 11 per cent to 22 per cent, reaching two billion people.[16] In this light, a report from the UK Government Office for Science recommends that green spaces should be both visible and accessible from every older person's home, ideally within 300 metres.[17]

Needless to say, the quality of green spaces is a key factor in their use. If poorly designed, managed and kept, the visitor's sense of security and general experience will be severely affected. Uninteresting, monotonous and neglected spaces tend to generate a downward spiral leading to their abandonment by most residents. Green spaces, therefore, must offer aesthetically pleasing experiences, activities for all ages, be well kept and safe.

The amount, distribution and quality of green spaces can contribute to reducing health inequalities in cities. Many observational studies have shown a positive correlation between greater access to green spaces and reduced health inequalities. In fact, the impact of the amount of green spaces on levels of health of nearby residents is stronger in lower socio-economic groups.[18] The relationship between social inequality and offer of high quality green spaces is historically perceived in urban settings. Quality green spaces tend to increase land prices in their vicinity and result in high-income groups locating there. In contrast, low-income groups may not have the means to move out to districts with a better offer.

Green spaces are usually highly valued by the public. In the UK, a survey conducted by CABE (Commission for Architecture and Built Environment) reported that 90 per cent of the respondents believe that green spaces improve people's quality of life.[19] In addition, people living close to green spaces tend to report higher levels of happiness.[20]

Even though clean air is considered to be a fundamental requirement for human health and well-being, air pollution is a growing problem. As reported by the UN's World Health Organization, it is in fact the world's largest single environmental health risk, being responsible for one in eight total deaths globally.[21] Its known pernicious effects on health include respiratory and cardiovascular diseases. The Environment Agency estimates that more than 90 per cent of people in European cities are breathing dangerous air, making air pollution the number one environmental cause of premature death in the EU.[22] The rapid urban growth of Asian mega-cities in recent decades was accompanied by an exponential increase in air pollution. In December 2015, Beijing issued the first pollution red alert when smog reached forty times more than the safe levels in some areas, forcing millions of vehicles off roads and prompting the closure of schools and factories.

Recent studies proved that green spaces have the capacity to substantially improve air quality. For instance, it is considered that a tree-lined street can reduce indoor pollution by 90 per cent compared with a street without trees,[23] and that the larger the green space and the closer to the source of pollution, the greater the benefits to air quality.[24] Trees are considered more effective than shorter vegetation in improving air condition, whose effect can be supplemented by bushes and grasses.[25]

Noise pollution is another important environmental problem in urban centres, leading to higher levels of stress, mental illness and low productivity. Furthermore, noise adversely impacts on local ecology and public amenity. Green space planning again can contribute to noise abatement in cities. The location of green spaces as buffer zones between areas to be protected and sources of noise has been a common strategy in planning history. Also, efficient planting as barriers or shelters for pedestrians can lessen the effect of noise.

There is strong evidence to support that the creation of networks of high-quality green and blue spaces, including green routes leading to main destinations, should become a priority in planning today. The network should range from regional to local scales and be overlaid with the traffic network and public and private transport networks. This would allow for a well-connected structure encompassing a variety of sizes and types of green spaces as well as activities and personal experiences in nature. Consideration must be given to the needs of residents, who should be involved in co-designing their green spaces.

Since its inception the green wedge model aimed at driving large green spaces from the countryside into the core of urban settings near to where people lived. The body of evidence discussed so far shows that the combination of size, proximity and ease of access is fortuitous in attracting people to green areas and in improving health in cities. The importance of integrating this body of evidence into planning greener cities is evident. If indeed access to nature is a fundamental need of human beings, providing numerous positive psychological and physical benefits, the application of the green wedge idea to both existing and new urban settings has the potential to significantly improve the lives of people across the globe.

The birth of urban design and the 'Star City'

The postmodern criticism of undefined large open spaces and the focus on urbanity in the fields of architecture and urban studies devolved to a great degree the discussions about green space planning to landscape architecture and ecology. The emergence of urban design as a disciplinary field was marked by a return to townscape. Urban Design, trying to establish itself between the fields of architecture and town planning with the crisis of the project of modernity, soon aimed at defining parameters for the creation of place-specific and place-generating proposals no larger than the city scale. The role of empirical analyses and phenomenological experience of place infused its foundational discourses in the 1960s and 1970s, such as Kevin Lynch's *Image of the City* from 1960, Jane Jacobs' *Death and Life of Great American Cities* from 1961 and Gordon Cullen's *Concise Townscape* from the same year. The return to the idea of type, as opposed to model, appeared in the works by Rossi, *Architecture of the City* in 1966, and Venturi and Scott Brown, *Learning from Las Vegas* in 1972. The need to resolve the dichotomy between planning voids and 'solids' in cities was dealt with by Rowe and Koetter's *Collage city* from 1978, while Koolhaas in *Delirious New York* from 1978 focused on the dazzling power of New York as the contemporary metropolis *par excellence*. In these instaurational texts, green spaces are severely minimized both as objects of theory and as instruments of urban design practice.

A significant counter to this trend came from landscape architecture. Ian McHarg in *Design with Nature*, from 1969, called for an integrative way of thinking which applied a novel ecological assessment method with regional planning. In this line of thought, McHarg was suspicious of the forceful establishment of geometrical models of green space planning and argued that the distribution of open space must respond to natural processes. He questioned the actions of the 'geometric planner' proposing that 'the city be ringed with a green circle in which green activities – agriculture, institutions and the like – are preserved or even introduced', as this may not be the most suitable location for 'green activities'. In addition, he recapped that urbanization processes tended to densify within resulting in 'open space [being] most abundant where people are scarcest'.[26] He suggested instead that:

> Optimally, one would wish for two systems within the metropolitan region – one the pattern of natural processes preserved in open space, the other the pattern of urban development. If these were interfused, one could satisfy the provision of open space for the population.[27]

In so doing, the land reserved for open space would be derived from the analysis of natural processes and be intrinsically suitable for 'green' purposes. The 'interfusion' proposed resonated with many of the aims of those involved in proposing green wedges, particularly with the attempts to promote a balanced relationship between man and nature. The solution would be in looking to nature first and then planning accordingly.

For Lewis Mumford, now from a cultural perspective, the understanding of human settlement in harmony with nature also needed to emerge out of the scale of the region. He urged that 'we must treat the whole region as a potential park area' and that it was a task of planners to ensure that a generous and well-conceived regional network of green spaces became features of future cities:

> In the cities of the future, ribbons of green must run through every quarter, forming a continuous web of garden and mall, widening at the edge of the city into protective greenbelts, so that landscape and garden will become an integral part of urban no less than rural life, for both weekday and holiday users.[28]

Green wedges appear as a viable solution again. Mumford referred to them as 'ribbons of green (...) widening at the edge of the city'. Contrary to the idea of the metropolis, his ideas were instrumental in the reconfiguration of large urban agglomerations into smaller, defined, community areas. The question of large green spaces, and their geometries, which to some extent was addressed by Mumford, will reappear in the discourses from the standpoint of urban design. For instance, Christopher Alexander in A Pattern Language addressed the dilemma of how to let cities grow but still offer easy access to intra-urban green space and the countryside. For Alexander, the large city 'becomes good for life only when it contains a great density of interactions', but in sprawling it tends to distance men from the countryside. In line with Geddes's and Mumford's approaches, he considered that 'our need for contact with the countryside runs too deep, it is a biological necessity'. As a consequence, 'with the breakdown of contact between city dwellers and the countryside, the cities become prisons'.[29] The model that would 're-establish and maintain proper connection between city and country' should be based on keeping 'interlocking fingers of farmland and urban land, even at the centre of the metropolis'.[30] Alexander suggested that city fingers should be at most 1 mile (1.6 kilometres) wide so as to allow every inhabitant to access the countryside within a 10-minute walk, while the minimum width of the green fingers would also be 1 mile, determined by the minimum acceptable size for a typical farm. According to him, agricultural valleys should be considered as key elements in this network. It must be noted that Alexander's recommendations about city form did not imply a top-down application of models, but were to be achieved as hopeful results of mediated bottom-up processes.

A strong return to urban models in foundational urban design texts is seen in Lynch's book *Theory of Good City Form* from 1981. This work aimed to identify the best forms of urban settlement through the examination of existing models. 'The Star' model is the first to be mentioned. He described it as a city with a strong centre, radial transport arteries and green wedges taking up the remaining space between the built areas. In line with previous discourses, Lynch also stressed their importance in creating a green channel directly out into the countryside, providing routes for pedestrians, cyclists and even horse riders. He acknowledged the proclaimed benefits of this model, notwithstanding the inherent difficulties in its implementation:

> The 'green wedge' idea is almost the reverse of the greenbelt concept. In this view, open space should penetrate into the heart of a settlement and radiate outward to the periphery. Thus all developed land will have open space nearby, although there will be less of it toward the center, as the rays converge. Open spaces are linked together, and connect to the rural environs of a city, however distant. Yet growth at the periphery, along the major access routes, is never blocked.[31]

Lynch focused on the link between the transport system, form of development and disposition of green spaces in the definition of this model. Cliff Moughtin also described the model, drawing attention to the mounting importance of cross-connections as the wedges widen towards the countryside.[32]

New ways to look at links to the countryside and channels of greenery within the city emerged with the ecological movement and subsequent debates on sustainability. Concepts such as 'greenways', 'green corridors', 'landscape corridors' and 'green infrastructure' emerged and have been contributing to promoting a more systemic integration of ecology, planning and urban design within the framework of the sustainability agenda.

Green infrastructure

The creation of a network of green spaces within an urban plan has been receiving extensive attention. Initially referred to as a 'park system', the idea of a network of interconnected green spaces has a long standing tradition in planning history. Recently, focus on the combined values and benefits of such networks for nature and human beings has led to a redefinition of the idea into what has been termed green infrastructure (GI).

The dual opposition between an anthropocentric and a 'naturalistic' view of green networks is being questioned.[33] A key characteristic of green infrastructure is its ability to deliver a wide range of ecosystem services and perform several functions in the same location.[34] Ecosystem services refer to the range of benefits provided by ecosystems, including the provision of food, water, climate regulation, flood control, protection against soil erosion and intangible benefits such as those related to recreational, cultural and spiritual activities.[35] There is evidence suggesting that an integrated approach in the planning and management of ecosystem services at multiple scales is essential. These include the regional, city and local scales.[36]

Several authors have delved into the benefits of green infrastructures.[37] These tend to be identified in the domains of social, ecological, environmental and economic benefits for clarity of argument, but should be seen as intertwined. In terms of their social aspects, they can help enhance the inhabitants' health, shape city form and control sprawl, improve the connectivity of the urban fabric, offer attractive high-quality places for people, provide psychological and physical benefits of access to green spaces, enhance tourism and so on. Main contributions of green infrastructure to ecology are the protection and promotion of biodiversity and natural settings as well as the establishment and enhancement of ecological corridors. Urbanization generally leads to fragmentation and decrease of areas used as ecological habitats, which in turn can cause local extinction of species. In Europe, for instance, 30 per cent of land is moderately or highly fragmented. Ecological corridors can help reconnect isolated natural areas across the wider landscape. In so doing, they can increase the mobility of wildlife and restore services that a healthy ecosystem can provide.[38] Better air quality, the reduction of the urban heat island effect, minimization of acid rain occurrences, urban thermal regulation, promotion of airflow leading to cooling and removal of pollutants, carbon storage, protection against soil erosion, reduction in flood risk and surface water runoff, and the protection of clean water and water tables are some of the environmental benefits identified. Economic benefits relate to added economic value to places, the generation of renewable energy and resources, rainwater harvesting, accommodation of waste treatment and recycling, general agriculture and sustainable food production, among others.

More and more green infrastructures have been used to help mitigate the potential effects of climate change. Rising global average temperatures are predicted to impact on climate and weather patterns. Desertification processes and water scarcity are just some of the potential consequences. These in turn are predicted to damage agricultural production and transform ecological systems. In cities, the increased risk of severe storms and droughts, floods, heat waves, the urban heat island effect – among others – are just some of the expected challenges.[39] Defining ways in which green infrastructures can contribute to a resilient future has become imperative. Further research is needed in this field, but it is recognized that they can help reduce the overall temperature in urban environments, minimize or reverse desertification processes, alleviate the impact of severe floods by contributing to sustainable urban drainage systems (SUDS), provide 'soft' solutions for coastal protection, minimize heat island effects, store carbon, improve air quality and enhance ecosystems resilience, among others.[40] In any case, they must be part of comprehensive solutions for city-regions.

Green wedges have played key roles in green infrastructure projects across all the aforementioned domains. Their significance in regional and city plans will be analysed in the next chapters, but it is worth noting here that green wedges are now part of numerous green infrastructure strategies in the world (see Table 5.1 for examples in the UK).[41]

Table 5.1 Green wedges in green infrastructure strategies in the UK

Year	Reference	Place	Author	Notes
1987	Leicestershire Structure Plan	Leicestershire, UK	Leicestershire County Council	Green wedge policies Subsequent plans maintain policies on green wedges
2002	Doncaster Core Strategy	Doncaster, UK	Doncaster Metropolitan Borough Council	Seven green wedges designated
2008	Chelmsford Core Strategy and Development Control Policies	Chelmsford, UK	Chelmsford City Council	Green Wedge designation of the valleys and floodplain of the Rivers Chelmer and Can

Year	Reference	Place	Author	Notes
2008	Harrogate District Local Plan	Harrogate, UK	Harrogate Borough Council	Green wedges designation
2009	East Midlands Regional Plan	East Midlands, UK	Government Office for East Midlands	'Green Wedges serve useful strategic planning functions in preventing the merging of settlements, guiding development form and providing a "green lung" into urban areas, and acts as a recreational resource'
2010	Liverpool Green Infrastructure Strategy	Liverpool, UK	The Mersey Forest	Green infrastructure plan
2014	Harlow Local Development Plan	Harlow, UK	Harlow Council	Pursuit of a more interconnected network with green wedges and fingers

Landscape Ecology

Steeped in complexity theory and systems thinking, landscape ecology emerged in the 1980s. From this standpoint, the concept of landscape is understood as a heterogeneous land area composed of a cluster of interacting ecosystems that is repeated. Landscape ecology focuses on the shared characteristics of landscapes: structure, function and change. It argues that all landscapes share a common structure based on the concepts of patches, corridors and a background matrix. Patches are defined as non-linear surface areas differing from their surroundings, corridors being distinctive linear strips of land and the matrix being the most extensive and most connected background element.[42]

In the context of regional and city planning, green wedges would often constitute corridors and matrixes. It is however imperative to consider analyses at multiple scales as they are likely to contain a range of elements performing different structural functions. Considering a green wedge, for instance, as a landscape entity, a series of patches and corridors within its borders may be found.

Forman and Godron define three types of corridor structure: line, strip and stream corridors. Considering these structures, green wedges tend to present a hybrid or an in-between condition, being often of the first type, the line, when within, for instance, dense urban settings and of the second type, the strip, when they widen towards the outskirts. The stream corridor borders water courses, varying in width. Time and again water courses become the spines of green wedges, as can be seen for example in Melbourne and Hamburg. The implications of the corridor width for ecological diversity are important to highlight in order to further explore how green wedges may support ecological services. In corridors, there tends to be a change in species composition from the centre to the edges and it is expected that the wider the corridor, the more likely it is to contain favourable habitats for more species. As such, the definition of minimum widths of green wedges, as appropriate, so that they are wide enough to support an interior environment is likely to have a positive effect on wildlife.[43] Furthermore, high levels of connectivity along and across green wedges lead to stronger ecological corridors. Since the matrix is considered to be the most connected element of the landscape, its predominant characteristics can vary extensively in any given case. Woodland and rural land are only two of the predominant conditions in green wedges.

At city and regional scale, the pattern of green wedges against the built-up area presents a boundary with a high perimeter-to-area ratio, which 'is characteristic of systems with considerable interchanges of energy, materials or organisms with the surroundings'.[44] As such, the potential for exchanges between the built-up areas and green wedges is high. In this light, it could be argued that the propitiousness of integrating socio-ecological services, manmade structures and activities with nature given by the model ought to be one of its main characteristics today.

Landscape Urbanism

Landscape Urbanism can be defined as a master planning approach that locates the landscape at the heart of the process, according to Waldheim, replacing architecture as the 'basic building block of contemporary urbanism'.[45] This notion can be traced back to Olmsted and the American park system tradition and has been reconfigured and presented as an alternative to modernist planning and neo-traditionalist new urbanism movement.

The influence of systems thinking on landscape urbanism can be seen in its defence of dynamic planning processes leading to change over static form, as well as on the need to consider the interactions of socio-economic, cultural and ecological dimensions alongside one another. The *a priori* rejection of the opposition between city and nature in landscape urbanism resonates with contemporary discourses on green infrastructure projects as discussed and positive planning of large green spaces. This approach has found immediate applicability in urban regeneration projects involving large-scale infrastructures and derelict brownfield sites.

Sustainability and resilience in face of climate change

The United Nations predicts that the world's population will reach ten billion people in 2050 and that the proportion of urban dwellers will increase from 50 to 70 per cent of the total population. For a start, this would mean that seven billion people would live in urban areas. Today, two-thirds of all Europeans already live in towns and cities. Along with the fact that cities are responsible for 80 per cent of world's total CO_2 emission, it is worth mentioning that as our Human Development Index increases, so does our ecological footprint. There will be a need to accommodate many more urban inhabitants, promote better living conditions across the world, and at the same time drastically reduce emissions and our ecological footprint. It is known that growing urbanization tends to put pressure on open spaces. An increase in urban encroachment onto green spaces and building on green field sites have been evident across the world during the last fifty years and may still exacerbate to accommodate our need for urban dwellings if clear policies and strategies to counteract this trend are not put in place. Equating these seemingly disparate needs and expectations evidently pose considerable difficulties. In any case, towns and cities need to be part of the solution.

If the construction of the modern age had been based on the predominance of industrial development and urbanization, a shift in perception started with the oil crisis of the 1970s. It questioned the model of economic growth based on fossil fuels and high levels of consumption and waste generation. Since then, annual demand on resources exceeds what the planet can regenerate.[46]

The realization that our actions could indeed lead to the destruction of the planet (climate change) and that further prolonged reliance on fossil fuels could not be sustained led to a crisis of industrial society and a search for more holistic approaches towards urban development and the protection of the environment. The Brundtland Report *Our Common Future*, which faced the task defined by the UN to set forth a 'global agenda for change', became a fundamental reference in the articulation of a new paradigm. 'Sustainability' was presented as having three pillars: economic, social and environmental, and 'sustainable development' as the development that 'meets the need of the present without compromising the ability of future generations to meet their own needs'.[47] Rio 92 Agenda 21, the Aalborg Charter in 1994, the Kyoto Protocol in 1998, Johannesburg in 2002 and Rio +20 debated ways to reduce our demand on the planet and different ideas on ecological development. More recently discussions around how to define indicators and parameters to construct sustainable cities and urban spaces have manifested themselves in planning and urban design.

It is widely accepted that urban sustainability needs to be at the core of contemporary modes of planning and design. Echenique identifies different contemporary strategies of urban growth: compaction, dispersal and structured expansion.[48] Proponents of the compact city aim to increase density in inner urban areas to minimize land use, reduce the need for travel and promote urban vitality and diversity. According to this strategy, development should be concentrated on brownfield sites whenever possible, as opposed to greenfield sites.[49] Dispersal, on the other hand, distributes development across larger areas, often at regional scale, in connection to transport axes, reflecting the demand for space, proximity to the countryside and/or jobs. Structured expansion happens by planned peripheral development in existing cities.[50] Needless to say, combinations and variations of these approaches have been applied to varying degrees in contemporary planning, as will be discussed in the next chapters.

A large amount of research has been done into the relation between urban form and sustainability indicators, which is now being filtered through to the retrofit and construction of new developments.[51] Terms such as 'eco-city', 'eco-town', 'green city', 'eco-district', among others, have labelled numerous projects from neighbourhood to regional scale.[52] Further definitions of the concept of sustainable development have benefitted from a reiterative process of research and experimentation. The list of criteria and recommendations for sustainable developments is almost as large as the number of authors addressing the topic. However, as Naess noted, these discourses tend to concentrate on the creation of enhanced living conditions in close contact with nature and on reduction of energy use, waste and emissions coupled with closed-loop processes in which resources transformed into waste become resources again.[53] More specifically, these discourses, in varying levels, generate solutions that tend to attempt to forge an integrative view of the different sub-systems involved in the construction of the urban system; consider in articulation local, city and regional scales; promote greater access to quality green space, including wildlife habitats and corridors; engage in sustainable food production; promote medium-high density; integrate development with public transport; promote cycling, walking and outdoor recreation; adopt mixed-use solutions; aim for diversity as well as attempt to meet indicators related to resource efficiency, waste management and ecological footprint.

Recently the concept of resilience has been intertwined with that of sustainability, as cities need to be prepared to face the predicted impacts of climate change.[54] Stemming from ecology, resilience theory shifts the understanding of ecosystems as closed, stable and predictable systems functioning according to a linear model of development to the recognition of their open, complex, self-organising and changeable nature. Resilience has been defined as the capacity of a system to adapt and regenerate in the face of disturbance and changing conditions, while retaining its function, structure, identity and feedback.[55] However, in the concept of resilience, disturbances also open up opportunities for adaptation and change through the emergence of new trajectories.[56] As a framework for an integrative socio-ecological approach, resilience has been applied to city planning and the planning of large green structures. This approach suggests the overcoming of old dichotomies between the man-made and nature, arguing for a dynamic relationship between both, each one impacting the other. Resilient societies are those that are able to effectively absorb large shocks and contain the components needed for renewal and reorganization, being able thus to respond to external disturbances through adaptive capacity. Folke et al. propose that to build adaptive capacity, societies need to consider socio-ecological systems together, live with change and uncertainty, nurture diversity, combine different types of knowledge for learning and create opportunities for self-organization.[57]

Recent discourses have identified some of the roles that green spaces can play in promoting sustainable and resilient cities, but more investigation on this subject is still needed.[58] As Erixon et al. stated, resilience thinking – by acknowledging complexity, change and mutability as inherent to ecosystems – could offer large green space planning a path for more proactive and dynamic approaches.[59] First, the authors argue, the interconnectedness and interdependence of man and nature should be better acknowledged. Second, there is a need to better understand how processes and features at different scales can affect each other, which leads to the fact that considering different scales cohesively can help build resilience. Finally, they maintain that adaptive capacity is a pre-requisite for resilience. In this respect, high diversity is fundamental both in terms of absorbing disturbances and in regenerating and re-organizing itself after such disturbances. High diversity increases the range of possibilities that a system has to keep its functions and structures or to adapt and find new states.[60] Consequently, non-integrative solutions – for instance nature reserves that exclude functions other than biological to avoid disturbance to the wildlife habitats – which do not take into consideration the implications for socio-cultural activities can have a detrimental impact on the socio-spatial cohesiveness of communities. In terms of preservation, it is now recognized that nature protection is not always best achieved through a 'leave as it is' approach, but that dynamic approaches can indeed promote enhanced socio-economic sustainability.[61] This in turn can lead to creative generative processes.

6

Towards Sustainable and Resilient City-regions

This chapter analyses the roles of green wedges in leading contemporary city-region visions for sustainable and resilient urban futures. The case studies selected are Stockholm, which won the first award of European Green Capital in 2010; Copenhagen, the award winner in 2014; Helsinki, a frontrunner in the execution of major integrated urban transformations; the Randstad region, which is attempting to reinvent the concept of the Green Heart into a green and blue delta; Melbourne, considered one of the most liveable cities in the world, and Freiburg, one of the greenest. For all these global cities, proactive planning for the development of polycentric networked city-regions leading up to 2020–50 is at the core of preparing for expected and potential mutable scenarios.

Stockholm: Blue and green wedges

The Swedish planning system concentrates power in the hands of the municipalities, which are required to produce and have a current municipal comprehensive plan. They serve as guidance for detailed plans, which are then legally binding. The State can intervene should a municipal plan be deemed detrimental to areas beyond its boundaries. Regional planning bodies work with municipalities to define a regional plan to coordinate a shared vision for the region in question.[1] In the case of Stockholm region, the regional plan encompasses the areas of twenty six municipalities, covering a population of more than 2 million people. Consequently, a large number of stakeholders need to work together for a common framework to be achieved and observed in the municipal land use plans.

The Regional Development Plan for the Stockholm Region (RUFS 2010) sets out the direction for Stockholm's region up to 2030. The vision is no short of ambition: to become Europe's most attractive metropolitan region.[2] The key driver here is the growth forecast, as Stockholm is preparing to receive 600,000 more people by 2030. Aside from equating a larger, healthier and happier population, five other challenges were identified: to be a small but internationally leading region, to improve security, to reduce the impact of climate change while still promoting growth, to enhance capacity and to 'open up' the region. To meet these challenges, Stockholm region aims to become a leading growth region, more open and accessible and with a good resource-efficient living environment. The planning strategies identified for sustainable development include strengthening the region's polycentric structure, densifying around transport hubs and improving the green wedge structure.

In this vision for 2030, Stockholm builds on its planning tradition of polycentric corridor development with green wedges. The objective of making the urban structure denser and polycentric is intended to generate a more attractive urban environment close to public transport, encroaching as little as possible on green wedges. On account of this, in addition to the central core, eight outer regional cores are to be strengthened. In the light of the forecasted population growth, the choice for infill development for the creation of a dense polycentric urban structure is not unusual. It is intended to provide conditions for growth avoiding sprawl, for the safeguarding of green spaces and the enhancement of urban liveliness, traffic efficiency and the distribution of facilities. For that, the alignment between the transport infrastructure and hubs – by means of the intensification and diversification of functions and activities around stations – and an increased housing and high-quality green space offer becomes a necessity. In addition, the interconnectivity of the central area with the regional cores, as well as their cross-connectivity, is going to be developed.

The fact that the region's population is growing increases the demand not only for housing and services, but also for high-quality green spaces. These areas play an important role in ensuring the region's attractiveness. Central to that is the definition of a tiered green and blue infrastructure for the region, encompassing regional, city and local scales. In this context, the largely uninterrupted nature of the region's ten large green wedges is foremost. As they cross municipal boundaries, regional cooperation has been necessary for the development of a shared holistic view of challenges, existing values and potentialities.

Today, Stockholm's green wedges are the main elements of the region's green and blue infrastructure. The Regional Development Plan for the

Stockholm Region presents a clear commitment to safeguard, improve the accessibility and quality of the green wedges and the shoreline. There has been a historical process of development and consolidation of Stockholm's green wedges, which led to them being considered world-unique and of incalculable value, and, therefore, of fundamental importance for the region.[3] According to Bette Malmros, regional planner from the department of 'Growth and Regional Planning Management' of Stockholm County Council, 'the green wedges are here to stay'.[4]

Building on Stockholm region's structure, new development is to be concentrated within or adjacent to existing built-up areas, along axes of growth. As such, the eight regional cores are located on transport axes and planned to be the centres of gravity for new development. They are to be in relative proximity to at least one green wedge. This strategy is also intended to minimize encroachment on the green wedges.

Since the 1952 plan until the 1990s, Stockholm had been shifting between the idea of green wedges and green belts. In the last decades, a move towards the former became predominant in regional planning studies for the Swedish capital. This was based on the fact that the city had grown along radial lines of traffic, avoiding rocky areas, floodplains and agricultural fields, which generated the star-shaped form it has today with green and blue wedges. Furthermore, historically, the Crown, the military and the State owned a large proportion of the areas pertaining to green wedges, which kept them largely undeveloped. Recently, there has been an increase in the amount of green wedge land owned by the municipalities.

Stockholm region possesses ten green wedges: Järva, Rösjö, Angarn, Bogesund, Nacka-Värmdö, Tyresta, Hanveden, Bornsjö, Ekerö and Görväln (Figure 6.1). These follow to a great extent the definition of green wedges contained in the 1952 plan. For instance, the axis between Haga Park and Järva highlighted in the post-war plan has taken today the shape of the Järva wedge, containing the world's first urban national park. Stockholm region's historically developed coherent urban structure has determined the conditions of existence of the green wedges. A fundamental contemporary preoccupation is that the interaction between these large-scale green areas and the urban structure be increased and enhanced. The report *När, vad och hur? Svaga samband i Stockholmsregionens gröna kilar* is an important step in this direction, since it presents recommendations to the municipalities into how to keep the wedges coherent and, at the same time, increase the interaction between the green and the urban structures.

According to the RUFS 2010, 'every green wedge should be held together and its functions and qualities should be retained and improved'.[5] The plan stated that a green wedge should be at least 500 metres wide, as this would

FIGURE 6.1 *Stockholm's Regional green structure, green asset core map, 2010.* Source: *The new Regional Development Plan for the Stockholm Region (RUFS 2010), map 21, 165. Courtesy of The Growth and Regional Planning Administration in Stockholm County Council.*

provide visitors with a sense of seclusion in nature, as well as the possibility of experiencing varied landscapes. Besides, this is considered to support the proliferation of different edge and interior ecological habitats.[6]

While biodiversity was the main theme during the 1990s, the subsequent plans for the green and blue infrastructure of Stockholm included a wider range of functions. Stockholm County Council identified the green wedges' main functions (Figure 6.2) mostly around recreation and biodiversity. Other functions such environmental management and mitigation of the impacts of climate change are becoming more prominent.[7] The region's green wedges are the setting for many recreational activities, both active, such as hiking, cycling or sports practised at open-air recreational centres, and passive, focused more on the contact with the natural environment in its variety of landscapes, from

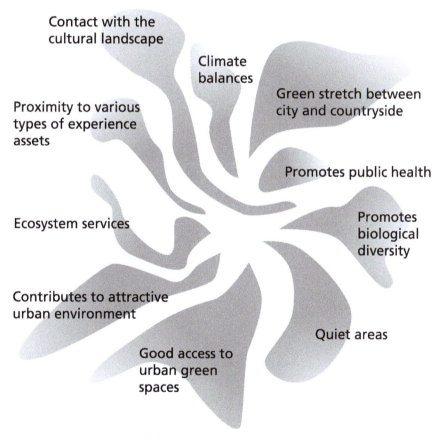

FIGURE 6.2 *Diagram of functions of Stockholm's green wedges.* Source: *The new Regional Development Plan for the Stockholm Region (RUFS 2010), 2010, 147. Courtesy of The Growth and Regional Planning Administration in Stockholm County Council.*

wilder to more urban. In ecological and environmental terms, these wedges are home to important forested areas acting as significant ecological corridors, as is the case of the Järva and the Tyreste wedges. Stockholm region presents high levels of ecological connectivity, mostly due to the continuity of green wedges extending from the countryside and forested areas into the city core. This allows almost every inhabitant of the region close access to large green spaces. Moreover, some species are still found in the inner area of Stockholm which otherwise would not be there.[8]

Although the agricultural function is not predominant in Stockholm region's green wedges, it is expected that it may become more so in subsequent plans for the region.[9] Nonetheless, it is worth pointing out that certain sections of the green wedges contain allotments, as can be seen in the vicinity of Hammarbybacken ski slope in the Nacka-Värmdö wedge. These allotments not only address matters of local food production and associated environmental and sustainability benefits, but also have a significant role to play in building community spirit and social integration. The roles of green wedges in absorbing rainwater and protecting sensitive basins and watercourses cannot be overlooked (particularly around Lake Mälaren). They also improve air quality, provide air exchange and climate equalization for the innermost parts of Stockholm, among other roles. In terms of resilience to future challenges due to climate change, more research needs to be done to better assess how green wedges can contribute here, for instance in evaluating their part in accommodating SUDS in a scenario of more frequent and stronger storms.[10] It has been argued recently that socio-ecological systems are interdependent and that cities can do much more to integrate ecosystem services in the built environment through complementary land use and urban green structure planning.[11] Stockholm's approach to integrating social values, ecological considerations and environmental needs has put the region at the forefront of knowledge about green wedges.

A specific contribution of the green wedges of Stockholm to knowledge of large green structure planning is the development of a methodology for the assessment of their social values and the public's expectations. The methodology is one of the outcomes of the research led by Malmros, which involved in-depth interviews, focus groups and a case-study approach. It identified seven types of values ascribed to green wedges by the public across a range of landscapes from the most undeveloped to the most developed. They were: 'untouched green spaces', 'woodland harmony', 'open views and open landscapes', 'biodiversity and lessons from nature', 'cultural history and living rural environments', 'activities and challenges' and 'facilities and meeting places'. The results were mapped using GIS, which matched the values with specific areas. The research showed that beauty, quietness and the experience of being in a natural environment were particularly cherished, especially in the first three categories; while activities and gathering places were particularly relevant in the latter categories.[12] This points to the need of planning and managing the green wedges for a multiplicity of spatial configurations and experiences to cater for the different users' needs. Although the literature is generally consistent in supporting the positive link between green areas and their proximity to users, this work showed that the proximity of parts of green wedges to urban settings and traffic arteries needs to be considered in relation to the different expected experiences within these green spaces. The strong correlation between place and experiences thus requires a careful consideration of the impact that nearby urban settings and man-made disturbances may have and planning for appropriate solutions to each circumstance. Malmros' research informed the development of the green and blue infrastructure strategy for the region, leading to the proposals in the RUFS 2010, and was highly influential in the study of social values of green spaces in other cities.

Another significant contribution found in Stockholm's approach to the future of green wedges relates to the definition of 'green asset cores'. This concept addresses the social values of green wedges and their qualities of place, as they signify sites of special natural, cultural, historic or aesthetic importance. Every wedge is to contain asset cores, which should be a few square kilometres in size as a minimum. They are recognized as the most valuable parts of any given green wedge. Here value is understood in its qualitative dimension. Enhancing the attractiveness of green wedges, and therefore their use and perceived value, by strengthening existing and developing new cores where needed, a virtuous cycle of use by the population, creation of emotional attachment and identity building is generated, which in turn helps safeguarding these spaces. The plan, therefore, sees the improvement and creation of green asset cores as crucial for the strengthening of the whole green infrastructure of Stockholm. An implemented example can be found in the Järva wedge (Figure 6.3), which presents a variety of well-connected high-quality landscapes, stretching from the shore at Djurgården (Figure 6.4) through the Haga Park (Figure 6.5) to Lake Mälaren in the north.[13]

A number of projects are addressing the accessibility of and connectivity to and across green wedges. In the pursuit of a balanced transport infrastructure, the plan proposes the improvement of the radial axes and connections across them. If this may lead to negative impacts on the cohesiveness of green wedges and the quality of place around these interventions, an integrated approach and well-thought through plans can minimize the potential drawbacks and even enhance their connectivity. Public access to green wedges is to be strengthened by the establishment of public transport 'green stations', which would be those within a radius of 500 metres of a green wedge. Similarly, a

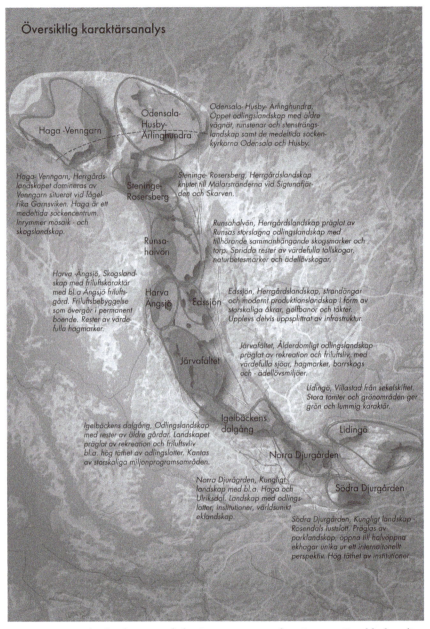

FIGURE 6.3 *The landscapes of the Järva green wedge.* Source: *Stockholms läns landsting, 2012, 53. Courtesy of The Growth and Regional Planning Administration in Stockholm County Council.*

FIGURE 6.4 *View of Djurgården.*

number of piers with public transport provide direct access to coastal areas
and the archipelago.

The thinner areas of green wedges (narrower than 500 metres), usually
occurring in the proximity of urban centres or transport infrastructure, are
referred to as 'weak green links'. In certain areas, they play an important role in
providing continuity within a green wedge, which otherwise would be broken
down. An interesting example is found in the connections between Hammarby
Sjöstad, one of the most well known sustainable urban extensions in Europe,[14]
and the Nacka-Värmdö green wedge through two 'ecoducts' (Figure 6.6) over
the Södra Länken highway, one in the vicinity of an existing oak woodland
and another near the Hammarbybacken ski slope. From there they reach the
heart of Hammarby Sjöstad through green fingers. The 'ecoducts' are green
footbridges that not only give residents and visitors a direct connection to the
green wedge (Figure 6.7), but also work as wildlife corridors.[15]

Mapping a variety of types of links from strong to weak – according to
their capability of keeping the wedge continuous, attracting people and
in circumstances serving as wildlife corridors – is a clear step forward in
articulating strategies for the improvement of the quality of green wedges
and synergies between them and their urban surroundings. The weak green
links – locations where there is a severe challenge in ensuring the connectivity
of specific areas within a green wedge, such as highway crossings – therefore,

(a)

(b)

FIGURE 6.5 *Views of Haga Park.*

FIGURE 6.6 *View of an 'ecoduct' connecting Hammarby Sjöstad to the Nacka-Värmdö green wedge.*

FIGURE 6.7 *View of the Nacka-Värmdö green wedge.*

are deemed of strategic relevance and action to strengthen them are set as priorities.

Stockholm region counts with over 20,000 islands. This geographical condition is a particularity of Stockholm, presenting it with locations of special aesthetic attractiveness, recreational experiences and ecosystems.[16] Despite its attractiveness, Stockholm's coastal location increases the region's vulnerability in face of global warming and climate change. Preoccupations over the supply of drinking water and the prospect of an upsurge in more frequent droughts, floods and severe weather-related events are becoming prominent in discourses related to water management.

The blue spaces plan – comprised of coastal areas, lakes, groundwater and watercourses – addresses the region's recreational needs and aims to improve Stockholm's resilience by broadly committing to safeguarding and developing assets, protecting key landscapes and securing drinking water resources. The region intends to protect and develop the blue asset cores through a similar strategy to that envisioned for the protection and development of green asset cores. This would involve areas along the coast and within the archipelago. Rainwater absorption and infiltration to water tables is a key consideration and protection areas include lakes and their catchment areas. And, while greater attention has been paid to green wedges in the regional and city plans, the blue infrastructure is likely to receive more attention in the following plans. Further integration with the green wedges can help in this process by providing large permeable land and in filtering and directing storm water as part of sustainable urban drainage systems. To ensure that Stockholm capitalizes on its socio-ecological systems and remains resilient in face of environmental threats, a stronger integrative approach including both green and blue infrastructure must be developed.

The RUFS 2010 has a special section highlighting its contribution to the sustainability of the region. A holistic perspective was sought across all the objectives in the plan, which was deemed to increase the possibilities of success in meeting its expectations. It was found that, in general terms, the choices made in the plan would lead the region to a number of environmental advantages.[17] First of all, the dense urban structure proposed would entail less total demand for development of sections of the existing green spaces. Regarding the green and blue infrastructures specifically, a number of indicators were used to model the impact of the plan. In spite of the potentialities of green wedges to make major contributions in this regard, the indicators used are limited and mostly refer to the safeguarding of green wedges, the proximity of population to these green spaces and the level of encroachment on green wedges and the shoreline. The plan projects that, if implemented properly, the percentage of the population that has access to a green wedge within a 1,000 metres or 2,500 metres of their homes would be roughly maintained in 2030, at 48 and 80 per cent, respectively (a drop of 1 per cent from the current status). Given the increase in population expected, this is seen as a very positive result.

Similarly to the regional plan, the Stockholm City Plan 2010 provides guidance on development strategies for sustainable growth for the city, including overall use of land and water. It shares the regional plan's notion of a polycentric and interconnected city-region, building on the strategy of densification for the inner city and proposing the concentration of sustainable growth around the nine strategic nodes (Figure 6.8).[18]

Compared to the previous municipal plan, the treatment of green wedges in the Stockholm City Plan 2010 is more flexible. While the former was unyielding about inner-city densification and the preservation of the city's large green spaces, the latter has assumed a stance that acknowledges that some physical

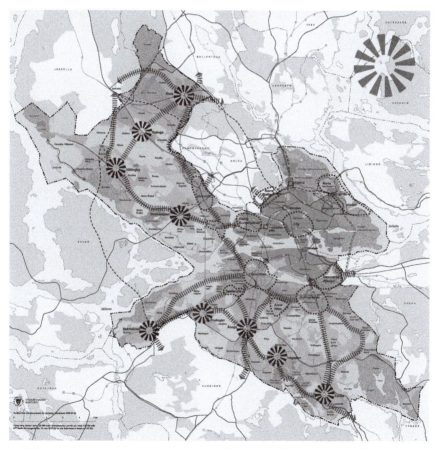

FIGURE 6.8 *Stockholm City Plan 2010 map.* Source: *The City Planning Administration (2010). Courtesy of Stockholm City Planning Administration.*

changes in the green wedges can enhance them and their surroundings.[19] In turn, this approach resonates with research on resilience thinking applied to large-scale green structures as discussed before, inasmuch as a more flexible and positive approach to the planning and management of green wedges may promote the interconnectedness of socio-ecological ecosystems and accommodate complexity, change and multi-scale interactions.[20] Arguably in line with research about the need for human interaction in cities, place-making and liveability – characteristic of recent urban design thinking[21] – the City Planning Administration aims to enhance the connectivity between certain districts divided by green wedges, countering their perceived lack of safety and dullness. The strategies envisaged included the creation or enhancement of green pedestrian and cycle corridors between neighbourhoods and access by public transport; the introductions or enhancement of 'green meeting points', such as allotments, communal gardens and playgrounds; and the development of key sections with buildings with active ground floors.[22] These could be implemented conjointly or in isolation, depending on the specificity of each case. In landscape ecology terms, 'green asset cores' and 'green meeting points' can be related to the concept of mini-patches within the landscape. Likewise, 'green links' can be associated with the notion of corridors.

The City Planning Administration is currently implementing these ideas along the axis of the neighbourhoods of Farsta, Fagersjö and Rågsved. The area connects to the regional Hanveden green wedge in the south through the Magelungen lake. The proposal combines the three strategies mentioned before: including improved public transport, green routes and better access to water and greenery. A variety of outdoor recreational activities are indicated across the area. In addition, the proposal suggests the construction of buildings along the main traffic arteries between Farsta and Fagersjö, strengthening this connection (Figure 6.9).

Green wedges may pose challenges not only to the physical connectivity of a city, but also to its social cohesion. The Järva area, located in the northwest Stockholm, is an interesting example of a contested space, where social and physical integration are put to check. The Vision for Järva 2030, which sits within the general Vision 2030 for Stockholm, is a long-term programme by the City of Stockholm and other stakeholders to promote sustainable development in the area.[23] Here the districts of Kista, Tensta and Rinkeby are separated by the Järvafältet, a section of the Järva wedge. Kista, one of the nine strategic nodes for sustainable development identified in the City Plan, is an important IT centre. Tensta and Rinkeby were built between 1965 and 1975 as part of the Swedish government Million Homes Programme. It was largely influenced by the post-war discussions on suburban planning and reinterpretations of modernism. Socio-economic problems became evident in these areas, which are some of the most socially segregated suburbs of Stockholm.

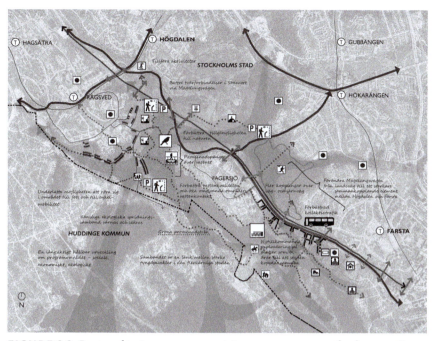

FIGURE 6.9 *Proposal to improve connectivity across a green wedge between Farsta and Fagersjö. Courtesy of Stockholm City Planning Administration.*

Lack of connectivity across and along Järvafältet, interruptions by lines of traffic with associated noise and pollution and poor quality of open space are challenges to be overcome. Most of Järvafältet consists of open fields, grazing meadows and former agricultural areas.[24] Patches of woodland, allotment gardens, sports fields and other activities can also be found. Due to these circumstances, it currently acts as a barrier to integration, heightening the effect of social segregation.[25]

To reverse this process, the City of Stockholm has shown a strong commitment to develop an integrated approach for Järva involving retrofit of building stock, new sustainable development, multiple forms of governance and the transformation of the open spaces (Figure 6.10). Planned interventions around Järvafältet encompass improvements to the connectivity of the street and footpath networks and the strengthening of the edges between the urban fabric and the green wedge, for instance through the construction of hallmark buildings, which can increase legibility and boost local identity and sense of pride.[26] The positive planning within the green wedge considers the establishment of green asset cores, where inexistent, or their enhancement, activating routes and unlocking the quality of place in key zones.

A notable planned urban intervention in the area is the Stockholmsporten project, at the proposed intersection of two European motorways, E18 and

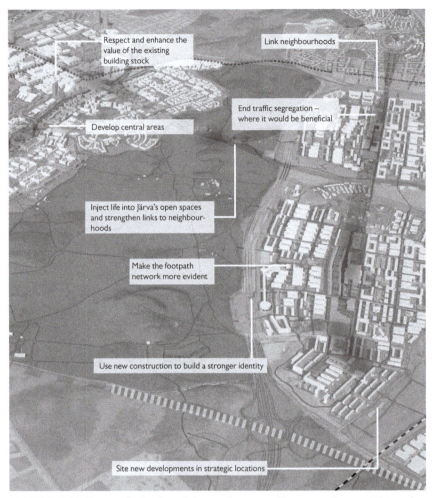

Respect and enhance the
value of the existing
building stock

Link neighbourhoods

End traffic segregation –
where it would be beneficial

Develop central areas

Inject life into Järva's open spaces
and strengthen links to neighbourhoods

Make the footpath
network more evident

Use new construction to build a stronger identity

Site new developments in strategic locations

FIGURE 6.10 *Proposals for Järvafältet and surrounding areas.* Source: *Vision for Järva 2030, 13. Courtesy of the City of Stockholm.*

E4. BIG was the competition winner with the entry 'Energy Valley', which articulates infrastructure, existing districts and the Järvafältet into a new reinvented landscape (Figure 6.11). A floating solar-powered reflective sphere marks this new gateway into Stockholm. Other projects include Rinkeby Terrace and Tensta Terrace. They bridge over the E18 motorway, providing housing, public terraces overlooking Järvafältet and direct connections to it.

As can be seen, the projection of Stockholm as 'Europe's most attractive metropolitan region' involves an integrative and multidisciplinary mode of thinking. Their proactive planning from the region to local scale encapsulates a vision of the future that encounters in green wedges potent and energizing instruments for its attainment.

(a)

(b)

(c)

FIGURE 6.11 *Views of Stockholmsporten project. Courtesy of BIG – Bjarke Ingels Group.*

The Copenhagen Finger Plan: The development of a model

Ever since the 1947 Finger Plan, Copenhagen has been the clearest and most consolidated example of the implementation of the green wedge idea. Differently from cities like Stockholm, Helsinki or Freiburg where natural conditions such as mountainous terrain and watercourses helped generate and keep green wedges, in the case of Copenhagen these are down to the confidence in the application of this planning idea. As discussed previously, the focus on organizing development around nodal points along public transport routes while keeping the resultant green wedges, characteristic of Copenhagen's approach, became an international reference to regional planning. In a recent Danish planning document, the Finger Plan structure has been considered 'a piece of living heritage that we owe to future generations to take care of'.[27] Today, Copenhagen is a leading city in terms of planning quality, urban design and urban sustainability.[28] Copenhagen's perception as a green city can be reasonably attributed to the dynamic and forward-looking consolidation of green wedges over the last seventy years. The green wedges to date continue to fundamentally structure the city's green infrastructure.

It is worth summarizing key recent past references in the development of Copenhagen's regional structure for a better appreciation of its current situation. The Regional Plan 1989 not only pursued the original Finger Plan's concepts of organizing development along the fingers, densification around the train stations and the preservation of the green wedges, but also brought to the fore ecological and environmental considerations.[29] The Regional Plan 2005 broadly followed the same structure. In 2006 the Danish government published a National Planning Report that listed clear goals for holistic development plans, including the maintenance of the difference between the city and the country, the integration of transport infrastructure and planning and that 'planning must be based on respect for nature and the environment'.[30] In 2007 the Revised Planning Act restructured the Danish planning system. The Ministry of Environment became responsible for defining a comprehensive framework for regional and municipal planning. The Regional Councils have since been responsible for preparing regional plans that, in coordination with the municipalities, describe a vision for the region. In turn, the municipal plans comprise a framework for the detailed local plans.[31] As per the very nature of Copenhagen's regional structure, crossing many municipal boundaries, communication and integration between regional planning and local plans therefore has become crucial. It is worth noting that the Planning Act includes special rules on planning in Greater Copenhagen in order that it maintains the main principles of the finger structure and that green wedges are not converted into 'urban zones'.[32] The same year the Finger Plan 2007 and thirty-four municipal plans replaced the Regional Plan 2005. Also in 2007, Copenhagen launched a vision for the city called Eco-Metropole, aiming to be world leader in terms of environmental initiatives by 2015. The four main areas of the programme concentrated on cycling, environmental policy, green and blue infrastructure, cleanliness and health. The programme highlighted that a 'sustainable city is also a city in harmony with nature' and that the green and blue infrastructure would bind the city together. To become a green and blue city, Copenhagen intended to enhance the amount of green and blue spaces, as well as their connectivity and ease of access. As discussed earlier, there is strong evidence linking proximity to green spaces and well-being.[33] In this light, the goals were that 90 per cent of residents would be able to walk to a park (compared to 60 per cent in 2007), beach or a sea swimming pool in under 15 minutes and that they would visit these spaces twice as often than they did in 2007 (which was every other day, for 1 hour). Regarding the city's ambition to become a clean and healthy city, the goals included becoming free from health-damaging noise and achieving high levels of air cleanliness.

In turn, the Finger Plan 2007 acted as a framework for the metropolitan region of Copenhagen, having as its main aim to coordinate development with the regional traffic and green infrastructures in order to enhance the region's quality of life and attractiveness. Copenhagen is a key player in the international competition between cities and, as noted in the plan, the quality of the environment is today considered a prerequisite to attract investment and skilled workers.

In the Finger Plan 2007, the region was divided into four geographical areas: the internal metropolitan area (the 'Palm'), the outer metropolitan area ('Urban Fingers'), the green wedges and the rest of the metropolitan area. The fingers were named, from north to south: Helsingør, Hillerød, Farum, Frederikssund, Roskilde and Køge. The plan presented a tiered green wedge structure comprised of the outer northern landscapes and the areas of Hjortespring, Vallensbæk and Vestskoven; the inner green wedges and coastal green wedges.

The plan reinforced the finger structure, where urban development could occur, and the preservation of green wedges. Development areas close to stations and municipal centres were fostered. An example of that can be seen in the plan's regulation as to the location of new large office buildings, which should be within 600 metres of railway stations, reinforcing thus the local nodes and the usage of public transport. Green wedges were to be safeguarded from large buildings, from encroachment and be mainly used for urban forests and recreation, although agricultural use was also deemed possible. As a matter of fact, the transformation of farmland into parkland, sports fields, woodland and allotments has been occurring for decades, mainly in the southern wedges.[34]

The population forecast for Denmark is an increase of 350,000 inhabitants by 2030, and another 300,000 by 2050. Notwithstanding this scenario of growth, Copenhagen is working towards ambitious environmental targets. At the same time as it is planning to accommodate 110,000 inhabitants more, requiring the construction of 6.8 square kilometres of 'new city', Copenhagen intends to become carbon neutral by 2025.[35] It is in this context that a new Finger Plan was published in 2013. The main objectives of the Finger Plan 2013 were to update the plan from 2007, to create a coherent network of more open areas and green connections in the metropolitan area, to improve housing opportunities and to support sustainable development.

The attractiveness of Copenhagen is intrinsically related to its green wedges; to quote the plan: 'modern citizens demand green cities, with plenty of parks and urban forests'.[36] Regarding the green wedges, their main purpose has been to ensure that large peri-urban landscapes are kept free from urban development, offering public access to relatively undisturbed recreational areas a few minutes from every citizen's residence. A recent study about the recreational experiences of residents in green spaces in the Copenhagen region, based on Stockholm's social values methodology, found similar results to those in Sweden. They were also classified in seven categories, from most natural to most urban: 'wilderness', 'feeling of the forest', 'panoramic views, water, and scenery', 'biodiversity and land form', 'cultural history', 'activity and challenge' and 'service and gathering'. It was noted that the more the green wedges penetrate the urban fabric, the more they acquire the character of urban parks, hence the dominant experiences relate more often to the last two categories. At the urban fringe and further away, where more forested and agricultural areas predominate, the experiences tend to be more related to the first four categories.[37] Proximity to forests is highly important, as this is the most preferred recreational environment in Denmark. However, for the visitor to fully appreciate them, silence and the sense of isolation from urban disturbances are considered essential. As is the case in Stockholm, there is a preoccupation to avoid noise in the wedges, both related to activities and proximity to disturbance sources such as motorways, in order to ensure that a sense of isolation and connection to nature may occur in a quiet environment. The study, therefore, makes recommendations regarding the creation of buffer zones for the most natural green spaces and the creation of limits to the noise levels in these areas (45 dB for wilderness and 55 dB for 'feeling of the forest').[38]

The definition of the outer, inner and coastal green wedges is maintained from the 2007 plan, but it is worth noting that a particularity of the Finger Plan 2013 (Figure 6.12) is the creation of 'city green wedges' (Figure 6.13) – including the ring of old fortifications, the Damhussøen and the lowlands

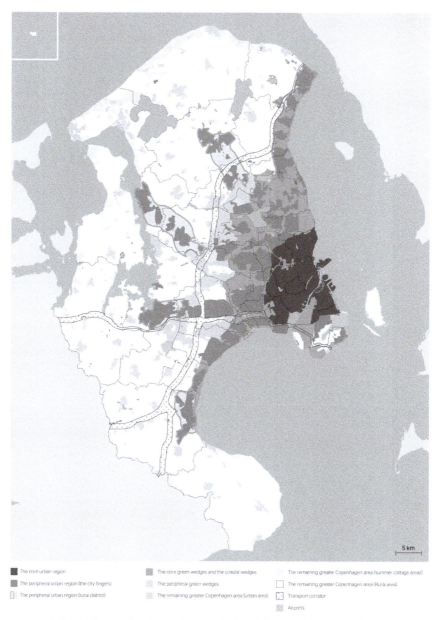

FIGURE 6.12 *Finger Plan 2013.* Source: *Mijoministeriet Naturstyrelsen, 2013, 13. Courtesy of Danish Business Authority.*

along Harrestrup stream – and an overall regional green path network. Also worldwide famous for cycle use, Copenhagen has a Green Cycle Route strategy involving the construction of a network of over 115 kilometres of cycle routes running along green and blue spaces.[39] The integration of this

Green urban wedges

The core green wedges and the coastal wedges

FIGURE 6.13 *The 'City Wedges' and Coastal Wedges.* Source: *Mijoministeriet Naturstyrelsen, 2013, 32. Courtesy of Danish Business Authority.*

network to the 'city green wedges' is contemplated and encouraged in the plan. In a city where the bicycle is a form of transport and almost half of the trips to work or to study are made using one, the articulation of a cycle strategy with green spaces carries on Copenhagen's tradition to integrate transport and green space planning.

Another novelty introduced by the plan, compared to previous plans for the region, was that green wedges could be used actively for climate change adaptation if this did not detract from their recreational use. Interventions falling into this category include the use of green wedges in the creation of SUDS. The Finger Plan 2013 allows for proactive planning involving the naturalization of water streams and the creation of artificial floodways, holding ponds and lakes, enhancing green wedges' potential to be used more effectively in climate change mitigation. Recreational, ecological and environmental benefits can be overlaid in the definition of SUDS – providing thus multiple benefits to the region and its residents.[40] The municipalities of Brøndby and Vallensbæk were some of the first to use this new prerogative, proposing the construction of a system of holding ponds along a transport corridor in the Vallensbæk wedge, integrated into a network of recreational spaces.[41]

Connectivity across the wedges has been an issue in Copenhagen. The backbone of the traffic structure comprises the radial S-train lines and ring roads. Public transport across fingers tended thus to be less prioritized. The proposed creation of a new tramline, 'Ring 3',[42] crossing the fingers will provide not only direct north–south connections but also better opportunities for the definition and consolidation of local centres. This corridor marks a transition from the dense inner urban area, the palm, to the fingers and green wedges. While it is clear that the new ring will enhance the accessibility of the green wedges, monitoring its impact on the wedges will be necessary.

Due to the association between the landscape quality and socio-economic processes, green wedges have largely developed independently, at different paces, presenting today different opportunities and challenges. The geographical characteristics and natural beauty of northern Copenhagen have attracted urban development since the beginning of the twentieth century. The high amenity value of its lakes, hills, forested landscapes and seaside (Figure 6.14) rendered them sought-after locations for the construction of second homes. Land value followed. In contrast, the flat and agricultural southern landscapes of the Vallensbæk and Vestskoven green wedges offered a much less attractive environment for settlement (Figure 6.15). One of such areas is the municipality of Brøndby, which comprises areas on both sides of the Vallensbæk green wedge, and where social and spatial fragmentation has been an issue for decades. Its municipal plan sets clear goals and strategies up to 2025, including urban development plans such as the densification and revitalization of Brøndby Strand central area and the overall improvement of the public realm. In a municipality that possesses many green areas and where most residents can access a green space within 300 metres of their homes, the task at hand is the issue of quality. Brøndby has implemented a consultative process and intends to prioritize the transformation of existing green areas based on the residents' values and experiences they wish to undergo when in a green space. To this

(a)

(b)

FIGURE 6.14 *Photographs of landscapes in the northern Copenhagen region*

end, improved green connections and a more varied selection of activities and landscapes will be implemented in the municipality's green spaces, including in the Vallensbæk green wedge, which will further benefit from the activation of edge conditions along motorways which border it, so that instead of being residual areas they become assets for everyday use.[43]

The demarcation of the green wedges is now done by the Danish Ministry of Business and Growth, but the responsibility to plan the green wedges remains down to the municipalities. Since green wedges are strictly

(a)

(b)

FIGURE 6.15 *Photographs of landscapes in the southern Copenhagen region*

regulated, the municipalities have to abide by those rules in their local plans. As the region grows along the fingers, new green wedge areas may have to be defined to ensure the continuity of the finger plan structure.

The green fingers of Helsinki

In 2000, the Land Use and Building Act defined the three-tiered planning structure of Finland: the regional plan, the master plan at city or district scale and the local development plan. In 2002, Helsinki published a master plan defining land use distribution, including housing, services, work and green spaces. One of the plan's central ideas was the strategic densification of the inner urban fabric along clear transport routes. In turn, the plan followed the logic that the denser the city is, the more important it is to provide quality green spaces of easy access to its citizens.[44]

In terms of the green space provision, the 2002 master plan consisted of an integrated system whose backbone was formed by green wedges (Figure 6.16). The main roles of the green spaces in the plan were recreational and ecological. In addition to the Central Park, which had already appeared in Saarinen's plan from the beginning of the twentieth century, the plan included other five: the West Park, Helsinki Park, Viikki-Kivikko Park, East Park and Vuosaari Park. Geography and land ownership have played a fundamental role in the pattern of occupation of Helsinki and the presence of green wedges today. Historically, development avoided the rocky formations and floodplains, occupying preferentially land where building was easier to carry out. Moreover, it is important to note that the city of Helsinki owns some 66 per cent of land within its boundaries and the State approximately 13 per cent, so in total public authorities own nearly 80 per cent of land.[45]

The West Park assumed a connecting role between central Helsinki and Nuuksio National Park. The Viikki-Kivikko and the Vuosaari Park played a similar role in connecting to the Sipoonkorpi National Park. The Helsinki Park was introduced by the Helsinki City Planning Department as a response to EU legislation on National Urban Parks. The park runs from the valley of the Vantaanjoki River in the north to the seashore and the archipelagos at the southern and eastern edges of the city centre. It encompasses thirteen nature conservation areas, recreational zones, pastures and other cultural landscapes.[46]

The Finnish capital faces many challenges, including population growth, international competition and the effects of climate change. As a response, Helsinki City Planning Department published the Helsinki City Plan 2013: Vision 2050. The city's vision involves being a lively and thriving international metropolis, recognized as a seaside city with appealing living options, sustainable mobility and an attractive recreational, natural and cultural

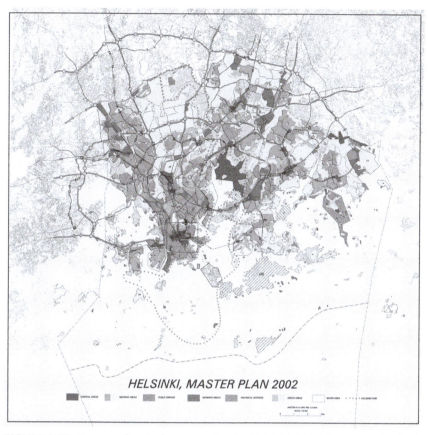

FIGURE 6.16 *Green wedges in the master plan for Helsinki, 2002. Courtesy of Helsinki City Planning Department.*

environment. With current population at 600,000 residents and the prospect of growth to 860,000 inhabitants by 2050, Helsinki intends to accommodate this population growth through the densification of the inner core, expansion of the delimitation of the central area and consolidation of regional and district cores. Helsinki of 2050 is to be comprised of ten large districts, each with its own positive image. The districts, in turn, would be formed of identifiable neighbourhoods containing their own cores. The expanded city centre would be the dominant core with more extensive range of services, facilities, housing and commerce. Development would be directed around the neighbourhood cores and between them.

The regional open space plan proposed for Helsinki operates on a number of levels. It is intended to help structure and organize the different districts, ensure access to green and blue spaces and contribute to climate change mitigation. By 2050, Helsinki is to become a 'green city by the sea'. While in

2002 the green and blue space strategy seemed to over-rely on large-scale green spaces, the vision of a 'green network city'[47] in 2050 is for a more comprehensive, complex and multi-scale open space structure embedding the patch-corridor-matrix approach from landscape ecology. This system includes national parks, regional recreational areas, green and blue wedges, district parks and green routes (Figure 6.17). The six wedges from the Master Plan 2002 were maintained as the backbone of the network. Since in a denser urban environment the importance of providing easy access to green spaces increases, the plan calls for proactively developing them as high-quality places and complementing the green space network with a wide range of typologies and scales. The plan's commitment to enhance the cohesiveness of the green wedges is worth noting, both in terms of the promotion of recreational spaces and ecological habitats and corridors.

The green network is aligned with the transport strategy. The transport network is expected to enhance access via public transport to green and blue spaces at all scales as well as to remodel the relationship between these spaces and high-speed vehicular routes. One of the most challenging difficulties of the green wedge model is the connection across the wider sections. In Helsinki, these spaces were often crossed by motorways in the 1960s and 1970s, their isolation being reinforced by the lack of a robust complementary public

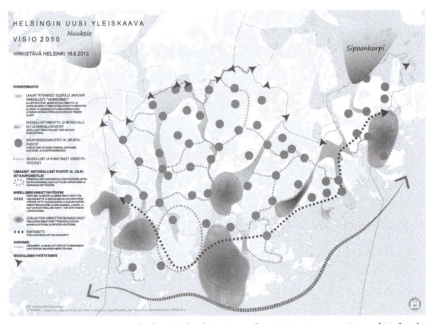

FIGURE 6.17 *Green and Blue Helsinki, vision for 2050.* Source: *City of Helsinki, 2013, 50–1. Courtesy of Helsinki City Planning Department.*

transport system. To counter it, a systemic interrelation of transport and green spaces networks has been devised. In addition, a remarkable strategy that Helsinki puts forward is the transformation of motorway-like areas into urban boulevards, such as the case of the 'Mannerheim boulevard' (Figure 6.18).

FIGURE 6.18 *Plan of an urban transformation proposed along motorway-like area in central Helsinki, 2015. Courtesy of Helsinki City Planning Department.*

This initiative will activate valuable and well-located areas, allow for strategic densification, promote places for people and improve connectivity along and across some of the green wedges (Figure 6.19).

Helsinki's Central Park is an example of an internationally recognized multifunctional green wedge that encapsulates the potentialities of proactive and positive planning. The park spans 11 kilometres, from the seashore to Helsinki Park, containing a range of distinctive sections with their own identities (Figure 6.20). In a country where all residents live within 10 kilometres of the sea, developing the seaside areas to meet the resident's expectations and needs is crucial. The Central Park's connection to the sea creates a continuous, and yet varied, landscape strengthening the links between green and blue spaces and putting in evidence the delicate relationship between urbanization and natural environment in the light of potential future climate-related changes. At its most urban section, the park is the site of a world-renowned cultural landscape including the Kiasma Museum of Contemporary Art, Helsinki Music Centre, the National Museum of Finland, Aalto's Finlandia Hall and the Finnish National Opera building (Figure 6.21). Further north, it includes sport facilities such as the

FIGURE 6.19 *Visualization of the Mannerheim boulevard.* Source: *City of Helsinki, 2013, 24–5. Courtesy of Helsinki City Planning Department, 3ᴰ Render/Raisa Kiljunen-Siirola, Essi Leino, Terhi Kwsisto, Alpo Tani, Tadani Rauramo.*

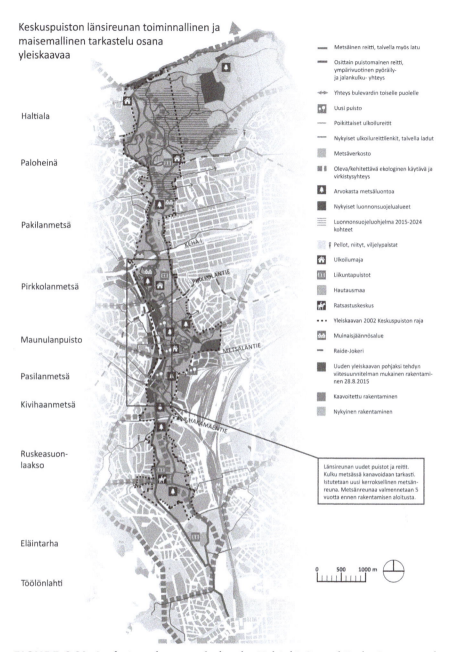

Keskuspuiston länsireunan toiminnallinen ja maisemallinen tarkastelu osana yleiskaavaa

Haltiala

Paloheinä

Pakilanmetsä

Pirkkolanmetsä

Maunulanpuisto

Pasilanmetsä

Kivihaanmetsä

Ruskeasuon-
laakso

Eläintarha

Töölönlahti

Metsäinen reitti, talvella myös latu

Osittain puistomainen reitti, ympärivuotinen pyöräily- ja jalankulku- yhteys

Yhteys bulevardin toiselle puolelle

Uusi puisto

Poikittaiset ulkoilureitit

Nykyiset ulkoilureittilenkit, talvella ladut

Metsäverkosto

Oleva/kehitettävä ekologinen käytävä ja virkistysyhteys

Arvokasta metsäluontoa

Nykyiset luonnonsuojelualueet

Luonnonsuojeluohjelma 2015-2024 kohteet

Pellot, niityt, viljelypalstat

Ulkoilumaja

Liikuntapuistot

Hautausmaa

Ratsastuskeskus

Yleiskaavan 2002 Keskuspuiston raja

Muinaisjäännösalue

Raide-Jokeri

Uuden yleiskaavan pohjaksi tehdyn viitesuunnitelman mukainen rakentaminen 28.8.2015

Kaavoitettu rakentaminen

Nykyinen rakentaminen

Länsireunan uudet puistot ja reitit. Kulku metsässä kanavoidaan tarkasti. Istutetaan uusi kerroksellinen metsän-reuna. Metsänreunaa valmennetaan 5 vuotta ennen rakentamisen aloitusta.

0   500   1000 m

FIGURE 6.20 *Analysis and proposals for the Helsinki Central Park. Courtesy of Helsinki City Planning Department.*

(a)

(b)

(c)

FIGURE 6.21 *Views of Helsinki's Central Park.*

1952 Olympic Stadium. Towards Helsinki Park, it gradually becomes more forested, accommodating gardens, playgrounds, allotments, equestrian and other sports facilities, gym equipment, walking and cycle routes and natural preservation zones.

A characteristic of Helsinki's green wedges is that they extend from the seashore into the hinterland. Green and blue wedges predominate in the city's vision for large-scale open spaces. Although wedges tend to open up towards the countryside, some wedges in Helsinki present an inverted geometry with their larger area opening up to the sea, such as the Viikki-Kivikko Park and the East Park.

A recent survey of general attitudes towards and benefits felt to be derived from green areas in Helsinki showed that outdoor recreation opportunities, contact with nature, stress relief and aesthetic experiences were considered to be the most important benefits. Forested areas were valued more than urban parks, which is a characteristic shared with the other Nordic countries.[48] Although outdoor recreation remains the principal function of green wedges, a more concentrated effort in developing a discourse on their importance for the promotion of a sustainable city and the mitigation of the impacts of climate change emerged.[49] Helsinki expects to reduce its greenhouse emissions by 30 per cent from the 1990 level by the year 2020, being emission-free by 2050. Besides the overarching strategies of densification of the city structure, promotion of sustainable transport and renewable energy, the plan considers also the contribution of large continuous green spaces to these efforts. They encompass, but are not restricted to, the protection of biodiversity, enhancement of ecological corridors, rainwater management, flood control and the resilience of seaside areas.

The city has just published a proposal for a new city plan (Figure 6.22).[50] The basic principles remain the same, such as that Helsinki should grow into a dense city with district and regional centres interconnected by rail. The central area is to expand along the motorway-like areas transformed into city boulevards. Helsinki reaffirms its commitment to be a green city, and the green wedges continue to be the fundamental backbone of the city's green infrastructure. They are conceptualized to accommodate a wide range of landscapes with significant recreational, cultural, ecological and environmental values, including a 'Forest Network'. 'Natural core areas' connected by ecological corridors have been identified, most of which are to be found in the green wedges. Transversal green links crossing the green wedges have been proposed to strengthen east–west connectivity for wildlife and human beings. Green nodes, such as neighbourhood parks, are to be found along the green links or in their close proximity.[51]

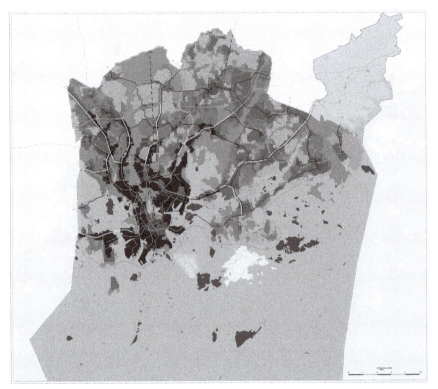

FIGURE 6.22 *New proposed city plan for Helsinki. Courtesy of Helsinki City Planning Department.*

Randstad: From Green Heart to Green-Blue Delta

'Concentrated deconcentration' was put in practice in the late 1970s and the early 1980s to avoid the Randstad becoming a continuous megalopolis and to protect the Green Heart. This meant the accommodation of nearly 500,000 people in designated overspill areas and strict development control in the villages within the Green Heart. In the late 1980s, debates about inner city decay meant the overturning of the previous approach and a focus on compact urban growth in brownfield as well as in greenfield sites close to urban areas.[52] VINEX, the Fourth Memorandum of Spatial Planning Extra in the Netherlands, pushed in this direction with a programme of construction including more than 800,000 new dwellings.

If in the beginning of the implementation of the Randstad-Green Heart model green wedges were mostly conceptualized as buffer zones between cities, in the early 2000s debates about the need for a more proactive planning of these spaces as regional parks began to take place. Some authors have pointed out the pendulous nature of how these green spaces have been seen, at times as elements of separation and more recently as recreational areas for the urban dweller.[53] This discussion has not yet been resolved. Today this polycentric urban region covers an area of 8,300 square kilometres, approximately 20 per cent of the Netherlands, and has a population of more than 7 million people, amounting to 45 per cent of the total population of the country. It is expected that the Randstad will need between 500,000 and a million new homes by 2040. In 2008 the government launched the 'Randstad 2040 Structural Vision' aiming to strengthen the international competitiveness of the region to attract businesses and employees, as well as to address the challenges of growth and resilience to climate change. This is part of the 'Randstad Urgent Programme' – a partnership of the government, municipalities and metropolitan regions. At the core of the view is the understanding that processes of specialization and concentration are fundamental for the promotion of the knowledge economy. Consolidation of existing built-up areas is a priority, nonetheless the vision does not exclude structural expansion and decentralization strategies should the need arise.

As noted, the quality of the living environment is a key factor in the international competitiveness of cities and regions, and in this respect green spaces have a crucial role to play. A report from the OECD concluded that the Randstad region fell short of the highest levels of international competitiveness and had as one of its main recommendations to make a 'better use' of the Green Heart. The OECD's interpretation of 'better use' however may seem controversial, since it involves the provision of housing within the boundaries of the Green Heart, but yes, coupled with more high-quality recreational landscapes.[54] In this regard, at the same time that the Randstad 2040 vision accentuates the need to consolidate its cities, it proposes changes to the surrounding landscapes and their relationship with urban areas. The historic definition of the Green Heart as an enclosed typology mostly dedicated to agriculture is questioned in face of pressure for development, the need for recreation in high-quality landscapes near residents and the contemporary challenges of resilience to climate change. The Green Heart, thus, is to be incorporated into a large green and blue delta (Figure 6.23) and the former buffer zones to assume the form of metropolitan parks, offering 'excellent' green and blue spaces near cities.

The Green-Blue Delta consists of the river area, the Utrecht Heuvelrug, Low Holland, the Green Heart, the IJsselmeer area, the south-western delta and the coastal zone. Better integration with the green, blue and grey surrounding landscapes are aimed at strengthening the Green Heart's ecosystem services leading to improved landscape quality, more diversity and stronger climate resilience in the region. The main functions

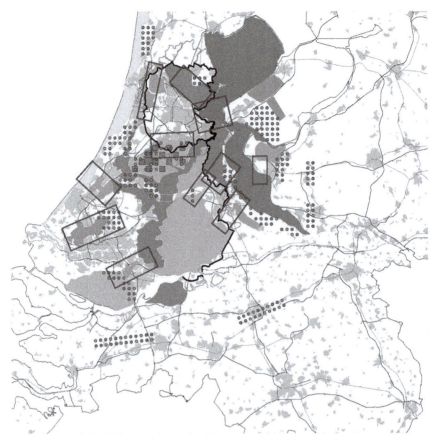

FIGURE 6.23 *Green and Blue Delta in Randstad, including areas for the metropolitan parks.* Source: *Dutch Minister of Housing, 2008, 37. Courtesy of the Ministry of Infrastructure and Environment of the Netherlands.*

allowed include agriculture, nature protection, 'the enjoyment of nature', water storage, urban agriculture, care functions and small-scale housing.[55] The vision adopts resilience thinking as a key driver in face of the need to adapt to and mitigate the effects of climate change. Protection against flooding is seen as a task not only for 'hard' engineering approaches, such as the established dyke around Randstad, but also for 'soft' strategies. The latter includes ensuring that construction in floodplains in a number of inland locations happens only if the highest level of water is taken into consideration. Allowing for the rise in the water level and the resultant salinization of the soil leads to the transformation of arable land in other kinds of landscape, including residential and recreational spaces.[56] Change, adaptability and coordination between multiple scales are called for in the strategy.

In the light of the need for more attractive high-quality green spaces for leisure and well-being near urban areas, the green wedges – formerly acting as buffer zones – are to become metropolitan parks and be integrated into the green and blue regional network. New housing areas would be placed near them. In order to enhance the wedges' spatial qualities and diversity of use, a shift towards their positive planning is entailed and recreational functions are to become more pronounced. Whether there should be a sharp contrast between city, countryside and the new metropolitan parks, or if indeed hybridism is to be pursued, is under debate.[57] While some areas would be preserved due to their socio-ecological and economic values, the possibility of change associated with positive planning is strongly considered.

An area contemplated for such transformation can be found in Midden-Delfand, between The Hague and Rotterdam. A new housing area is planned to be located on its eastern end. This will become one of the starting points of a green wedge that radiates out towards the Nieuwe Waterweg canal. This area has recently been the object of stimulating proposals, such as the 'Park Supermarket' (Figure 6.24) idea by van Bergen Kolpa Architects with Alterra Wageninge, which aspire to define a landscape for the twenty-first century around the production of food and the recreational needs of the Randstad. Another example is the Deltapoort project, adopted in 2012 for the area between Rotterdam and Dordrecht, which presents a comprehensive vision for a metropolitan park spanning the period up to 2025.[58]

FIGURE 6.24 *Image of Park Supermarket. Courtesy of Van Bergen Kolpa Architects.*

Melbourne towards 2030

The persisting scenario of population and urban growth pervading many large Australian cities led to a shift in paradigm from suburbanization to compaction. Over the last decades Australia's planning policy has been developing strategies for sustainable growth by reducing urban sprawl through the promotion of inwards growth and its concentration around strategic hubs located along public transport routes. Not only can this be seen in the Melbourne 2030 plan, but also in *The 30-year Plan for Greater Adelaide*, in *Canberra Spatial Plan* and in *A plan for growing Sydney*.[59]

Released in 2002, Melbourne 2030 comes after a period of relaxation in metropolitan-wide planning controls, which led to increased suburbanization and associated erosion of Melbourne's green wedges.[60] The premise of population growth for Melbourne of 1 million by 2030 determined the need to establish this long-term vision. However, already in 2008 this projection was updated indicating that 1.8 million additional people are likely to need to be accommodated in Metropolitan Melbourne by 2036.[61]

The plan covered thirty-one municipalities and aimed to manage sustainable urban growth and consolidate the city's international competitiveness and reputation as one of the most liveable cities in the world. The main spatial planning structure proposed builds on the 1960s corridor-wedge model, relying on densification around mixed-use 'activity centres' along public transport routes and the preservation of green wedges. The shift from a city-centric 'hub and spoke' model to a more dynamic networked city-region is pursued (Figure 6.25).[62] The activity centres are hierarchical in scale and classified as Principal, Major and Neighbourhood. Their location in close proximity to transport hubs would strengthen urban mobility by public transport. Neighbourhood activity centres would have a catchment area of between 400 and 500 metres serving the neighbouring residents and workers at walking and cycling distances and providing focal points for the different communities.

The plan included twelve green wedges, which formed an arc around metropolitan Melbourne. Although in some cases they connected to inner urban green and blue spaces, they were designated outside the Urban Growth Boundary – in parts resembling a green belt. The green wedges are known as Werribee South, Western Plains South, Western Plains North, Sunbury, Whittlesea, Nilumbik, Manningham, Yarra Valley and Yarra and Dandenong Ranges, Southern Ranges, South East, Westernport and Mornington Peninsula. The plan indicated clearly that green wedges were not just another type of park, but 'active, living areas' that host non-urban activities.[63] These would include the traditional functions of agriculture, recreation and conservation

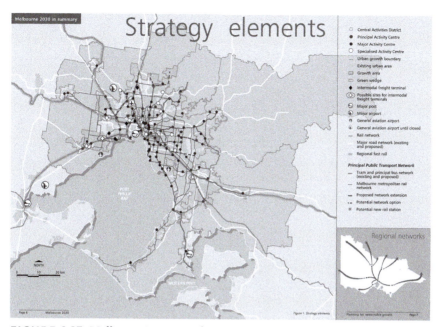

FIGURE 6.25 *Melbourne's strategy for 2030.* Source: *State of Victoria, 2002, 6-7. Courtesy of A/Executive Director, Planning Implementation.*

areas, but also uses that other cities tend not to be so open in associating with green wedges, such as airports, sewage treatment plans, waste disposal sites and quarries.[64]

Melbourne 2030 required that councils produce a Green Wedge Management Plan (GWMP) for green wedge land in their jurisdiction, which should present a shared vision, actions and a management strategy for the green wedge in question. The GWMPs vary in focus and scope, but broadly address the social, economic and environmental pillars of sustainability. The social functions of the green wedges have been mostly delineated around the creation of networks of green space (as exemplified by Kingston GWMP),[65] the need for recreation in nature, the opportunity to host community cohesion activities and the preservation of cultural heritage. The economic benefits generally relate to the significance that green wedges have in agricultural production and tourism, and associated job creation. In this respect, for some areas intensive farming remains at the heart of the vision, as is the case put forward in the Westernport GWMP.[66] And although farming across the green wedges is still a significant industry, decline in total farm holdings can be seen. For example, in their respective green wedge land, the Yarra Ranges Council[67] lost 22 per cent of farmland between 1994 and 2006 and Brimbank City Council forecasts that soon agriculture will occur only by 'lifestyle or hobby'.[68] Possible motives include increased land values due to their attractiveness for residential use, recreation and tourism; the need for larger farm sizes and structures to cope with the demand and to accommodate seasonal workers, which may not be possible on green wedge land; and the volatility of weather conditions, which is due to increase with climate change.[69] The principal environmental functions of Melbourne's green wedges elaborated in the GWMPs address the protection of biodiversity and renewable and non-renewable resources, as well as water security – by safeguarding water catchment areas and water tables. An emerging discourse about the roles that green wedges can play in combating the effects of climate change is observed. The expected changes include less rainfall and run-off resulting in reduced water supply and surface water flows, more heat waves, changes in habitat suitability, increased risk of fires, increased frequency and severity of storms and shifting seasonal boundaries with associated impact on agricultural production.[70] Green wedge land is seen as important in tackling these issues through the protection of creeks, river valleys and permeable land (with associated impact on water tables), as well as in thermal regulation, enhancement of ecological habitats and wildlife corridors, and development of new farming practices, among others.

Plan Melbourne 2014, a metropolitan planning strategy, was launched to help guide Melbourne's growth and change over the next thirty to forty years. Its vision is for Melbourne to become 'a global city of opportunity and choice'. The plan predicts that Melbourne's population will grow from 4.3 million to around 7.7 million by 2051, requiring that 1.6 million new dwellings be built in the metropolitan region.[71] The plan capitalizes on the notion of a highly connected metropolitan region, with strong employment centres as key nodes on the transport network. Although densification remains central to Melbourne's future, suburbs would be protected from significant housing densification. This would be ensured by an expanded central area capable of accommodating medium-to-high density developments, planned development in greenfield sites and urban regeneration of brownfield sites. Melbourne is to be transformed into a city of '20-minute neighbourhoods', where people would have access to a range of local services within 20 minutes from home.[72] Although not much is said about the green wedges, it is intended that they are protected and enhanced. To this end, while the Melbourne 2030 plan defined an Urban Growth Boundary excluding landscape and conservation areas from development, Plan Melbourne 2014 intends to lock in a permanent boundary for Melbourne's metropolitan built-up area in order to protect the values of non-urban land and to promote agricultural production.[73] The green wedges' main functions remain spread across the social, economic and environmental pillars of sustainability, including agriculture, protection of water catchment areas, promotion of biodiversity, recreation, tourism and landscape conservation.[74]

Freiburg: The green wedge and the mountain–valley systems

Freiburg promotes itself as a 'green city' due not only to its ecological credentials developed since the 1970s, but also to its vision of integrating greenery and urban development at regional and city scales. The city, with a growing population of approximately 230,000 inhabitants, is located on the western fringe of the Black Forest in southwest Germany, near France and Switzerland. In the late nineteenth century and early twentieth century, the city saw significant population and urban growth. Severely destroyed in the Second World War, it was rebuilt mainly following the pre-war layout, albeit roads were widened to allow for the implementation of tramways. In the 1970s most of the town centre became pedestrianized, displaying the city's strong focus on place quality, public transport and ecological initiatives. As Scheurer and Newman noted, this showcase of a car-free environment, coupled with advanced standards of resource efficiency and renewable energy, generated a powerful paradigm of ideal sustainable neighbourhood developments of the future.[75]

In the 1980s, the municipality developed a proposal for Freiburg entitled 'Fünffingerplan', the 'Five-finger plan', set out to define five radial green wedges between the axes of development. These wedges would be located in the open spaces left over from development from the open countryside into the inner city, in the areas of Mooswald, Schlossberg, Sternwald, Schöenberg and the western area of the Dreisam valley, including Dietenbach. The model was further developed to accommodate a green ring that would demarcate the central area, intersecting the green wedges.[76]

The Open Space Plan 2020+, published in 2005, aimed at updating the green wedge model inherited from the 1980s. The leading principle of the proposal is maintaining the frame of the green wedges, but articulating them to the development of a polycentric urban structure and an expanded regional interconnected network of green spaces.[77] The green wedges' continuity and connectivity to the city and to other green areas are to be maintained. Their quality is also to be enhanced. A dense network of connections and other green spaces would complement the wedges.

Freiburg's strategic location, climate, positive image and employability rates have been generating an influx of residents. By 2030, Freiburg expects that up to 50,000 inhabitants will be added to its population. To accommodate this, the city would need to build approximately 14,600 homes, which it intends to do through the densification of key areas and the construction of a new district: Dietenbach.[78] After the world-renowned examples of Rieselfeld and Vauban, this new district is anticipated to set advanced standards for sustainable development. Despite the challenges, the city aims to reduce its

CO_2 emissions by 50 per cent by 2030 and achieve a 100 per cent of energy from renewable sources by 2050.

Freiburg has a clear strategy to ensure that its policies not only lead to a balanced and enhanced relationship between urban and natural environments, and consequently to an enhanced quality of life and international attractiveness, but also act as drivers of economic growth.[79] In this respect, the city has been advocating a conjoined development of the three pillars of sustainability – having become today a reference in urban sustainability. Freiburg's 'green city' slogan captures how the city values the integration of building and nature. With 43 per cent of Freiburg made up of woodland, the city is one of the largest forest-owners in Germany. The green infrastructure for Freiburg involves an array of typologies at different scales. Due to its geographical location and topographical condition, the urban development of Freiburg avoided the mountainous areas in favour of the river valleys. This in turn generated a belt of greenery around Freiburg with numerous penetrating wedges. Today, 660 hectares of green space extend from the outskirts into the core of the city.[80] This can be seen in how the Schauinsland area, located in the Southern Black Forest Nature Reserve, stretches for approximately 15 kilometres to reach into Freiburg through the wooded hill of Sternwald. Likewise, the Schlossberg, on the north side of the Dreisam River, links the Black Forest with the centre of Freiburg.

In the context of the current importance of forested areas in the perceived attractiveness of cities, Freiburg ranks high. The Schauinsland is a major recreational feature for residents and tourists. Up until 1954, silver had been mined in the mountain. Today it acts as one of the gateways into the Black Forest; with incalculable amenity value, it offers beautiful views, access to quiet wooded areas and opportunities for active recreation such as hiking, hill climbing and skiing. Similarly, the Schlossberg is a section of the Black Forest wedged directly into the east of Freiburg's Old Town. It also serves as a wooded retreat and place for active recreation. The remnants of historic fortifications on its summit, once of strategic importance to control the entrance to the Dreisam River Valley, enrich the user's experience. The southern and northeastern fringes of the Schlossberg present a transitional zone of wooded and cultivated slopes merging into the cityscapes. The Schlossberg is directly connected to the city centre via the Stadtgarten through footbridges. In this case, the winding landscape of the hill leads into the more formal arrangement of the Stadtgarten, to then reach the built-up areas of the inner city. Views across the valley (Figure 6.26) and into Freiburg are statements of the interconnectedness between the city and nature, of a sense of belonging to the wider geographical condition of the region. In fact, the Schauinsland and the Schlossberg are the largest continuous open spaces in Freiburg and among the largest in Germany itself.[81]

Green wedge situations are highlighted in the Landscape Plan 2020. The landscape integration of built structures and green spaces involves the

FIGURE 6.26 *View of Freiburg from the Schlossberg.*

penetration of the latter into the urban areas. In addition to its scenic value, the continuous and unfragmented nature of certain spaces is important to generate ecological corridors running from the open country to the city. In this regard, they would reconnect biotopes that may have been isolated due to development and urban encroachment.[82] A national network of biotopes was introduced in 2002 and was followed by Biotopes Network Plan for Freiburg in 2003, which became referential to the city's Landscape Plan 2020.[83]

The city's symbiotic relationship with the Black Forest is worth noting on many levels. Freiburg's urban fabric, pressed between the Schauinsland and the Schlossberg, extends partially into the Dreisam Valley. Sternwald, Schlossberg and the Dreisam Valley constitute parts of a regional green wedge into Freiburg, fulfilling crucial environmental functions. Apart from acting as valuable recreational areas and ecological habitats, they help inject fresh air from the Black Forest into Freiburg. With the prospect of climate change, as the city is the sunniest and warmest in Germany, the role of green spaces in regulating its air quality and temperature becomes even more important. Recent research shows that near-surface air temperature is increasing and heat waves are likely to intensify.[84] It is known that in non-action scenarios, the effects of urban heat islands will become more severe.[85]

Fortunately, the particular geographical position of Freiburg between the Upper Rhine Plain and the Dreisam Valley creates a mountain–valley wind system known as Höllental, which is of fundamental importance to Freiburg's thermal regulation and air quality. The Sternwald, the Schlossberg and the Dreisam Valley funnel fresh air from the Black Forest into Freiburg. These winds are created by solar radiation. During the day the sun heats up the mountain slopes and the air above them, generating an upslope movement. At night, as the slopes and the air cool down, the air sinks into the valley, flushing into Freiburg. This occurs during approximately 70 per cent of the year (Figure 6.27).[86] Regarding air quality, morning up-valley winds lead the polluted air from Freiburg to the Black Forest.[87] Conversely, at night, the effect of this wind system is proven to decisively improve the city's air quality during periods of the year bringing clean air from the Black Forest. The Land Use Plan 2020 has determined that air movement corridors must be excluded from future building activities that could interfere with the air flow in and out of the city.

This chapter has examined the importance of green wedges in key contemporary polycentric city-region visions (Table 6.1). These cases have shown integrative approaches in which urbanization and the provision of high-quality green spaces do not exclude each other. Significant population growth is expected and is considered a spark for proactive planning for positive change. The densification of the inner areas and district nodes along main public transport routes is a strategy seen in all cases. These examples also show that the provision of quality green spaces, their distribution and ease of access are absolute requirements of contemporary cities and regions. On top of the commonly associated benefits of green spaces to recreation, health, ecology and environment, they become key assets of attractiveness in competitive global cities, both for professionals and investment. Ideas of hybrid networks of green space predominate in the discourses.

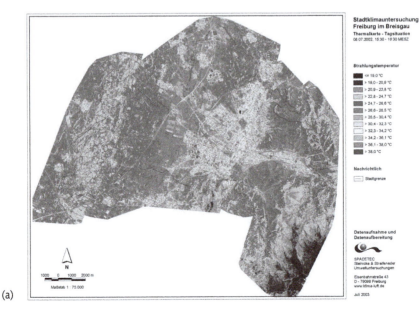

(a)

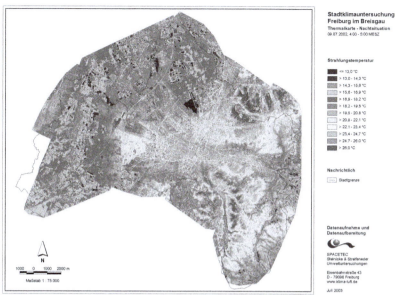

(b)

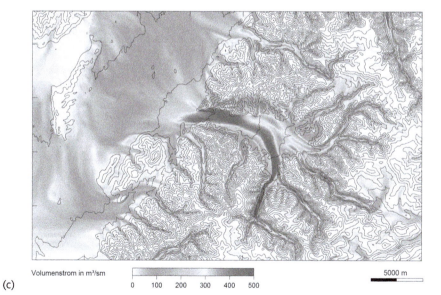

(c)

FIGURE 6.27 *Urban climate analysis of Freiburg (a) on a summer day and (b) night, and (c) a map showing cold air volume flow from the Black Forest into the city. Courtesy of the City of Freiburg.*

Table 6.1 Green wedges in the networked city-region

Year	Reference	Place	Author	Notes
1981	*Theory of good city form*	Generic	K. Lynch	Reference to the 'Star' city or the green wedge idea
1996	*Urban design: green dimensions*	Generic	C. Moughtin	'Star' city The importance of cross-connections as the wedges widen
2002	Melbourne 2030	Melbourne, Australia	State of Victoria	Protection and improvement of green wedges Green Wedge Management plans need to be developed and updated regularly
2006	Landscape Plan 2020	Freiburg I. Br., Germany	City of Freiburg	Green wedges are key for thermal regulation and air exchange
2007 and 2013	Finger Plan	Copenhagen, Denmark	Danish Ministry of the Environment	Development of the corridor-wedge model City wedges
2008	Randstad 2040 Structural Vision	Randstad, the Netherlands	Ministry of Infrastructure and Environment of the Netherlands	Positive planning of green wedges into metropolitan parks
2010	Regional Development Plan for the Stockholm Region	Stockholm, Sweden	Stockholm County Council	Ten green wedges Leading region in the planning of green wedges Green asset cores and social values
2010	Stockholm City Plan	Stockholm, Sweden	Stockholm City Planning Administration	Positive planning of green wedges
2013 and 2015	Helsinki City Plan 2013: Vision 2050	Helsinki, Finland	Helsinki City Planning Department	Motorways into boulevards Positive planning of green wedges

7

Green Wedges: From the City-region to the Neighbourhood

A multi-scale approach is today a requirement of planning. Different jurisdictions and planning administration levels are required to cooperate in order to efficiently tackle societal challenges and augment the chances to capitalize on opportunities for improved environments. While the previous chapter centred on city-region interactions, this chapter focuses on the relationships between city, districts and local scales. For clarity, however, it must be observed that the regional scale is also referred to here whenever necessary for contextualization. The chapter starts with analyses of the case studies of Hamburg, Milan and Songzhuang Arts and Agriculture city; and in the sequence focuses on the districts of Viikki, in Helsinki, Rieselfeld and Vauban in Freiburg; on Dunsfold Park, a new neighbourhood in the UK and on the application of the idea as a typology of green space in la Sagrera Linear Park in Barcelona.

Hamburg green network plan

Hamburg, the 2011 European Green Capital winner, launched a comprehensive strategy to remain in the world's top tier of 'green cities'. The prospect of climate change is a driver for change. The city set out to meet a number of quality of life and environmental targets, including cutting its carbon emissions by 40 per cent by 2020 and by 80 per cent by 2050. This will involve becoming car-free in the next fifteen to twenty years.[1]

Part of the strategy includes a redefinition of a green infrastructure plan. The *GrünesNetzHamburg* (Green Network Hamburg) plan draws from Schumacher's vision from 1919 crystallized in his leaf-city diagram and from Oelsner's green-belt plan from 1925. The former argued for the definition of axes of development intercalated with green wedges, which would penetrate from the countryside into the urban core, and the latter was centred on the creation of two green belts. Since the 1960s, these ideas have dominated the plans for the city. If originally the green wedges were seen mainly as public recreational zones close to residential areas, in the 1980s their ecological and environmental functions started to be delineated. Green wedges became important owing to their role in enabling improved habitat connectivity, helping preserve distinctive landscapes and because of their contribution to air exchange and temperature regulation.[2] In 1985, the Landscape Axes strategy was drawn up (Figure 7.1), focusing on these radial green spaces. In the open space plan for Hamburg adopted in 1997, the green wedges were complemented by the two aforementioned green belts. This strategy became part of the Landscape Programme, which determined Hamburg's aims for the environment and open space provision.[3]

In 2004, the wedges from the Landscape Axes strategy and the two belts were further detailed and became the basis of the 2013 Green Network (Figure 7.2). They were complemented by other key recreational areas, such as

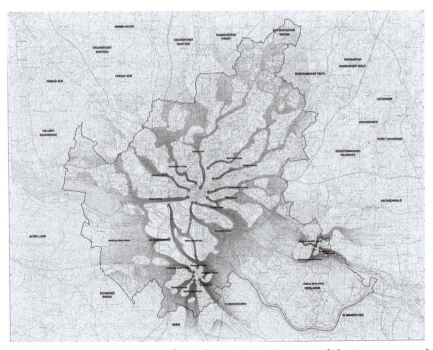

FIGURE 7.1 *Landscape Axes of Hamburg, 1985. Courtesy of the Department of Environment and Energy, City of Hamburg (Freie und Hansestadt Hamburg, BUE Behörde für Umwelt und Energie, Amt Naturschutz, Grünplanung und Energie, Abteilung Landschaftsplanung und Stadtgrün).*

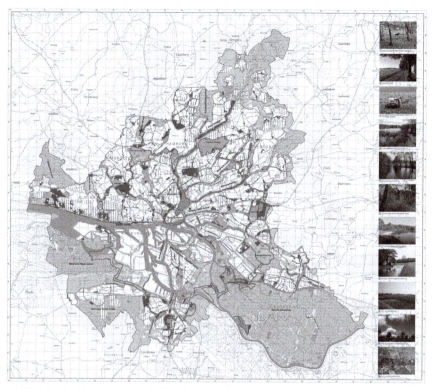

FIGURE 7.2 *Green Network plan for Hamburg, 2013. Courtesy of the Department of Environment and Energy, City of Hamburg (Freie und Hansestadt Hamburg, BUE Behörde für Umwelt und Energie, Amt Naturschutz, Grünplanung und Energie, Abteilung Landschaftsplanung und Stadtgrün).*

urban parks, and by an interconnected system of smaller green open spaces and green links. The green wedges range from 18 to 25 kilometres in length and cover from open country and woodlands in the periphery to urban parks, sports grounds, green corridors and tree-lined streets as they approach the inner city. To a large extent they follow natural features, such as the axes of the rivers Elbe, Alster and Osterbek. As the green wedges reach the inner parts of the city, they become thinner, more tortuous and make use of trees, bushes and lawns in an attempt to remain unbroken. A common reservation against the green wedge idea refers to its applicability to densely built-up areas. Hamburg's example shows that the variability in the width and types of green spaces, or green features, along the axes of green wedges imparts flexibility to a green wedge model, allowing its implementation across urban fabrics of very different characteristics.

Regarding Hamburg's green belts, the first is located approximately 1 kilometre away from the city hall on the grounds of the old city wall, connecting the majority of the green wedges. Recreational areas, such as the Elbpark, predominate in the first belt. The second forms a circle at 8 kilometres from the city hall and runs for 90 kilometres. Despite its dimension, the second green belt presents high continuity and consists mainly of parks, allotments and woodland.

Hamburg's Green Network further includes around eight district parks, thirty borough parks, 130 neighbourhood parks and more than 35,000 allotments. In addition, approximately 250,000 trees line the city's streets. Altogether, almost half of the city's area is dedicated to green and blue spaces. Future development of the network will concentrate on improving the quality of place and the connectivity of the wedges and rings.

The experience of Hamburg shows that combining historical green spaces, geographical features and newly created greenery even in the most urbanized areas of the city can succeed if there is political will and public support. The green network addresses Hamburg's vision of a healthy and sustainable city and in so doing puts it at the forefront of urban sustainability today.

The Raggi Verdi of Milan

How can the green wedges idea be applied to a densely built-up city? What are the strategies that can be used to adapt the model to suit the particularities of a dense *urbe*? Milan is a case in which a dense historic centre was no impediment to the definition of a plan that included several long radial green spaces penetrating from the surrounding hinterland into the innermost parts of the city.

Milan is a compact city with a strong industrial past. It counts with approximately 1.3 million inhabitants in a space of only 180 square kilometres. In the last decades, the city has experienced an intense process of deindustrialization and population decline, not only leaving an economic gap to be filled, but also prompting the city to rethink its spatial configuration and pursue new identities. In this light, the restructuring of brownfield sites became one of the focuses of interventions in the 1990s. Alongside it, interventions in green spaces also became one of the strategies pursued for the transformation of the city, particularly with the proposal of the *Nove parchi per Milano*. Given the city's compact configuration with few open spaces, the realization that it could nevertheless be restructured through a better articulation and definition of its existing open spaces and newly proposed 'voids' paid dividends in subsequent plans for the metropolitan region.

The *Raggi Verdi* (Green Rays) plan, initiated by the Associazione Interessi Metropolitani (AIM) and the landscape firm LAND in 2003, followed this pathway in redefining Milan's image and relationship with nature. If, in the collective imagination, Milan was not a green city, it should become one. This green network plan included eight radial green spaces – labelled 'green rays' (Figure 7.3) – that extended from the city centre outwards, intersecting the metropolitan green belt.

The 'green ways' would act as green wedges connecting and activating the city's open spaces.[4] Andreas Kipar defined them as 'channels crossing the solid matter of the city', as environmental axes bringing a 'new sense of nature to the city centre and a new urbanity outwards'.[5] They were to follow the radial structure of the city and were distributed evenly, covering each administrative zone. The Raggi Verdi plan aspired to create a network that would allow residents to flow freely through the green wedges, reaching the green belt and the countryside beyond. Due to Milan's compact urban fabric, the green wedges in the city centre were necessarily narrower and mostly defined by trees and bushes (Figure 7.4); but with their average length of 7–12 kilometres, they were planned to span a

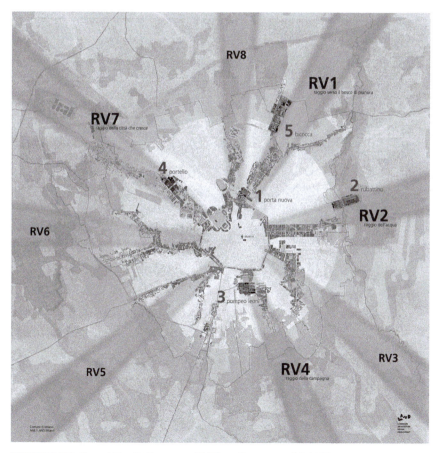

FIGURE 7.3 *Raggi Verdi diagram of Milan. Courtesy of LAND.*

(a)

(b)

FIGURE 7.4 *Illustrations of Raggi Verdi in inner Milan. Courtesy of LAND.*

variety of scales and landscapes as they radiate out, including large parks in the periphery and the green belt. The green belt would link the green wedges up and would encompass the nine parks surrounding Milan – including the regional parks of Parco Agricolo Sud and Parco Nord – offering 72 kilometres of linear parks. The ecological function is also highlighted as of foremost importance. The system of green spaces would provide the necessary connectivity to form ecological corridors, potentializing thus the emergence of habitats across the metropolitan area.

In 2005, the Comune di Milano incorporated the Raggi Verdi plan into its Plan for the Governance of the Territory (PGT).[6] Some of the key partners involved in the development of the PGT were studio Metrogramma, Id-Lab, Mediobanca and LAND. Metrogramma was responsible for the general structure plan and the intention was to promote a sustainable, systems-based, polycentric and dense city. Growing the city inwards is, as seen in previous case studies, a shared motto. As Bullivant highlighted, the plan embodied a research-based framework for a city in dynamic equilibrium.[7] This paradigm assumed the overcoming of isolated enclaves and moved towards a more interconnected city-region, where the centre–periphery relationship can be overcome in the direction of a more balanced distribution of activities across the different centres.[8] In this process, the reorganization of Milan's open spaces into a network is the basis upon which much of the expected permeability and connectivity can happen. The Green Plan (PdV) presented the guidelines for the green infrastructure as part of this general framework.

The current PGT sets out the objectives for 2030 and reinforces the approach to densify inwards. Alongside it, the quest for creating voids by subtraction from the mass of buildings remains a strategy to enhance the green network plan, the *Raggi Verdi* being its defining elements.[9] The vision is for a city that 'lives in greenery', easy to reach and move around, and with plentiful new services and spaces for all. As far as the concept of living in greenery is concerned, the plan holds up as models the Scandinavian cities, particularly in regard to the large amount of green spaces available to their residents.[10] The commitment is to achieve over 50 square kilometres of green spaces until 2030, lifting the ratio of 8 square metres per inhabitant found in the 1980s to 30 square metres.

Strategies for redeveloping both brownfield sites and open spaces were articulated. An example of this is the Porta Nuova project, which is the largest urban regeneration project ever attempted in Milan. The project is a mixed-use high-density scheme including an urban park, in an area of 290,000 square metres adjacent to the Garibaldi station. It connects the neighbourhoods of Garibaldi, Varesine and Isola. The first green ray crosses the Porta Nuova project, articulating it to the proposed green network on its way to the North Park. The seventh green ray, the Fiera Ray, encapsulates an axis of transformation that includes the City Life project – with iconic buildings by Isozaki, Hadid and Libeskind – and the Portello Park, leading out to the Fiera di Milano.

Milan is a fascinating example of urban transformation led by energizing landscapes. The malleable way in which green wedges, or green rays, were proposed – from the open territories in the hinterland to the narrow inner city spaces – serve, as in the case of Hamburg, as examples of a resourceful application of the idea to compact urban environments.

Songzhuang Arts and Agriculture city: A new form of urban–rural relationship

In the master plan of Songzhuang Arts and Agriculture city, by Sasaki Associates, a robust vision to articulate agriculture, parkland and development has been achieved. Located on 4,000 hectares on the outskirts of Beijing, Songzhuang's plan is based on a grid-like network, with a series of self-sustaining districts organized around a central agricultural green wedge (Figure 7.5). Assuming a corridor structure, this wedge accommodates traditional and new forms of agricultural production, as well as research into agricultural products and processes. In fact, the plan calls for the preservation of 98 per cent of existing agricultural land as either productive farmland or functional landscape

(a)

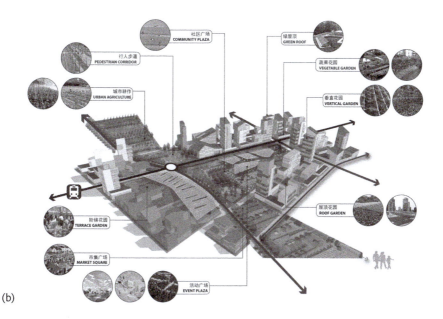

(b)

(c)

FIGURE 7.5 *(a) Master plan for Songzhuang, (b) diagram and (c) view of integrated landscape, 2012. Courtesy of Sasaki Associates.*

infrastructure. Numerous innovative edge conditions have been developed at the intersection of the green wedge with the built-up area, merging and re-configuring the relationship between the urban and the rural.[11]

Recreational and ecological green and blue corridors cross the plan, providing enhanced connectivity among the different elements of the landscape. The plan sought to restore the ecology of the site and nurture new habitats, especially along the Chaobai River corridor. A network of canals is provided, contributing to landscape quality, irrigation of the fields and biodiversity. With approximately 70 per cent of China's population living in urban areas by 2035, this plan offers an effective solution for the integration of the urban and the rural domains.[12]

Green wedges at multiple scales: Viikki

The site is located 8 kilometres from the centre of Helsinki, on the southern end of the Viikki-Kivikko wedge, which stretches from a nature conservation area near the inner bay to the Sipoonkorpi National Park in the north. Instigated by the publication of the Brundtland Report in 1987, sustainable development at municipal level was promoted in Finland in the 1990s, leading to the 'Eco-Community' initiative. Established by the Ministry of the Environment and the Finnish Association of Architects, this project prompted the identification of several areas for new ecological experimental developments across the country. In 1994 it was decided that Viikki would become the pilot area for the Eco-Community project.

The main objective of the local plan for Viikki was to deeply integrate built and natural environment in the creation of a new ecological housing area and adjacent science park, with reduced consumption of natural resources in both the construction phase and after occupancy. In addition, the development was to result in a model for future sustainable development. The proposal was to accommodate more than 15,000 residents, 7,000–8,000 workplaces and 6,000 students by 2015. The overall plan for the area is based on the green wedge model (Figure 7.6), with two districts connected by a major green wedge and a minor forested green wedge between residential areas to the east. A green buffer protects the development along the motorway to the north and northwest, where it connects to the science park. Green fingers and green routes penetrate the residential zones, connecting them to the main green spaces.

The major green wedge acts as a central park (Figure 7.7), stretching from its most urban end through to the nature conservation area to the south, and in so doing to the main Viikki-Kivikko wedge. The northern, and narrower, end contains a civic square, commerce and a church. A sports and recreational zone is located at the core of this wedge, where it connects with the forested area to the east. The Horticultural Centre, which defines the southeast edge of the central park and contains approximately 140 allotments, is meant to promote urban farming and social activities.[13] The remainder of this wedge is a multiuse recreational area, including two patches of woodland in its transition to the nature reservation zone. On its southwest edge, a dense zone of vegetation was planted to serve as a wind barrier.

FIGURE 7.6 *Plan of the Latokartano area. Courtesy of Helsinki City Planning Department.*

A competition for the southernmost area of the site, known as Eco-Viikki, was launched in 1994, seeking ecological visions and model solutions for a 23-hectare residential area for 1,700 inhabitants. The winning proposal, by architect Petri Laaksonen, according to the competition organizers, 'stood out from the other entries due particularly to its unique urban structure and implementation of ecological principles'.[14] The plan replicated the idea of green wedges, which now penetrated between 'home zones' – rows of urban blocks organized along central precincts (Figure 7.8). This strategy not only visually broke up the built form, but also ensured that every plot had direct access to a 'mini' green wedge for recreation, gardening and food growing.

An environmental impact report was drawn up alongside the development of the detailed master plan. Regarding the change in the landscape character, it was considered that the transformation of the previously cultivated fields into meadows or allotments would improve the birdlife habitat in the area. By the same token, the green wedges would evolve into ecological habitats supporting a rich variety of species.[15] These open space areas constitute an integral part of Viikki's storm-water management system. The surface water run-off from the blocks is led to the green wedges and from them to Viikinoja

(a)

(b)

FIGURE 7.7 *Views of the central green wedge in Viikki.*

brook, which was created on the western edge of Eco-Viikki. Residents can reuse run-off water through rainwater wells and hand pumps. This was an important consideration also to keep the surface water run-off that flows towards the nature conservation area as clean as possible.[16]

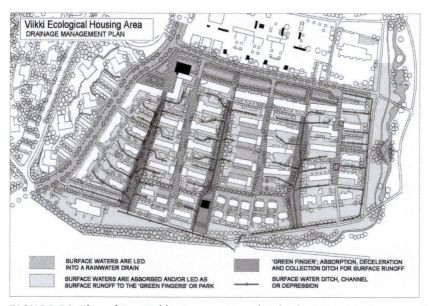

FIGURE 7.8 *Plan of Eco-Viikki.* Source: *City of Helsinki, 2005, 16. Courtesy of Helsinki City Planning Department.*

In summary, the implementation of the green wedge model in Viikki presents a tiered approach, from the scale of the district to the level of the block. The major green wedge acts as a focal point, offering a variety of functions and activities related to the promotion of sustainable and healthy living, such as sports facilities, recreation areas and urban farming. At the neighbourhood and block level, the idea is scaled down to offer semi-public spaces directly related to the private homes. In a resident's survey from 2003, this was considered to be one of the best features of the area.[17] In addition, the enhancement of diverse ecological habitats as well as the definition of a sustainable urban drainage system integrated with the provision of open spaces to the residents contributed significantly to meet the initial expectations for the area. Ecologically conscious architecture completes the urban character of Viikki, which has indeed become one of the most significant recent examples of sustainable development.

Rieselfeld

The development of the new districts of Rieselfeld and Vauban in Freiburg were responses to the housing demand from the late 1980s. Rieselfeld is located in the vicinity of the Dreisam Valley green wedge on a former sewage works site in the west of the city. The vision for Rieselfeld encompassed a dense, diverse, mixed-use district in close connection with nature and integrated with the city centre by light rail. The district was not to become a solely residential suburb, but a sustainable development with homes, jobs, facilities, commerce and a network of open spaces. Public engagement occurred strongly since the earliest stages of planning, leading to a comparatively higher sense of community ownership and identity.

After a planning competition, the implementation phase began in 1994 and was completed in 2012. The district covers an area of 70 hectares and is home to approximately 10,500 people. The fan-shaped plan, narrow in its eastern connection to the city, opens up to the aforementioned green wedge that is today a 250-hectare nature reserve. In so doing, it avoids the noise from the city, while benefiting from a larger frontage with the green wedge. A light rail line runs through a boulevard in the centre of the development, along which most of the commercial units and facilities are located. A strong sense of urbanity is found there, as the density is higher than on the periphery of the district, and active frontages and the presence of the tram generate urban life. Across Rieselfeld, 90 per cent of the buildings are tall, of up to five storeys. Shorter units can be found along the northern and southern edges.[18] A north–south green wedge traverses the plan in its central area.

The green and blue infrastructure plan for Rieselfeld includes the two green wedges, green buffer zones, green fingers along streams, communal courtyards, squares, tree-lined streets and gardens (Figure 7.9). Amenity value, recreation, ecological habitats, water management, food production and air quality are their predominant roles. The nature reserve, although immediately outside the development area, is connected to Rieselfeld (Figure 7.10). It is predominantly comprised of woodland and agricultural fields. A nature trail linking the different landscapes up helps visitors explore the area. Due to the radial character of the plan and the use of green fingers, tree-lined streets and green courtyards, the development blends in with the green wedge. This happens most noticeably in the green courtyards in the immediate vicinity of the entrance to the nature trail as well as in the stretches of woodland along the southern and northern borders of Rieselfeld, where it meets the north–south green wedge. These buffer zones delimit the development, creating transitional zones to the adjacent areas, and reduce the impact of noise from the surrounding roads.

As has been noted, a north–south green wedge reaches from the nearby countryside into the central square of Rieselfeld. Located on the north side of the main boulevard, it contains a district meeting centre and a church. The green wedge's south and eastern border are mostly defined by large educational and sports facilities. In addition it contains wooded areas and recreation grounds leading northwards towards the plains of Käslebach and Dietenbach. As the Höllental system does not reach Rieselfeld, strategies to benefit from other sources of ventilation were needed. In this respect, this central green wedge capitalizes on the north–south wind help promoting air flow into the denser areas. However, the creation of a new district in

Leisure area "WaldSeck"
Nature reserve with an "experience nature" path
Day nursery for children
Children's centre
Extension primary school
Station for firebrigade equipment
Sports kindergarten
Ecumenic churches
Gymnasium
Social meeting centre with rooms for children and young adults, and youth work
Independent Waldorf school
Primary school
Secondary school with sports hall
Sports club facilities
Children's center
Day nursery for children
Tram

Opfinger Straße

Town Planning Concept: Projektgemeinschaft Rieselfeld, Freiburg

Besançon-Allee

FIGURE 7.9 *Plan of Rieselfeld, 1994. Courtesy of the City of Freiburg.*

FIGURE 7.10 *Aerial photograph of Rieselfeld. Courtesy of the City of Freiburg.*

Dietenbach poses questions about the preservation of the coherence of that section of the green wedge.[19]

Rieselfeld has been under development for over twenty years. The interrelation between careful planning, community participation and methods of delivery has indeed made it a model of sustainable district development. The articulation of the urban structure with the transport system and green infrastructure was key for its success. The existing green wedge, to a great extent natural and agricultural in character, and the more urban north–south green wedge created the backbone of the green infrastructure for Rieselfeld, which, complemented by the other aforementioned typologies, generated a cohesive network supporting a number of ecosystem services in the district.

Vauban

Built on the grounds of former French barracks, which came into municipal ownership in the early 1990s, Vauban covers an area of 40 hectares and accommodates 5,500 residents.[20] It is located in the south of Freiburg, 3 kilometres away from the city centre. It sits on the footsteps of the Schönberg green wedge highlighted in the Five Finger Plan.

From the start, Vauban was seen as an opportunity for the creation of a model sustainable district with strong public participation. This manifested itself in the conceptualization of a compact, low-energy, mixed-use, car-reduced, walkable district well served by public transport (light rail) and high-quality open spaces. In 1994 an ideas competition was launched, which was won by architects Kohlhoff & Kohlhoff. By 1998, the first citizens arrived.[21] Similarly to Rieselfeld, the plan is structured along the main axis (Vaubanallee) defined by the light tramway. On Vauban's eastern side, former barracks were predominantly converted into student accommodation. New build ranged from 2 to 4 storeys, with taller structures along the central axis. However, unlike Rieselfeld, Vauban presents a less urban character throughout, with increased openness and buildings of smaller scale. Trees and front gardens often border the residential streets, which present well-proportioned street canyons and traffic-reducing measures, enhancing their sense of place and at the same time helping to visually unify the district. Parking is only permitted in one of the multi-storey parking buildings at the periphery. A market square and facilities such as nurseries, schools and civic meeting places were built alongside the private development. Vauban took the lead in promoting renewable energy. The buildings have to meet strict low-energy standards and most display solar panels. The district showcases today the world's first passive apartment block, and first PlusEnergy house (Heliotrope), commercial building (Sun Ship) and housing community (Solar Settlement).

The open space network for Vauban integrates green and blue spaces at varying scales. At city scale it benefits from its proximity to the Schönberg Mountain, which is part of the Black Forest (Figure 7.11). Largely wooded, its northern slopes present a rural character reaching the nature reserve along Dorfbach stream, at the southern border of Vauban. The Dorfbach stream is a nature preservation area of significant value for the protection of ecological habitats and as an ecological corridor. In addition, it serves as a recreation area and is a transitional zone between Vauban and the areas beyond. From there, three green fingers penetrate the district's central area, not only providing green routes between Vauban and the green wedge, but also directing slope winds around the district helping the circulation of air. The green fingers also serve as parks for the residents and include playgrounds, relaxation areas and allotments.

The tree-lined central axis, covered in lawn where the light rail tracks are, can be considered a green spine connecting the central spaces and helping with air movement. Natural creeks and swales form a part of the network contributing to the creation of ecological habitats and corridors. The strong presence of greenery throughout the residential areas – including courtyards, green streets and routes – complements the network at local level. There is a clear approach to keep the appearance of the green spaces natural, with close to none manicured treatment of the different landscapes. The residents' participation in the planning and design phases forged this approach and was particularly relevant in the preservation of existing old trees and the promotion of soft landscapes and activities within the green fingers.[22]

Vauban showed an early coming together of top-down and bottom-up processes, which potentialized its initial aspirations to become a model

FIGURE 7.11 *View of Vauban's green connection to the Schönberg Mountain.*

sustainable district. The green infrastructure is at the core of the physical and social articulation of the district. Working at city and local levels, it benefits from a careful relationship with the surrounding hills and slopes. In the planning tradition of Freiburg, this network contributes to the microclimate, responds to ecological and environmental concerns and helps define an image of sustainability directly associated with a green liveable city.

The neighbourhood scale: Dunsfold Park, UK

The provision of a green infrastructure plan can be found in most urban design proposals of a scale equal to or larger than that of a neighbourhood. The Dunsfold Park exemplifies well such a case. The master plan is for the transformation of a Second World War aerodrome in Surrey, England, into a new eco-village of 2,600 homes. Currently, 86 per cent of the site is brownfield land. Dunsfold Park, master planned by Pollard Thomas Edwards architects, aims to be one of Britain's first zero-carbon settlements. It would be set within the background of a 350-acre (1.42-square kilometre) country park. One of the plan's main objectives is the delivery of high-quality landscapes with enhanced biodiversity. The proposal includes a linear central park, replacing an existing runaway, and three green wedges (Figure 7.12) connecting the village centre

FIGURE 7.12 *Plan of Dunsfold Park, 2015. Courtesy of Pollard Thomas Edwards/ Dunsfold Airport Ltd.*

to the surrounding country park and countryside beyond.[23] They are conceived to provide nearby recreational spaces, wildlife habitats and corridors and to contribute to a sustainable urban drainage system for the whole site.

The green wedge as a typology: La Sagrera Linear Park

In 2011 the European Union adopted a new strategy to halt biodiversity loss and restore ecosystems where possible. Moreover, it also highlighted the value of ecosystem services. Key targets for 2020 included better protection and restoration of ecosystems and the services they provide, improved use of green infrastructure, sustainable agriculture and forestry and a greater EU contribution to preventing global biodiversity loss. In fact, the strategy calls for a development of 'a green infrastructure for Europe'.[24] In line with this directive, Barcelona has developed the *Plan del Verde y de la Biodiversidad 2020* (Plan of Greenery and Biodiversity 2020). This is a comprehensive re-naturing programme aimed at capitalizing on Barcelona's potential to become a green city model. The main concepts of the proposed green infrastructure are re-naturalization and connectivity, which would be achieved by 'spaces of opportunity' and green urban corridors. The first involves the identification and action upon a variety of spaces in order to re-naturalize them. The latter, as identified in landscape ecology theory, are to be continuous stretches of greenery reconnecting patches of formerly isolated landscapes.[25] One of such corridors includes La Sagrera Linear Park. Besides linking the mountains to the sea, the park will generate numerous ecological habitats, strengthening Barcelona's ecosystem services.

La Sagrera Linear Park, by Alday Jover, RCR and West 8, is a complete requalification of an old railway line into an energising new multi-functional green axis. It blends layers of underground rail infrastructure and motorways with a large park on the surface. The park is planned to comprise varied landscapes accommodating transport nodes and cultural and sports facilities. In addition, it will connect districts historically separated by the presence of the railway. Here, landscape acts as a medium for the articulation of infrastructure, city and architecture. Through such a reconfiguration of a major industrial artery, a gesture is made towards a greener Barcelona. La Sagrera Linear Park is to become the largest park in the city, running for almost 4 kilometres and with an area of more than 40 hectares. The park is configured as a large green wedge opening up to mountainous landscapes in the north (Figure 7.13). One of the main concepts here was to allow a pedestrian or cyclist to be able to move unobstructed from the historic core all the way to the Catalan Pyrenees

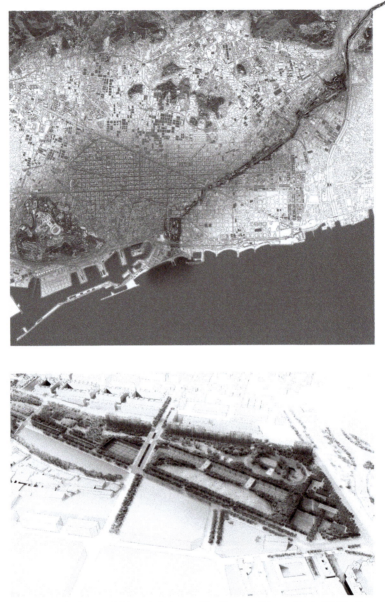

(a)

(b)

FIGURE 7.13 *(a) Plan and (b) aerial view of La Sagrera Linear Park, 2011. Courtesy of West 8. ©Aldayjover, RCR, West 8 and SBDA.*

in a green landscape. The widest part of the green wedge would become a gateway into Barcelona, welcoming those arriving from the north.[26]

The pursuit of sustainable and resilient city-regions must involve strategic and well-detailed actions at city, district and local scales. This chapter has shown that integrative and multiple-scale planning with high-quality delivery is fundamental (Table 7.1). Various visions of green cities are evident in contemporary planning discourse. In those, green wedges have received new definitions of use, form and potentialities – a process that, certainly, will continue in the years to come.

Table 7.1 Examples of green wedges at city, district and neighbourhood scales

Year	Reference	Place	Author	Notes
1994	Viikki	Helsinki, Finland	Various	Green wedges at multiple scales
1994	Rieselfeld	Freiburg, Germany	City of Freiburg i. Br	Connection to city green wedge Local central green wedge
2003	Raggi Verdi	Milan, Italy	AIM and LAND	Eight green wedges Flexibility of the wedges as they reach the inner city
2005	Green space ordinance	Münster, Germany	City of Münster	Three green rings and seven green wedges
2011	La Sagrera Linear Park	Barcelona, Spain	Alday Jover, RCR and West 8	4-kilometre long green wedge connecting linking mountains and the sea
2012	Songzhuang Arts and Agriculture city	Songzhuang, China	Sasaki Associates	Central green wedge accommodating traditional and new forms of agricultural production, as well as research into agricultural products and processes Innovative edge conditions
2013	Green Network	Hamburg, Germany	City of Hamburg	Hybrid model Flexibility of the wedges as they reach the inner city
2014	Vision for Järva 2030	Stockholm, Sweden	City of Stockholm	Various proposal to improve the area surrounding Järvafältet
2015	Plan of Dunsfold Park	Cranleigh, UK	Pollard Thomas Edwards	Three green wedges connecting the village centre to the surrounding country park and countryside Part of the SUDS for the site

Green Wedge Urbanism: Past, Present and Future

The green wedge idea: From the city scale to the polycentric region

The objectives of this book were twofold. First, to construct a history of the green wedge idea in planning discourse and practice and, in so doing, help forge a more comprehensive and integrated historiography of urban and green space planning. Central to our argument is the fact that, despite the lack of attention received by the literature, green wedges have played fundamental roles in the envisaging of the future of our towns, cities and regions, and that the history of this idea would offer valuable insights into the potentiality of green wedges today. Secondly, the book aimed to explore how the green wedge idea could contribute to the integration of cities and nature, leading towards an improved quality of life and more sustainable and resilient places.

Transnational exchanges fomented by the circulation of key individuals, plans and publications, and by the participation in professional events, forged the diffusion and development of the green wedge idea. The diverse spatial-temporal events and structures relating to its reception presented themselves as overlapping layers of complexity. Different local conditions, such as stages in the process of industrialization and growth of cities, led to syncopated focuses on the relevance of green space planning and consequently to asynchronous developments of the green wedge idea, particularly in the cases of some Latin American, Asian and African cities. Yet, the idea's main definitions and diverse applications have gravitated throughout history and different geographical locations towards certain recognizable features and functions.

A difficulty inherent in appreciating this process of diffusion and development is that of terminology. While the term 'green wedge' was consciously used and defined by many actors referring to both a wedge-like green space and to a planning model, a multiplicity of terms such as 'radial park' or 'green finger', when referring to the former, or 'star city', when considering the latter, were also concomitantly used.

Since its initial conception, the green wedge idea has developed in response to key planning preoccupations and, in turn, has itself shaped planning debates. It emerged from an empirical observation of the radial growth of modern cities. Although towns and cities were craving for intra-urban green spaces in the nineteenth century, the leftover spaces between development along traffic arteries typical of the period were originally seen as negative spaces and barely considered as part of the urban life. The insight to revert these voids into positive urban green spaces radically transformed the potentialities of park systems. Eberstadt's defence of the green wedge as the most adequate means of modern green space planning led to the definition of a model that would be replicated and adapted for many years. At this inaugural moment, the green wedge model is positioned in direct opposition to that of the green belt, and aimed at providing the most needed balance between built-up areas and open spaces, integrating transport and park system planning, connecting the city to the countryside, offering open air recreational spaces near where people lived and funnelling fresh air right into the core of cities flashing out pollution in turn. The model, often embedded with symbolic meaning, represented the hoped-for reconnection between city and countryside, man and nature, in other words, the promise of a better society in harmony with its environment. From this original model, others followed.

The second iteration of the green wedge model incorporated the notion of a green belt, resolving the initial opposition between belts and wedges. In plans for locations where outwards urban growth was not necessarily an issue, green belts tended to be absent, whereas where urban containment was opted for, this was often done through the means of a green belt. The British contribution here was crucial. An anti-metropolitan feeling combined with Howard's garden city ideal and the pressure from rural preservationists made the articulation of belts and wedges a win–win situation. By the interwar period, this model would reach significant international recognition. The main functions and characteristics of these green spaces remained similar to those of the first model, while the functionalist views of the sanitary capabilities of green spaces were emphasized.

The green wedge idea, first established theoretically for a largely monocentric city, soon acquired regional scope. Yet, it would be only in the plans for the post-war period that the proposition that cities needed to be reconfigured through the definition of neighbourhoods and districts that a sense of polycentrism would be marked. Taken a step further, polycentrism involved satellite towns or regional centres. It is in this perspective that the *Greater London Plan 1944* defined yet another model. Based on the wedges-belt one, the third green wedge model accommodates the idea of satellite towns surrounding the main city. In the case of London, it was made manifest in the application of the wedges-belt model to the city and the proposition of the new towns surrounding it. In a bellicose context, spacious planning found in green wedges a worthy ally. Green wedges would help prevent the spreading of fire due to bombing and be turned into agricultural zones in the event of food shortage.

The fourth model encompassed the regional scale in the form of corridors of development along rail traffic lines with interspersing green wedges. The corridor-wedge model was enunciated in the *Copenhagen Finger Plan 1947* and further pursued internationally in the 1960s and 1970s. This meant a significant shift upwards in scale for green wedges, which tended to comprise large tracts of land. The agricultural function becomes consolidated. In this period, green wedges also become used for a function that traditionally belonged to green belts: as buffer zones between towns – in this case located along the corridors of development.

The need to accommodate growth, the search for effective ways to provide green spaces for urban dwellers and the will to consider the regional scale have been constant planning concerns. These have been at the base of the formulation of the green wedge concept and its multiple models. As the models developed, they in turn framed planning debates by putting in evidence the potentialities of radial structures, the possibility of balancing green and grey urban spaces and the promotion of a particular articulation of the urban and the countryside. With the new discourses of sustainability and resilience, plans have been able to capitalize on established green wedge characteristics as well as to develop new layers of meaning, functions and roles.

Today, the idea of the polycentric city (or city-region) is pervasive. The development of complexity theory and systems thinking led to modes of planning that promote the intrinsic relationships among the different urban systems and the integration of ecosystem services into urbanism. The emergence of the 'networked' city, thus, brings together social, cultural, ecological and environmental factors into the planning of cohesive and integrated traffic systems, green and blue space networks and urban development, as seen, for instance, in the cases of Helsinki and Stockholm. In the fifth model green wedges remain the main large-scale structural axes of green space planning, which are complemented by a network of green and blue spaces at multiple scales that balance the provision across the city. This results in much improved connectivity across the green wedges without compromising their cohesiveness. In this model there tends to be a stronger connection between the open space network and the other urban systems.

A variety of functions have been associated with green wedges in this model, most recently including uses intended to mitigate the impacts of climate change. As a typology, the green wedge has been able to leave its mark in many cities, still performing most of its main functions, as is the case of La Sagrera Linear Park in Barcelona.

Towards a theory of green wedge urbanism

This study has provided a comprehensive account of the history of green wedges in urbanism and its practice to date. As an attempt to synthesize this knowledge for future applications, this section offers a theory of green wedge urbanism. In so doing, it formulates ten principles upon which the practice of green wedge urbanism can be based:

1. Balanced relationship between built-up areas and green wedges
2. Connection between the city and the countryside
3. Continuity of the green wedges
4. Public access and use
5. Positive planning and design for high-quality environments
6. Systemic integration into a comprehensive plan
7. The integration of ecosystem services
8. Permeability of the edges and cross connections
9. A multi-scale approach
10. Flexibility of form

Balanced relationship between built-up areas and green wedges

One of the fundamental objectives of the green wedge idea has continuously been to balance the urban and nature, city and the countryside. Green wedges can be used to break up the mass of buildings in towns and cities, and in so doing help define the identity of neighbourhoods, districts and cities. Besides, they can provide easy access to nature throughout the urban fabric. Research shows that numerous benefits are associated with contact with quality green spaces, and it is unquestionable that the application of this planning idea allows the population an enhanced degree of proximity to those. For instance, the majority of the population in cities well known for the implementation of green wedges lives within 1,000 metres from green areas, such as Stockholm (97 per cent), Helsinki (91 per cent) and Copenhagen (80 per cent); this proportion is much lower in some other cities that are only starting to implement it, such as Barcelona (70 per cent), Hamburg (68 per cent) and Milan (47 per cent).[1] The provision of high-quality green and blue spaces, their appropriate distribution and ease of access are requirements of contemporary cities rather than just 'nice to have'. They are assets of attractiveness in competitive global cities. This acknowledgement is a common feature of the city-region plans analysed in this book.

Connection between the city and the countryside

This has been across history another fundamental principle associated with green wedges. Symbolic and utilitarian reasons for the objective of linking the city and the countryside (or non-urban areas) could be identified. This study has showed that in moments of crises allegorical manifestations of the role of green wedges came to the fore indicating a search for a brighter future and a longing for the ideal harmony between man and nature and city and the countryside. This can be seen, for instance, in Stasse and de Bruyne's paper and Geddes's evocation of the star-like city, in Bruno Taut's Die Stadtkrone and in the radical plans for London for the post-war period. Such a symbolic association is also present in more recent views, as is the case of Stockholm. In addition, if connection to nature is a human need and cities have grown further away from the countryside, green wedges have contributed to re-establishing such a link.

The green and blue connections provided by green wedges from the hinterland to the city core allow for increased presence of wildlife even in the most urbanized areas, as Copenhagen can demonstrate. Such connections maximize the opportunities for ecological corridors and habitats, potentially strengthening socio-ecological relationships in and around cities. Furthermore, novel approaches to redefining established categories of urban, suburban and rural could be explored, especially regarding food production.

Continuity of the green wedges

The continuity of green wedges must be maximized across the wider landscape. Highly continuous landscapes can help reconnect isolated ecological habitats and strengthen ecological corridors. They also offer residents the possibility to explore and experience a variety of landscapes and activities in nature. The level of connectivity within a green wedge has a direct impact on the previous principle. Abercrombie was just one of the many who highlighted the value of uninterrupted pleasant green connections from the city to the countryside. Infrastructure elements crossing green wedges, such as railways and motorways, pose challenges to their continuity. Holistic assessments of how the different urban systems impact on one another should include how the continuity of green wedges is to be achieved and enhanced. Stockholm's identification of a hierarchy of weak links along green wedges and integrative strategies to improve these connections, such as 'ecoducts', can certainly offer insights to other cities.

Public access and use

Access to green wedges should be as much as possible public. In all cases studied, they were conceived for the benefit of the entire population – for instance the Finger Plan 2013 has a strict policy against new large privatizations of the green wedges in and around Copenhagen.

Private control of land has been repeatedly a hindrance to the implementation of green wedges. A recent report in the UK argued that greater public control of land use and the definition of effective mechanisms to capture and share the benefits of land value uplift due to development can help create opportunities for bold strategic investment.[2] This could include the provision of green wedges and associated infrastructure.

As the case of Melbourne has shown, some uses may require controlled access, such as intensive farming or an airport. These cases need to be monitored in relation to the rest of green wedge land and recreational use must be explicitly included whenever possible. Lack of accessibility and use by the population lead to a minimal social value. Resident's lack of identification with these spaces, in turn, can provoke a vicious circle of lack of care and maintenance. The loss of green space area is more likely in these circumstances, as low public opinion may not offer sufficient pressure for their safeguarding. Conversely, facilitating access, promoting the use and improving the quality of green wedges increases the possibility of keeping them continuous and relevant to residents and visitors.

Positive planning and design for high-quality environments

There must be a proactive approach in the planning of large-scale green structures for the creation and enhancement of high-quality places that address contemporary needs and challenges. Positive planning is crucial to up-keep the relevance of green spaces and to unlock their qualities of place.

Negative planning, focused on avoiding change at all costs, by its own nature renounces the possibility of promoting positive transformations. In the case of England, for instance, London's green belt and a number of 'strategic gaps' between towns are locked in a straightjacket of non-action. Certainly this approach has its role in localized circumstances, but a wholesome 'freezing' of land is wasteful. There are many shades between 'saving' green spaces and 'giving them up' for development. Immobilizing urban green spaces as a way to preserve them blocks the possibility of change and in so doing their ability to adapt to the changing societal needs. Adding values, experimenting in the definition of activities and interactions, and proposing hybrids can support generative processes. Adaptive capacity and diversity are prerequisites for resilience. Policies that support flexibility, dynamism and change should be encouraged to make our large green spaces, and therefore our cities, more adaptable and responsive to our changing needs. For that to happen, top-down and bottom-up need to meet and control and decision-making must be negotiated. In this process, public participation must be included.

In the cities and regions analysed in Part Two, proactive planning is at the core of preparing for expected and potential mutable scenarios, setting goals and strategies for the period leading to 2030–50. Examples of that can be seen in the Randstad's transformation of former buffer zones into metropolitan parks, the visions behind the GWMP's of the Melbourne region, the planning and enhancement of green asset cores and green meeting points in Stockholm and Helsinki's establishment of natural green core areas within green wedges.

Systemic integration into a comprehensive plan

A holistic approach considering the various urban systems (i.e. public transport, green infrastructure and land use) in conjunction is needed. This approach argues for a dynamic relationship between systems, each one impacting the other. To maximize the green wedges' contributions to improving urban living conditions, they should be whenever possible articulated into a green and blue infrastructure strategy, in turn part of a comprehensive spatial plan.

The development of planning models from monocentrism to polycentrism has made the role of public transport axes and their articulation to green wedges ever more important. The response to growth of the cities and regions studied focuses on strategic densification and structured expansion, promoting an inward growth and consolidation and definition of multiple urban cores along transport axes. This strategy in turn helps safeguard existing intra-urban open spaces and fringe zones under pressure and strengthens public transport system and the use of facilities, services and commercial activities.

The integration of ecosystem services

A systemic integration of ecosystem services should be pursued to potentialize their multiple benefits. The need for urban development and the safeguarding of intra-urban green spaces has been historically put in a dualist opposition. However, the systemic and jointly consideration of the urban and nature can lead to a more sustainable and resilient future. Research has shown that a holistic integration of social, ecological, environmental and economic systems in flexible frameworks tends to enhance urban vitality and resilience.[3] Green wedges can provide a full range of ecosystem services – such as food provision, forest areas, protection of water catchment areas, coastal locations, minimization of flooding, climate regulation, improvement in air quality, ecological habitats and corridors and recreational spaces.

The cases analysed in this book evidence a growing commitment to making better use of green wedges' ecosystem services as part of overarching strategies. For example, Helsinki has shown a more integrated approach between socio-ecological systems in the last plan, which led to strategies to improve the green wedges and connections to them; the Randstad has completely redefined the Green Heart into a green and blue delta; in the Copenhagen region, climate change adaptation has become one of the official functions of green wedges; and Freiburg has implemented renewable energy production from wind turbines in sections of its green wedges.

Permeability of the edges and cross connections

The edges of green wedges should be permeable and carefully planned and designed for appropriate interaction between the built-up and open areas. However, porosity into green wedges may need to be controlled due to sensitivity of edge ecological habitats or other concerns. The high perimeter-to-area ratio that characterizes green wedge models favours exchanges between the inside and outside of green wedges. Enhancing mutual socio-ecological services along the edges of green wedges can capitalize on this distinctiveness of these models.

The transformation of many edges from a motorway condition to that of a boulevard, as can be seen in Helsinki, greatly enhances the permeability towards the green wedges, facilitating thus their use and development of social values. The programme of interventions established for the area in and around Järvafältet in Stockholm, including for instance Stockholmsporten and Rinkeby Terrace, shows how a comprehensive and integrative planning approach including infrastructure, urban design, architecture and landscape architecture can provide an enhanced framework for the positive transformation of the relationship between a green wedge and the rest of the city-region.

The wider ends of green wedges, usually on the outskirts, pose particular difficulties for physical integration, as the bands of development tend to be considerably further apart compared to those along the narrower ends. Poor transversal connections in the former sections have thus more disruptive implications to cities. Numerous attempts to address transversal connectivity have been seen in this book, including Helsinki's green links across the green wedges, Copenhagen's Ring 3 light rail and Hamburg's green rings.

A multi-scale approach

Green wedges tend to cross distinct administrative boundaries and often present complex land ownership patterns. Dialogue, cooperation and the democratic definition of shared aims, principles and strategies within and across different jurisdictions are therefore important for the planning, implementation and management of green wedges.

Consistency and cross-scale interactions in the planning and design of green wedges can strengthen the benefits they can provide. For instance, Stockholm's regional strategy of enhancing the quality, continuity and connectivity of its green wedges is reinforced by very precise actions at city and neighbourhood scales, such as the creation of green meeting points, the numerous urban design proposals along the edge of Järvafältet, the ecoducts of Hammarby Sjöstad and the green cycle paths and pedestrian pathways of Farsta, Fagersjö and Rågsved. In Helsinki, Viikki showed the use of green wedges at varying scales – in its connection to Viikki-Kivikko wedge, as a central park for the district and as local green spaces between blocks. Rieselfeld also presented a similar approach. Attention to detail at every level must be pursued, including – and perhaps most importantly – at the scale of the user.

Flexibility of form

By their very nature, green wedges have historically been large-scale green structures spanning from the inner city to the countryside. As they approach the urban fringe they tend to widen up. Largeness is both an opportunity and a challenge. It is well documented that large-scale green spaces create enhanced conditions for ecological diversity and wildlife migration through the continuity of ecological corridors and facilitate the hosting of a variety of recreational and cultural landscapes, experiences, functions and activities. Nonetheless, the usual difficulties derived from large scale need to be addressed, such as multiple land ownership and legislative frameworks, varied pattern of land use and occupation, fragmentation due to development and infrastructure and lack of available open space along 'the path' of the green wedge.

A flexible implementation of green wedges in consolidated urban fabrics is necessary. Milan's Raggi Verdi plan and Hamburg's Green Network show that a range of scales and shapes of green spaces may be the key to ensure the continuity of green wedges from the countryside to the compact urban cores. While the former can accommodate larger green spaces, in their narrowest ends green wedges can merge with greenways, tree-lined streets with bushes, lawns and other green features.

Final words

The planning, implementation and management of green wedges require a commitment to a strategic vision and their long-term stewardship. The theory proposed here is not intended to be exhaustive or static, but to synthesize key driving principles to guide further development of theory and inform practice.

It is important to note that the application of green wedge urbanism principles to new and existing areas presupposes levels of adaptation or hybridism according to local circumstances. As seen, various attempts to implement green wedges across the period of study did not materialize as intended, let alone speculative proposals with little possibility of implementation from the start. This was frequently due to one or a combination of the following factors: multiple ownership of land, financial and legal implications in compulsory purchase of land, the difficulty in controlling development within urban areas, lack of political will and the cost of constructing or restructuring the urban fabric. Conversely, in general terms, the successful implementation of the green wedge models discussed earlier drew from strong public control of land or development rights, appropriate legal frameworks, political drive and adequate financial support. The difficulties to be overcome in some cases may have been various but, as this book has shown, the benefits were there for the taking.

The constant process of updating to current demands has demonstrated the flexibility of the green wedge idea and its capacity for reinvention. With the challenges associated with the prospect of significant global population growth, increasing concentration of people in urban settings and the consequences of climate change, an integrative approach to planning for greener environments is a necessity. Advancements in systems thinking may lead to the development of far more integrated urban models, consolidating nature as a fundamental part of urban life. In this scenario, it is fair to anticipate that green wedges will play even stronger roles in mitigating the impacts of climate change and in overall resilience strategies, as well as in providing high-quality ecosystem services and recreational green environments at residents' doorsteps.

This book intends to be a referential mark in the study of the history, theory and practice of green wedge urbanism. As such, it has attempted to draw from distinct sources from across the world spanning more than a century. It contributes decisively to the history of green space planning by shedding light on a so far under-investigated seminal idea that has had and continues to have relevance nationally and internationally. In doing so, the book argues for an integrated approach to the study of urban and green space planning. There is today a lively debate about re-naturing cities, since it can address multiple societal challenges and generate benefits such as the enhancement of health and well-being, sustainable urbanization, ecosystems and their services and resilience to climate change.[4] This book has evidenced how the various models derived from the green wedge idea can lead to strong re-naturing of cities and regions, making the idea a powerful tool in the construction of greener urban futures. No better results could this book achieve than be used as a source of knowledge and inspiration for the improvement of our environments.

Notes

Introduction

1 Later published as Ebenezer Howard, *Garden cities of to-morrow* (London: Faber, 1902).

2 See, for instance, Nicky Morrison, 'A green belt under pressure: The case of Cambridge, England', *Planning Practice & Research* 25, no. 2 (2010): 157–81; Kevin Thomas and Steve Littlewood, 'From green belts to green infrastructure? The evolution of a new concept in the emerging soft governance of spatial strategies', *Planning Practice and Research* 25, no. 2 (2010): 203–22.

3 Kate Barker, *Barker review of land use planning: Final report – recommendations* (Norwich: HMSO, 2006).

4 DCLG, *Local planning authority green belt: England 2013/14*, ed. Department for Communities and Local Government (London: DCLG, 2014).

5 Françoise Choay and Denise Bratton, *The rule and the model: On the theory of architecture and urbanism* (Cambridge, MA: MIT Press, 1997), 8.

6 Françoise Choay, *L'urbanisme, utopies et réalités: une anthologie* (Paris: Seuil, 1965), 20; Choay and Bratton, *The rule and the model: On the theory of architecture and urbanism*, 277.

7 Helen Rosenau, *The ideal city: Its architectural evolution*, 2nd ed. (London: Studio Vista, 1974), 16.

8 Bernard Lepetit, 'Propositions pour une pratique restreinte de l'interdisciplinarité', *Revue de Synthèse* 4, no. 3 (1990): 331–38.

9 Stephen Ward, *Planning and urban change* (London: Sage, 2004).

10 Raymond Grew, 'The case for comparing histories', *The American Historical Review* 85, no. 4 (1980): 769.

11 Marc Bloch, 'Comparaison', *Bulletin du Centre International de Synthèse*, no. 9 (1930): 34.

12 See the Introduction of Siegfried Giedion, *Space, time and architecture: The growth of a new tradition* (New York: Harvard University Press, 1942), 6.

Chapter 1

1 See Marc-Antoine Laugier, *Essay on architecture* (London: T. Osborne and Shipton, 1755); Gottfried Semper, *The four elements of architecture and other writings* (Cambridge: Cambridge University Press, 1989).

2 Rosenau, *The ideal city: Its architectural evolution*, 46.

3 Jürgen Habermas, 'Modernity: An unfinished project', in *Critical theory, the essential readings*, ed. David Ingram and Julia Simon Ingram (New York: Paragon House, 1991), 163.

4 Laugier, *Essay on architecture*, 248.

5 Ibid., 252.

6 For more information on the impression Karlsruhe caused in Loudon, see Ulrich Maximilian Schulmann, 'The hidden roots of the garden city idea: From John Sinclair to John Claudius Loudon', *Journal of Planning History* 2, no. 4 (2003): 291–310. Stübben also refers to it in his book: Joseph Stübben, *Der Städtebau. Handbuch der Architektur* (Braunschweig: Vieweg, 1890).

7 Claude-Nicolas Ledoux, *L'Architecture considerée sous le rapport de l'art, des moers et de la législation* (1804).

8 Julie Jefferies, 'The UK population: Past, present and future', in *Focus on people and migration*, ed. Roma Chappell (Norwich: Palgrave Macmillan, 2005), 3.

9 Friedrich Lenger, *Towards an urban nation: Germany since 1780* (Oxford: Berg, 2002), 71.

10 Brian Ladd, *Urban planning and civic order in Germany, 1860–1914* (Cambridge, MA; London: Harvard University Press, 1990), 15.

11 D. A. Johnson, *Planning the great metropolis: The 1929 regional plan of New York and its environs* (London: Spon, 1996), 13.

12 Anthony Sutcliffe, *British town planning: The formative years* (Leicester: Leicester University Press, 1981); William Ashworth, *The genesis of modern British town planning* (London: Routledge & Kegan Paul, 1954).

13 Peter Hall and Mark Tewdwr-Jones, *Urban and regional planning*, 5th ed. (London: Routledge, 2011), 15.

14 Cited by George Fletcher Chadwick, *The park and the town: Public landscape in the 19th and 20th centuries* (London: Architectural Press, 1966), 50–1.

15 Richard Phillips, *A morning walk from London to Kew* (London: J. Adlard, 1817), 30.

16 Cited by Gordon E. Cherry, *Cities and plans: The shaping of urban Britain in the nineteenth and twentieth centuries* (London: Edward Arnold, 1988), 55.

17 Lenger identifies four critical groups of the urban society: the followers of agrarian romanticism, interested in the preservation of the countryside and arts and crafts traditions; those believing in 'the city as the grave of the race', degenerating and killing city dwellers who often immigrated from the countryside; those opposing the technological advancements of the present for fear of losing the 'naturalness' of the past; and the sentimental ones, 'conjuring up of a better past'. See Friedrich Lenger, 'Building and perceiving the city: Germany around 1900', in *Towards an urban nation: Germany since 1780*, ed. Friedrich Lenger (Oxford: Berg, 2002), 98–9.

18 Franco Panzini, *Per i piaceri del popolo: l'evoluzione del giardino publico in Europa dalle origini al XX secolo* (Bologna: Zanichelli Editore, 1993).

19 Paolo Sica, *Historia del Urbanismo. Siglo XIX.* (Madrid: IEAL, 1980), 102.

20 Cherry, *Cities and plans: The shaping of urban Britain in the nineteenth and twentieth centuries*, 47.

21 Ladd, *Urban planning and civic order in Germany, 1860–1914*, 67.

22 John Claudius Loudon, 'Hints for breathing places for the metropolis, and for country towns and villages, on fixed principles', *The Gardener Magazine* v (1829): 686–90.

23 Schulmann, 'The hidden roots of the garden city idea: From John Sinclair to John Claudius Loudon', 302–7 and 291–310; Panzini, *Per i piaceri del popolo: l'evoluzione del giardino publico in Europa dalle origini al XX secolo*, 166–7.

24 Ladd, *Urban planning and civic order in Germany, 1860–1914*, 44. Siegfried Giedion, 'Chapter 3: City planning in the nineteenth century', in *Space, time and architecture: The growth of a new tradition* (New York: Harvard University Press, 1942).

25 Anthony Sutcliffe, *Towards the planned city: Germany, Britain, the United States and France 1780–1914* (Oxford: Basil Blackwell, 1981), 3; Gordon E Cherry, *The evolution of British town planning: A history of town planning in the United Kingdom during the 20th century and of the Royal Town Planning Institute, 1914–74* (Leighton Buzzard: L. Hill, 1974); Leonardo Benevolo, *The origins of modern town planning* (London: Routledge and Kegan Paul, 1967); Choay, *L'urbanisme, utopies et réalités: une anthologie*.

26 See also, G. Piccinato, *La construzione del l'urbanística Germania 1871–1914* (Roma: Officina, 1974); José Valdivia Luque, *Constructores de la ciudad contemporánea: aproximación disciplinar a través de los textos* (Madrid: Cie Inversiones Editoriales, 2004); Stephen Ward, 'What did the Germans ever do to us? A century of British learning about and imagining modern town planning', *Planning Perspectives* 25, no. 2 (2010): 117–40; Sutcliffe, *Towards the planned city: Germany, Britain, the United States and France 1780–1914*.

27 Franz-Josef Brüggemeier, 'Normal pollution: Industrialization, emissions and the concept of zoning in germany, 1800–1970', in *Towards an urban nation: Germany since 1780* (Oxford: Berg, 2002), 119.

28 Ladd, *Urban planning and civic order in Germany, 1860–1914*, 230.

29 Fritsch was an anti-Semite journalist. He used his model city to proclaim the harmful effects of large cities on morals and the health of the population and, ultimately, as Schubert noted, on the race. See Dirk Schubert, 'Theodor Fritsch and the German (völkische) version of the Garden City: The Garden City invented two years before Ebenezer Howard', *Planning Perspectives* 19, no. 1 (2004): 10.

30 Ibid., 25.

31 Ashworth, *The genesis of modern British town planning*; Gordon E. Cherry, *Pioneers in British planning* (London: Architectural Press, 1981); Cherry, *The evolution of British town planning: A history of town planning in the United Kingdom during the 20th century and of the Royal Town Planning Institute, 1914–74*.

32 Hall and Tewdwr-Jones, *Urban and regional planning*, 18.

33 Manfred Kühn and Ludger Gailing, 'From green belts to regional parks: History and challenges of suburban landscape planning in Berlin', in *Urban green belts in the twenty-first century*, ed. M. Amati (Ashgate, 2012), 185.

34 Stübben, *Der Städtebau. Handbuch der Architektur*, 226; Eugène Hénard, *Études sur les transformations de Paris*, ed. Jean-Louis Cohen (Paris: Editions L'Equerre, 1902 [1982]).

35 Ladd, *Urban planning and civic order in Germany, 1860–1914*, 85.

36 Ibid., 202–3.

37 Hegemann, 1930, 411–12, cited by Anthony McElligott, *The German urban experience, 1900–1945: Modernity and crisis* (London: Routledge, 2001).

38 Cherry, *The evolution of British town planning: A history of town planning in the United Kingdom during the 20th century and of the Royal Town Planning Institute, 1914–74*, 69.

39 Kühn and Gailing, 'From green belts to regional parks: History and challenges of suburban landscape planning in Berlin', 190.

40 Gordon E. Cherry, *Environmental planning, 1939–1969. Vol.2, National Parks and recreation in the countryside* (Peacetime history) (London: HMSO, 1975), 9–25.

41 Ladd, *Urban planning and civic order in Germany, 1860–1914*, 209. Original from Rolling, John. 'Liberals, socialists, and city government in imperial Germany: The case of Frankfurt am Main, 1900–1918'. PhD dissertation, University of Winsconsin-Madison, 1979, 68–70.

42 Patrick Geddes, *Cities in evolution*, Revised ed. (London: Williams & Norgate, 1915), 96–7.

43 Sonja Dümpelmann, 'The park international: Park system planning as an international phenomenon at the beginning of the twentieth century', *GHI Bulletin* no.37 (2005): 75.

44 Chadwick, *The park and the town: Public landscape in the 19th and 20th centuries*.

45 Francesco Dal Co, 'From parks to the region', in *The American city: From the civil war to the new deal*, ed. P. R. Baker, Dal Co Ciucci, F. D. Co, M. Manieri-Elia, M. Tafuri and B. L. La Penta (London: Granada, 1980), 141–293.

46 Frederick Law Olmsted, 'Public parks and the enlargement of towns', in *American Social Science Association,* Boston (25 February 1870), 10, https://catalog.hathitrust.org/Record/008726621.

47 Ibid., 13.

48 For a discussion about Olmsted's influence on American planning practice, see Jon A. Peterson, 'The birth of organized city planning in the United States, 1909–1910', *Journal of the American Planning Association* 75, no. 2 (2009): 123–33; Mario Manieri-Elia, 'Toward an "Imperial City": Daniel H. Burnham and the city beautiful movement', in *The American city: From the civil war to the new deal*, ed. P. R. Baker, Dal Co Ciucci, F. D. Co, M. Manieri-Elia, M. Tafuri and B. L. La Penta (London: Granada, 1980), 1–122.

49 Special Park Commission, 'Report of the Special park commission to the City council of Chicago on the subject of a metropolitan park system' (Chicago: Chicago Special Park Commission, 1905).

50 Daniel Burnham and Edward Bennett, *Plan of Chicago* (Chicago: The Commercial Club, 1909).

51 Panzini, *Per i piaceri del popolo: l'evoluzione del giardino publico in Europa dalle origini al XX secolo*, 287.

52 Hénard, *Études sur les transformations de Paris*.

53 J. C. N. Forestier, *Grandes villes et systèmes de parcs* (Paris: Hachette, 1906), 59. In this work Forestier defines the other elements of a park system: natural reserves, suburban parks, large urban parks, small parks, neighbourhood gardens and recreation areas.

54 Sonja Dümpelmann, 'Creating order with nature: Transatlantic transfer of ideas in park system planning in twentieth-century Washington D.C., Chicago, Berlin and Rome', *Planning Perspectives* 24, no. 2 (2009): 146.

55 William Whyte, 'The 1910 Royal Institute of British Architects' Conference: A focus for international town planning?', *Urban History* 39, no. 1 (2012): 149–65.

Chapter 2

1 This chapter is derived, in part, from an article published in *Planning Perspectives* on 25 August 2013, http://www.tandfonline.com/doi/abs/10.108 0/02665433.2013.824369 (accessed 9 September 2016).

2 In the case of England, the minutes of the RIBA Town Planning Committee meetings give a clear insight into how the United States and Germany were the main sources of inspiration in matters of town extension and park system planning. For instance, in July 1907, the Development of Towns and Suburbs Committee decided to send out letters to prominent planning figures such as Peabody in Boston, Miles Day in Philadelphia, McKim in New York, Carey in Buffalo and Stübben in Cologne asking for information on this subject. By October 1907, the committee was able to gather the much sought-after replies. See RIBA, *Minutes of the RIBA development of towns and suburbs subcommittee* (London: RIBA Archives, 1907).

3 He was a member of the RIBA and would later become the secretary of the 1910 RIBA Town Planning Conference. He was also one of the founders of the Town Planning Institute.

4 Henry Vaughan Lanchester, 'Park systems for great cities', *The Builder* 95 (1908): 343.

5 Ibid.

6 H. V. Lanchester Papers Collection, RIBA Archives, LaHe/1/3. Copies of Hénard's famous 'Plans Comparatifs' can be found in the collection.

7 *The Times*, 'Town planning', *The Times*, 19 February 1909.

8　Raymond Unwin, 'The Berlin exhibition of town planning', *The Builder* 99 (1910): 18.

9　The event included presentation sessions, exhibitions, site visits and social activities. Germany was by far the largest contributor to the exhibition – which was organized by Unwin – presenting plans for the Greater Berlin Competition, Munich, Cologne, Düsseldorf, Nuremberg and other cities. It was followed by the United States, with Burnham's Chicago plan; Great Britain, mostly featuring Letchworth, plans for garden suburbs, such as Hampstead, Bourneville and Port Sunlight, as well as Geddes' survey of Edinburgh; France, showcasing plans for Paris; and minor contributors, such as Italy, Sweden and other Scandinavian countries.

10　Arthur Crow, 'Town planning in relation to old and congested areas, with special reference to London', in *Town planning conference, London, 10–15 October 1910. Transactions*, ed. RIBA (London: RIBA, 1911)407–26.

11　G. L. Pepler, 'Greater London', in *Town planning conference, London, 10–15 October 1910. Transactions*, ed. RIBA (London: RIBA, 1911) 611–20.

12　F. S. Baker, 'Discussion – Cities of the present', in *Town planning conference, London, 10–15 October 1910. Transactions*, ed. RIBA (London: RIBA, 1911), 242.

13　C. M. Robinson, 'Cities of the present as representtive of a transition period in urban development – The evidence of standardised streets', in *Town planning conference, London, 10–15 October 1910. Transactions*, ed. RIBA (London: RIBA, 1911), 201–202.

14　Rudolf Eberstadt, 'Town planning in Germany: The Greater Berlin competition', in *Town planning conference, London, 10–15 October 1910. Transactions*, ed. RIBA (London: RIBA, 1911), 326.

15　Henry Vaughan Lanchester, 'Cause and effect in the modern city', in *Town planning conference, London, 10–15 October 1910. Transactions*, ed. RIBA (London: RIBA, 1911).

16　Henry Vaughan Lanchester, 'Informal meetings: Exhibition of lantern slides', in *Town planning conference, London, 10–15 October 1910. Transactions*, ed. RIBA (London: RIBA, 1911), 269.

17　John Brodie, 'Discussion', in *Town planning conference, London, 10–15 October 1910. Transactions*, ed. RIBA (London: RIBA, 1911), 238.

18　Werner Hegemann, 'Discussion', in *Town planning conference, London, 10–15 October 1910. Transactions*, ed. RIBA (London: RIBA, 1911), 240.

19　Thomas H. Mawson, 'Public parks and gardens: Their design and equipment', in *Town planning conference, London, 10–15 October 1910. Transactions*, ed. RIBA (London: RIBA, 1911), 435.

20　G. T. Plunkett, 'Open spaces and running waters', in *Town planning conference, London, 10–15 October 1910. Transactions*, ed. RIBA (London: RIBA, 1911) 465–75.

21　E. Stasse and H. de Bruyne, 'Bruxelles aux Champs', in *Town planning conference, London, 10–15 October 1910. Transactions*, ed. RIBA (London: RIBA, 1911), 648; See also Pieter Uyttenhove, 'The garden city education of

Belgium planners around the First World War', *Planning Perspectives* 5, no. 3 (1990): 271–83.

22 It is worth pointing out that this diffusion of the idea was mostly advocated by professionals involved with the Liverpool School of Architecture's Department of Civic Design.

23 Town Planning Review, 'Chronicle of passing events: St. Louis Outer Park, or public reservation district', *Town Planning Review* 1, no. 3 (1910): 263.

24 Patrick Abercrombie, 'Town planning schemes in America: Chicago', *Town Planning Review* no. 1: 58, 60.

25 'Washington and the proposals for its improvement', *Town Planning Review* 1, no. 2 (1910): 147.

26 'Town planning in Greater London: The need for co-operation', *Town Planning Review* 2, no. 4 (1912): 264.

27 Ibid.

28 Town Planning Review, 'Chronicle of passing events: York competition', *Town Planning Review* 6, no. 1 (1916).

29 See Gustav Langen, *Stadtplan und Wohnungsplan vom hygienischen Stadtpunkte* (Leipzig: Verlag von S. Hirzel, 1927); Gerhard Fehl, 'The Nazi garden city', in *The garden city: Past, present and future*, ed. Stephen Ward (London: Spon Press, 1992) 88–106.

30 Kühn and Gailing, 'From green belts to regional parks: History and challenges of suburban landscape planning in Berlin', 191.

31 Martin Wagner, 'Das sanitäre grün der Städte: ein Beitrag zur Freiflächentheorie' (1915).

32 NAI, 'Chaos and Order (1920–1927)', NAI, http://schatkamer.nai.nl/en/projects/chaos-en-orde (accessed 13 April 2015).

33 Nelson Peter Lewis, *Planning of the modern city: A review of principles governing city planning* (New York: John Wiley & Sons, 1916), 146.

34 Christiane Crasemann Collins, 'Urban interchange in the southern cone: Le Corbusier (1919) and Werner Hegemann (1931) in Argentina', *The Journal of the Society of Architectural Historians* 54, no. 2 (1995): 208–27.

35 See Johnson, *Planning the great metropolis*.

36 Thomas Adams, *The building of the city* (New York: Regional plan of New York and its environ, 1931), 443.

37 Johnson, *Planning the great metropolis*, 104.

38 Robert Schmidt, *Denkschrift betreffend Grundsätze zur Aufstellung eines General-Siedelungsplanes für den Regierungsbezirk Düsseldorf (rechtsrheinisch)* (Essen: Fredebeul & Koenen, 1912); see also Ursula Von Petz, 'Robert Schmidt and the public park policy in the Ruhr district, 1900–1930', *Planning Perspectives* 14, no. 2 (1999): 163–82.

39 Thomas Mawson, *Bolton as it is and as it might be* (Bolton: Tillotson and Son), 65–66.

40 Ibid.

41 See particularly Peter Hall, *Cities of tomorrow: An intellectual history of urban planning and design in the twentieth century* (Oxford: Blackwell, 1996), 142–87; Ward, *Planning and urban change*; Helen Meller, *Patrick Geddes: Social evolutionist and city planner* (London: Routledge, 1990).

42 London Society, 'London Society – Notes of their aims', 59 – cited by Mervyn Miller, 'The elusive green background: Raymond Unwin and the greater London regional plan', *Planning Perspectives* 4, no. 1 (1989): 19.

43 See Lucy Hewitt, 'Towards a greater urban geography: Regional planning and associational networks in London during the early twentieth century', *Planning Perspectives* 26 (2011): 551–68; Fabiano Lemes de Oliveira, 'Green wedges: Origins and development in Britain', *Planning Perspectives* 29, no. 3 (2014).

44 London Society, *Minutes of the London Society Committee* (London: London Society Archives, 1914).

45 Bruno Taut, *Die Stadtkrone* (Jena: Eugen Diederichs, 1919).

46 P. Wolf, *Städtebau: das Formproblem der Stadt in Vergangenheit und Zukunft* (Klinkhardt & Biermann, 1919), 85.

47 'Heiz- Kraftwerk Wettiner Platz (Westkraftwerk) – Funktional- sachliche Industriearchitektur', http://www.das-neue-dresden.de/heizkraftwerk-dresden-mitte.html (accessed 3 February 2016).

48 Robert Freestone, 'Exporting the garden city: Metropolitan images in Australia, 1900–1930', *Planning Perspectives* 1, no. 1 (1986): 81.

49 Metropolitan Town Planning Commission, *Plan of general development of Melbourne: Report of the metropolitan town planning commission* (Melbourne: Metropolitan Town Planning Commission, 1929), 199, 214 and between 28 and 29.

50 McElligott, *The German urban experience, 1900–1945: Modernity and crisis*, 100.

51 Cherry, *Cities and plans: The shaping of urban Britain in the nineteenth and twentieth centuries*.

52 G. L. Pepler, 'Open spaces', *Town Planning Review* 10, no. 1 (1923).

53 Barbara Szulczewska and Ewa Kaliszuk, 'Problems of green structure planning and management in Warsaw', in *Report of COST Action C11 – Greenstructure and urban planning: Final report,* ed. Ann Caroll Werquin, et al. (Luxembourg: Office for Official Publications of the European Communities, 2005).

54 Bolesław Malisz, 'Urban planning theory: Methods and results', in *City and regional planning in Poland*, ed. Jack C. Fischer (Ithaca, NY: Cornell University Press, 1966), 58.

55 Stanisław Różański, Stanisław Filipkowski, and Maria Buckiewiczówna, 'Plan ogólny Wielkiej Warszawy', *Architektura i Budownictwo* (1928): 431.

56 Grażyna Kodym-Kozaczko and Mieczysław Kozaczko, 'Master plan for Poznań (1931–1939) as compared with European theory and practice of city development', in *Modernism in Europe, modernism in Gdynia: Architecture of 1920s and 1930s and its protection*, ed. Robert Hirsch, Maria Jolanta

Sołtysik and Waldemar J. Affelt, *Poznań University of Technology* (Gdynia: The City of Gdynia, 2009), 107.

57 Ibid., 105–09.

58 Jósef Jankowski, 'Plany regulacyjne', *Dom, Osiedle, Mieszkanie*, no. 6 (1930): 15.

59 Leonard Tomaszewski, 'Urbanistyka w Z.S.R.R.', *Architektura i Budownictwo*, no. 8 (1931): 332.

60 Walter Koeppen, *Die Freiflächen der Stadtgemeinde Berlin-Denkschrift des Amtes für Stadtplanung*, vol. 2 (Berlin: Amt für Stadtplanung der Stadt Berlin, 1929), 10.

61 Miller, 'The elusive green background: Raymond Unwin and the greater London regional plan', 17. See also *The Times*, 1 January 1929; *The Times*, 12 August 1929.

62 GLRPC, *First report of the Greater London regional planning committee* (London: Greater London Regional Planning Committee, 1929), 15–17.

63 In a later publication, Robert Mattocks showed how Abercrombie and he also used the principle of combined park system models in their 1924 plan for Sheffield. See Robert Mattocks, 'The park system', *Town Planning Review* 17, no. 3 (1937): 161–83.

64 GLRPC, *Second report of the Greater London regional planning committee* (London: Greater London Regional Planning Committee, 1933), 32–33.

65 Jose Luis Sert, *Can our cities survive?: An A.B.C. of urban problems, their analysis, their solutions, based on the proposals formulated by the Congrès Internationaux d'Architecture Moderne* (Cambridge: Harvard University Press, 1942), 82. See also Architectural Review, July 1941, 33.

66 Alfred Agache, *A Cidade do Rio de Janeiro: Extensão, Remodelação e Embelezamento* (Paris: Foyer Brésilien editor, 1930).

67 Francisco Prestes Maia, *Estudo de um Plano de Avenidas para a Cidade de São Paulo* (São Paulo: PMSP, 1930).

68 Author's translation. See Agache, *A Cidade do Rio de Janeiro: Extensão, Remodelação e Embelezamento*, 206.

69 Maia, *Estudo de um Plano de Avenidas para a Cidade de São Paulo*, 1.

70 Ibid., 7.

71 Wil Zonneveld, 'A sea of houses: Preserving open space in an urbanised country', *Journal of Environmental Planning and Management* 50, no. 5 (2007): 661.

72 Patrick Abercrombie, *Town and country planning* (London: Oxford University Press, 1933), 147–48.

73 Anatole Kopp, *Town and revolution: Soviet architecture and city planning, 1917–1935* (London: Thames & Hudson, 1970).

74 From 'The Housing Question'. Cited by Nikolai Miliutin, *Sotsgorod: The problem of building socialist cities* (Cambridge: MIT Press, 1974), 60.

75 El Lissitzky, *Russia: An architecture for world revolution* (Cambridge: MIT Press, 1970), 59.

76 Karl Marx and Frederick Engels, *Manifest of the communist party* (Moscow: Progress Publishers, 1848), 17.

77 Friedrich Engels, *Die Lage der arbeitenden Klasse in England [The condition of the working class in England]* (Leipzig: Otto Wigand, 1845), 106.

78 Richard Stites, *Revolutionary dreams: Utopian vision and experimental life in the Russian revolution* (Oxford: Oxford University Press, 1989), 190–1.

79 See introduction by George R. Collins and William Alex, Miliutin, *Sotsgorod: The problem of building socialist cities*, 9.

80 Timothy Colton, *Moscow: Governing the socialist metropolis* (Cambridge: Harvard University Press, 1995), 224.

81 Ibid., 234. See also: Sergei Shestakov, *Bol'shaia Moskva [Large Moscow]* (Moskva: издание м.к.х, 1925).

82 Hénard, *Études sur les transformations de Paris*, 204–5.

83 Miliutin, *Sotsgorod: The problem of building socialist cities*, 11.

84 Colton, *Moscow: Governing the socialist metropolis*, 236.

85 Milka Bliznakov, 'The realization of Utopia: Western technology and Soviet Avant-Garde architecture', in *Reshaping Russian architecture: Western technology, utopian dreams*, ed. William C. Brumfield (Cambridge: Cambridge University Press, 1990), 151–2, 57.

86 Lissitzky, *Russia: An architecture for world revolution*.

87 Koos Bosma, 'New socialist cities: Foreign architects in the USSR 1920–1940', *Planning Perspectives* 29, no. 3 (2014): 307.

88 Ibid., 310.

89 It is worth noting that Soria y Mata's linear city model was adopted by many so-called Disurbanists as an example of a non-centralized way of occupying the territory.

90 See Le Corbusier's letter to Ginzburg in Kopp, *Town and revolution: Soviet architecture and city planning, 1917–1935*, 252.

91 Susan Buck-Morss, *Dreamworld and catastrophe: The passing of mass utopia in East and West* (Cambridge: MIT Press, 2000), 113–4.

92 Colton, *Moscow: Governing the socialist metropolis*, 241–4.

93 Among May's collaborators were Hans Schmidt and Arthur Korn. Bosma, 'New socialist cities: Foreign architects in the USSR 1920–1940', 315.

94 The Neighbourhood Unit concept was developed by Clarence Perry as part of the 1929 Regional Plan of New York and its Environs and would become one of the most recognized 'exports' of American planning theory. The concept proposed restructuring community life within a self-contained neighbourhood of between 5 and 9,000 inhabitants. Strategies to achieve this included the organization of the neighbourhood around a primary school or church, with adequate provision of playground and other green spaces and a hierarchical street network designed to minimize the traffic within the unit. The main thoroughfares would define their edges, along which commercial and district facilities would be located. In the planning for the post-war period in Europe, the concept would be adapted and combined to form districts, eventually leading to the configuration of the city in its totality and green wedges will be used around the units, alongside arterial roads, to reinforce their identities and often to separate them from the noise and pollution of main traffic lines and industrial zones.

95 Bosma, 'New socialist cities: Foreign architects in the USSR 1920–1940', 320.

96 Eric Mumford, *The Ciam discourse on urbanism, 1928–1960* (Cambridge: MIT Press, 2000), 59, 65.

Chapter 3

1 This chapter is derived in part from an article published in Town Planning Review in October 2015, http://online.liverpooluniversitypress.co.uk/doi/abs/10.3828/tpr.2015.30 (9 September 2016).

2 This was supported by Lord Reith, the Minister of Works and Planning between 1940 and 1942, who was responsible for reconstruction policy in order to make the replanning of damaged cities possible. See Ashworth, *The genesis of modern British town planning*, 227; Nick Tiratsoo, 'The reconstruction of blitzed British cities, 1945–55: Myths and reality', *Contemporary British History* 14, no. 1 (2000): 34; Junichi Hasegawa, 'The rise and fall of British reconstruction in 1940s Britain', *Twentieth Century British History* 10, no. 2 (1999): 138; Nicholas Bullock, *Building the post-war world modern architecture and reconstruction in Britain* (London: Routledge, 2002), 5.

3 D. E. Gibson, 'Problems of building reconstruction', *The Builder* (1940): 579.

4 The Builder, 'Town and country planning', *The Builder* no. 162 (1942): 333.

5 LCC, *London County Council. Memorandum on replanning and reconstuction of London, first draft* (London: London Metropolitan Archives, 1940a). The closest solution to the problem found the formulation of a legal framework to support the compulsory purchase of areas needed for reconstruction plans found in the publication of the Uthwatt Report.

6 LCC, London County Council. *Post-war reconstruction of London, notes of a conference held on 7th October 1940* (London: London Metropolitan Archives, 1940b), 1.

7 Stephen Ward, 'Soviet communism and the British planning movement: Rational learning or Utopian imagining?' *Planning Perspectives* 27, no. 4 (2012).

8 LCC, *London County Council. "Exhibition of the County of London Plan," 1943* (London: London Metropolitan Archives, 1943).

9 The group was formed in 1933 by four initial members: W. Coates, Maxwell Fry, P. Morton Shand and David Pleydell-Bouerie. Many other members will be accepted, at various times, such as William Tatton Brown, Arthur Korn, Graham Holford, Thomas Sharp and Ralph Tubbs. John R. Gold, 'The MARS plans for London, 1933–1942', *Town Planning Review* 66, no. 3 (1995): 245, 54.

10 Ibid., 249–53.

11 See '"Commoditie, firmenes and delight": Modernism, the mars group's "new architecture" exhibition (1938) and imagery of the urban future', *Planning Perspectives* 8, no. 4 (1993).

12 Ralph Tubbs, *Living in Cities* (London: Penguin, 1942), 31–32.

13 Ibid., 30.

14 Arthur Korn and Felix Samuely, 'A master plan for London: Based on research carried out by the town planning committee of the M.A.R.S. Group', *Architectural Review*, no. 91 (1942): 145.

15 Henry Vaughan Lanchester, 'An architect's view of reconstruction: The large city', *The Builder* 161 (1941): 569–70.

16 The Times, 'Mr A. Trystan Edwards', *The Times*, 3 February 1973. Lord Greenwood of Rossendale wrote that he and Unwin for some time run the country's public housing programme and that he was greatly influential to the Barlow Committee, the Scott Committee and the Reith Committee.

17 J47485, *A Hundred new towns for Britain: A scheme for national reconstruction* (London: Simpkin Marshall, 1934). See also The Times, 'Obituary: Mr A. Trystan Edwards: A town planning pioneer', *The Times*, 31 January 1973. He claimed that the Hundred New Towns Association was the first to introduce the idea of green wedges in model plans.

18 Arthur Trystan Edwards, 'A plan for "Greater London"', *The Builder* (1943): 129.

19 A note at the end of the article stated that the Hundred New Towns Association would submit the scheme to the London County Council and the Ministry of Town and Country Planning. Ibid.

20 P. J. Larkham, *The London Regional Reconstruction Committee: Architects, exhibitions, and post-war visions for replanning* (Birmingham: Birmingham City University, 2013), 2.

21 LRRC, *Greater London: Towards a master plan: The second interim report of the LRRC of the RIBA* (London: London Regional Reconstruction Committee, 1943), 4.

22 Ibid., 41.

23 Larkham, *The London Regional Reconstruction Committee: Architects, exhibitions, and post-war visions for replanning*, 15.

24 Emmanuel Marmaras and Anthony Sutcliffe, 'Planning for post-war London: The three independent plans, 1942–3', *Planning Perspectives* 9, no. 4 (1994): 444.

25 LCC, 'London County Council. Post-war reconstruction of London, notes of a conference held on 7th October 1940'. For a comprehensive analysis of the County of London Plan 1943 and the Greater London Plan 1944, see Fabiano Lemes de Oliveira, 'Abercrombie's green-wedge vision for London: The county of London Plan 1943 and the Greater London Plan 1944', *Town Planning Review* 86, no. 5 (2015).

26 LCC, 'London County Council. Memorandum on replanning and reconstuction of London, first draft'.

27 *London County Council. Memorandum by the architect, 6th December 1940* (London: London Metropolitan Archives, 1940c).

28 C. Latham, 'The planning problems of London: Lord Latham's survey', *The Builder* 162, no. 421–3 (1942).

29 LCC, *Interview with comptroller and Mr Miles, December 1940* (London: London Metropolitan Archives, 1940d), 2.

30 E. J. Carter and Erno Goldfinger, *The county of London plan explained by E. J. Carter and Erno Goldfinger* (London: Penguin Books, 1945).

31 LCC, *London County Council. Letter, 8th April 1941* (London: London Metropolitan Archives, 1941).

32 R. L. Reiss, 'The London plan and satellite town. Address to town and country planning association', *The Builder* no. 254 (1943).

33 J. Forshaw, 'Town planning and health. Mr Forshaw's Chadwick trust lecture', *The Builder* November–December: 14–15.

34 Cited by Sert, *Can our cities survive? An A.B.C. of urban problems, their analysis, their solutions, based on the proposals formulated by the Congrès Internationaux d'Architecture Moderne*, 82. See 'Park Planning', pt.IV, Town Planning Review, December 1938, 107.

35 LCC, *London County Council. County of London plan – housing density. Housing and Public Health Committee. Joint report by architect, chief assistant, valuer and comptroller of the council* (London: London Metropolitan Archives, 1944), 4.

36 'London County Council. "Exhibition of the County of London Plan", 1943'.

37 Patrick Abercrombie and J. Forshaw, *County of London Plan prepared for the LCC, 1943* (London: Macmillan, 1943), 42.

38 Ibid., 38.

39 Ibid., 39.

40 Ibid., 39–40.

41 Forshaw, 'Town planning and health. Mr Forshaw's Chadwick trust lecture', 15.

42 Abercrombie and Forshaw, *County of London Plan prepared for the LCC, 1943*, 39–40.

43 LCC, *London County Council. County of London Plan. Observations by government departments, Metropolitan Borough councils and other bodies – Open space proposals. Town Planning Committee. Report (12.10.44) by Architect (N.4)* (London: London Metropolitan Archives, 1944); TNA, *County of London Plan 1943: Consultation with the Ministry of Works* (London: The National Archives, 1943–4); *County of London Plan 1943: Consultation with the ministry of works* (London: The National Archives, 1943–6).

44 LCC, *London County Council. County of London Plan. Report (04.06.43) by chief officer of the Parks Department* (London: London Metropolitan Archives, 1943b), 118; Reiss, 'The London Plan and satellite town. Address to Town and Country Planning Association' 254; M. Cracknell, 'County of London Plan … a statement by the executive of the Town & Country Planning Association', *Town and Country Planning* 11 (1943).

45 LCC, *London County Council. County of London Plan. Parks Committee. Report (31.05.43) by Comptroller of the Council* (London: London Metropolitan Archives, 1943c), 2; *London County Council. County of London Plan. Observations by government departments, Metropolitan Borough councils and other bodies – Open space proposals. Town Planning Committee. Report (4.1.45) by comptroller of the council, A. R. Wood* (London: London Metropolitan Archives, 1945).

46 *London County Council. Town Planning Committee. Report by valuer (24.05.43)* (London: London Metropolitan Archives, 1943).

47 *London County Council. County of London Plan. Parks Committee. Report (31.05.43) by comptroller of the council*, 3.

48 *London County Council. County of London Plan. Observations by government departments, Metropolitan Borough councils and other bodies – Open space proposals. Town Planning Committee. Report (12.10.44) by Architect (N.4).*

49 *London County Council. County of London Plan. Town Planning Committee. Draft report of the Town Planning Committee, 11th June 1945. Eric Salmon, clerk of the council* (London: London Metropolitan Archives, 1945).

50 TNA, *Notes on a meeting between Mr Salmon, Professor Abercrombie, Mr Forshaw, Mr Pepler and HYL, 16th September 1941* (London: The National Archives, 1941c).

51 L. Silkin, 'London replanned: Decentralization of industry and population', *The Times*, 13 July 1943, 5.

52 Patrick Abercrombie, *Greater London plan, 1944: A report prepared on behalf of the Standing Conference on London Regional Planning* (London: HMSO, 1945), 97.

53 TNA, *Greater London Plan. Individual matters for comment, etc. Open spaces, 14 January 1944* (London: The National Archives, 1944), 2.

54 Abercrombie, *Greater London plan, 1944: A report prepared on behalf of the Standing Conference on London Regional Planning*, 103.

55 Ibid., 207–8.

56 TNA, *Greater London Plan. Individual matters for comment, etc. Open spaces, 14 January 1944*, 5.

57 J. P. Watson and P. Abercrombie, *A plan for Plymouth* (Plymouth: Plymouth City Council, 1943), 98–99.

58 Ministry of Town and Country Planning, *Greater London Plan, memorandum by the Ministry of Town and Country Planning on the report of the Advisory Committee for London Regional Planning* (London: London Metropolitan Archives, 1947), 13.

59 *Advisory committee for London regional planning. Open spaces sub-committee, 20th March 1946* (London: London Metropolitan Archives, 1946a).

60 *Greater London Plan – Open spaces and recreation areas. Memorandum prepared for interdepartmental committee by the Ministry of Town and Country Planning, 8th April 1946* (London: London Metropolitan Archives, 1946).

61 *Greater London Plan, memorandum by the Ministry of Town and Country Planning on the report of the Advisory Committee for London Regional Planning* 11.

62 Junichi Hasegawa, *Replanning the blitzed city centre: A comparative study of Bristol, Coventry and Southampton 1941–1950* (Buckingham: Open University Press, 1992), 5–6; 'The rise and fall of British reconstruction in 1940s Britain'.

63 M. Tichelar, 'The conflict over property rights during the Second World War: The Labour Party's abandonment of land nationalization', *Twentieth Century British History* 14 (2003): 177.

64 P. J. Larkham and K. D. Lilley, *Planning the 'City of Tomorrow'. British reconstruction planning, 1939–1952: An annotated bibliography* (Pickering: Inch's books, 2001), 1–6.

65 Stephen Essex and Mark Brayshay, 'Boldness diminished? The post-war battle to replan a bomb-damaged provincial city', *Urban History* 35, no. 03 (2008); Hasegawa, *Replanning the blitzed city centre: A comparative study of Bristol, Coventry and Southampton 1941–1950*.

66 R. Nicholas, *City of Manchester Plan, prepared for the City Council* (Norwich and London, 1945), 109.

67 Patsy Healey, *Urban Complexity and Spatial Strategies: Towards a relational planning for our times*, The RTPI Library Series (London: Routledge, 2007), 125.

68 Frederic James Osborn, *New towns after the war* (London: J. M. Dent and Sons Ltd., 1942).

69 Bullock, *Building the post-war world modern architecture and reconstruction in Britain*, 13.

70 New Towns Committee, *Final Report of the New Towns Committee (Command Paper 6876)* (1946), paragraph 60; Andrew Homer, 'Creating new communities: The role of the Neighbourhood unit in post-war British planning', *Contemporary British History* 14, no. 1 (2000): 66.

71 Hall and Tewdwr-Jones, *Urban and regional planning*, 68.

72 Frank Schaffer, 'The new town movement', in *New Towns: The British experience*, ed. H. Evans (London: C. Knight, 1972), 15.

73 Out of which 6 acres per 1,000 of population should be destined to active recreation, according to the National Playing Fields Association.

74 F. T. Burnett, 'Open space in new towns', *Journal of the Town Planning Institute* (1969): 259–60. However, despite the high overall ratios shown, no surveyed town reached the ratio suggested by the National Playing Fields Association of 6 acres of active recreation space to 1,000 people. The values ranged from 3.5 to 5.2 acres per 1,000 people.

75 Frederick Gibberd, 'Landscaping the New Town: Town-planning article with special reference to Harlow', *The Architectural Review* March (1948): 96.

76 *Final Report of the New Towns Committee,* Chapter 'Roads', paragraph 104.

77 New Towns Committee, *Final Report of the New Towns Committee (Command Paper 6876)*, Chapter VII. Landscape Treatment, paragraph 60.

78 Diamond Derek, 'New towns in their regional context', in *New Towns: The British Experience*, ed. H. Evans (London: C. Knight, 1972), 57.

79 A. C. Duff, *Britain's new towns: An experiment in living* (London: Pall Mall Press, 1961), 29.

80 Frederick Gibberd, *Harlow new town: A plan prepared for the Harlow Development Corportation* (London: HMSO, 1947); 'The master design; landscape; housing; the town centres', in *New Towns: The British experience*, ed. H. Evans (London: C. Knight, 1972).

81 'Landscaping the New Town: Town-planning article with special reference to Harlow', 85.

82 Ibid.

83 Gibberd, 'Landscaping the New Town: Town-planning article with special reference to Harlow'.

84 Lionel Brett Esher, *Interview, national life story collection: Architects' lives* (London: British Library, 1997–2007), Interview.

85 Ward, 'Soviet communism and the British planning movement: Rational learning or Utopian imagining?'

86 In India alone 118 new towns were built between 1949 and 1981. See Robert Home, *Of planting an planning: The making of British colonial cities* (London: Routledge, 2013), 208.

87 Ibid., 214–15.

88 A. Aran-glikson, 'The approach to planning in Israel', *Journal of the American Institute of Planners* 17, no. 1 (1951): 42.

89 Thomas Hall, ed., *Planning and urban growth in the Nordic Countries*, Studies in History, Planning and The Environment (London: E & FN Spon, 1991), 252.

90 Elke Sohn, 'Hans Bernhard Reichow and the concept of Stadtlandschaft in German planning', *Planning Perspectives* 18, no. 2 (2003).

91 See Hans Bernhard Reichow, *Organische Stadtbaukunst: von der Groflstadt zur Stadtlandschaft* (Braunschweig: Westermann, 1948); and Elke Sohn, 'Organicist concepts of city landscape in German planning after the second world war', *Landscape Research* 32, no. 4 (2007): 504.

92 'Hans Bernhard Reichow and the concept of Stadtlandschaft in German planning', 127.

93 See Barry A. Jackisch, 'The nature of Berlin: Green space and visions of a New German Capital, 1900–45', *Central European History* 47, no. 02 (2014).

94 Stanislaw Jankowski, 'Warsaw: Destruction, secret town planning, 1939–44, and postwar reconstruction', in *Rebuilding Europe's bombed cities*, ed. Jeffry M. Diefendorf (Basingstoke: Macmillan, 1990), 78.

95 Jeffry M. Diefendorf, *In the wake of war: The reconstruction of German cities after world war II* (Oxford: Oxford University Press, 1993), 192.

96 Gutschow had worked with Schumacher in the 1920s in Hamburg. See 'Konstanty Gutschow and the Reconstruction of Hamburg', in

Symposium: Continuity and change in Germany after 1945 (Madison: Brill Academic, 2001).

97 Takashi Watanabe, Marco Amati, Kenya Endo, and Makoto Yokohari, 'The abandonement of Tokyo's green belt and the search for a new discourse of preservation in Tokyo's suburbs', in *Urban green belts in the twenty-first century*, ed. Marco Amati (London: Ashgate, 2008).

98 Makoto Yokohari et al., 'Beyond greenbelts and zoning: A new planning concept for the environment of Asian mega-cities', *Landscape and Urban Planning* 47, no. 3–4 (2000): 161.

99 See Michael Buxton and Robin Goodman, 'Protecting Melbourne's green wedges – Fate of a public policy', in *Urban green belts in the twenty-first century*, ed. M. Amati (Dorchester: Ashgate, 2008).

100 See Mattocks, 'The park system'.

101 A. J. Brown, H. M. Sherrard and J. H. Shaw, *An introduction to town and country planning* (Melbourne: Angus and Robertson, 1969), 149.

102 Ibid., 150.

103 S. E. Sanders and A. J. Rabuck, *New city patterns: The analysis of and a technique for urban reintegration* (New York: Reinhold Publishing Corporation, 1946), 60–61.

104 Ibid., 196.

105 Malcom J. Proudfoot, 'New city patterns: The analysis of and a technique for urban reintegration', *Geographical Review* 37, no. 2 (1947): 350.

106 Cited in Jeffry M. Diefendorf, 'From Germany to America: Walter Gropius and Martin Wagner on Skyscrapers and the planning of healthy cities', *GHI Bulletin Supplement* 2 (2005): 37.

107 Ibid., 43.

108 Eric Mumford, 'CIAM urbanism after the Athens charter', *Planning Perspectives* 7, no. 4 (1992): 397.

109 Geddes, *Cities in evolution*.

110 Ludwig Hilberseimer, *The nature of cities: Origin, growth, and decline pattern and form planning problems* (Chicago: Paul Theobald, 1955), 193.

111 Ibid.

112 Ibid., 198.

113 Ibid., 201.

114 Ibid., 221.

115 Hans Blumenfeld, 'Theory of city form, past and present', *Journal of the Society of Architectural Historians* 8, no. 3–4 (1949): 16. See also 'Hans Blumenfeld', http://www.transatlanticperspectives.org/entry.php?rec=12 (accessed 18 December 2015).

116 'On the growth of metropolitan areas', *Social Forces* 28, no. 1 (1949): 63.

117 For the situation in Britain, see Hall and Tewdwr-Jones, *Urban and regional planning*, 55–79; for the case of Germany, see Diefendorf, *In the wake of war: The reconstruction of German cities after world war II*.

Chapter 4

1   Hall, *Planning and urban growth in the Nordic countries*, 251.

2   Bo Larsson and Ole Thomassen, 'Urban planning in Denmark', in *Planning and urban growth in the Nordic countries*, ed. Thomas Hall (London: E ... FN Spon, 1991), 21.

3   Henrik Vejre, Jørgen Primdahl, and Jesper Brandt, 'The Copenhagen Finger Plan: Keeping a green space structure by a simple planning metaphor', in *Europe's living landscapes. Essays on exploring our identity in the countryside*, ed. G. B. M. Pedroli, A. M. van Doorn, G. D. Blust, D. M. Wascher and F. Bunce (KNNV Publishing, 2007), 316, http://www.uniscape .eu/pageImg.php?idCont=962 ... idSez=20 ... idlink=100 ... lang=en (accessed 9 September 2016).

4   Egnsplankontoret, *Skitseforslag til egnsplan for Storkøbenhavn* (Copenhagen: Egnsplankontoret, 1948), 19.

5   Steen Eiler Rasmussen and Peter Bredsdorff, *Copenhagen Regional Plan: A summary of the preliminary proposal 1948–49* (Copenhagen: Tutein ... Koch, 1949), 8.

6   Ole Caspersen, Cecil Konijnendijk, and Anton Olafsson, 'Green space planning and land use: An assessment of urban regional and green structure planning in Greater Copenhagen', *Geografisk Tidsskrift-Danish Journal of Geography* 106, no. 2 (2006): 10.

7   This was due to the fact that the implementation of the Finger Plan was from the start easier to implement in the southwest, where land was flat and largely available, than in the northeast, where intense development had already occurred. Hans Thor Andersen and John Jorgensen, 'City profile: Copenhagen', *Cities* 12, no. 1 (1995): 16.

8   Vejre et al., 'The Copenhagen Finger Plan: Keeping a green space structure by a simple planning metaphor', 315.

9   Bredsdorff, *Copenhagen Regional Plan: A summary of the preliminary proposal 1948–49*, 3.

10 Erik Lorange and Jan Eivind Myhre, 'Urban planning in Norway', in *Planning and urban growth in the Nordic countries*, ed. Thomas Hall (London: E ... FN Spon, 1991), 148.

11 Stockholms stad, *Generalplan för Stockholm* (Stockholm, 1952), 151.

12 Ibid., 335.

13 Thomas Hall, 'Urban planning in Sweden', in *Planning and urban growth in the Nordic countries*, ed. Thomas Hall (London: E ... FN Spon, 1991), 221.

14 Helsingin Kaupungin, *Helsingin yleiskaavaehdotus: Laadittu asemakaavaosastolla 1953–1960* (Helsinki: Tilgmann, 1960).

15 See Fabiano Lemes de Oliveira, *Modelos Urbanísticos Modernos e Parques Urbanos: as Relações entre Urbanismo e Paisagismo em São Paulo na Primeira Metade do Século XX* (Polytecnic School of Catalonia, 2008).

16 Henrique Lefevre, 'Planejamento e problemas de São Paulo', *Revista de Engenharia* 11, no. 126 (1953): 142.

17 Carlos Lodi, 'O Plano Diretor de São Paulo', *Revista de Engenharia Municipal*, no. 8 (1957): 19.

18 Jerry B. Schneider, *Transit and the polycentric City* (Washington, DC: University of Washington, 1981), 130.

19 See R. W. Archer, 'New towns to metrotowns and regional cities 1', *The American Journal of Economics and Sociology* 28, no. 3 (1969): 260.

20 Schneider, 'Transit and the polycentric city', 195.

21 Ibid., 168–69.

22 Chicago Daily News, 'An end to urban sprawl: 3 plans for Chicago's future', *Chicago Daily News*, 10 December 1966.

23 MHLG, *The South East Study 1961–1981*, ed. Ministry of Housing and Local Government (London: HMSO, 1964), 7.

24 Ibid., 89.

25 Ibid., 53–56.

26 Ibid., 89–90.

27 Ibid., 91.

28 Ibid.

29 Colin Buchanan and Partners, *South Hampshire study* (London: HMSO, 1966), 95–6.

30 Ibid., 99.

31 Ibid., 113.

32 Peter Hall, *London 2000* (London: Faber and Faber, 1971), 163.

33 South East Economic Planning Council, *A strategy for the South East: A first report by the South East Economic Planning Council*, ed. Department of Economic Affairs (London: HMSO, 1967), 6–7.

34 Ibid., 8–9.

35 Ibid., 44.

36 J. Brian McLoughlin, *Shaping Melbourne's future? Town planning, the state and civil society* (Melbourne: Cambridge University Press, 1992), 45.

37 Melbourne and Metropolitan Board of Works, *Planning policies for the Melbourne metropolitan region* (Melbourne, 1971), 12.

38 Buxton and Goodman, 'Protecting Melbourne's green wedges – Fate of a public policy', 65.

39 James M. Rubenstein, *The French new towns* (Baltimore: The John Hopkins University Press, 1978), 2.

40 D. Burtenshaw, M. Bateman, and G. J. Ashworth, *The city in West Europe* (Chichester: John Wiley & Sons, 1981), 192–93, 255–60.

41 National Museum in Norway, *Forms of freedom – African Independence and Nordic Models. The Nordic Pavilion exhibition at the Biennale Architettura di Venezia* (Venice: La Biennale di Venezia, 2014).

42 Gerald Burke, *Greenheart metropolis: Planning the Western Netherlands* (London: MacMillan, 1966), 2.

43 Lewis Mumford, *The city in history: Its origins, its transformations, and its prospects* (London: Secker ... Warburg, 1961).

44 Burke, *Greenheart metropolis: Planning the Western Netherlands*, 6.

Chapter 5

1 Rodney H. Matsuoka and Rachel Kaplan, 'People needs in the urban landscape: Analysis of landscape and urban planning contributions', *Landscape and Urban Planning* 84, no. 1 (2008): 9.

2 Rachel Kaplan and Stephen Kaplan, *The experience of nature: A psychological perspective* (Cambridge: Cambridge University Press, 1989).

3 Anna Chiesura, 'The role of urban parks for the sustainable city', *Landscape and Urban Planning* 68, no. 1 (2004): 132.

4 Patrik Grahnand Ulrika A. Stigsdotter, 'Landscape planning and stress', *Urban Forestry & Urban Greening* 2, no. 1 (2003): 1–18.

5 Giuseppe Carrus et al., 'Relations between naturalness and perceived restorativeness of different urban green spaces', *Psyecology* 4, no. 3 (2013): 227–44.

6 Liisa Tyrväinen et al., 'The influence of urban green environments on stress relief measures: A field experiment', *Journal of Environmental Psychology* 38 (2014): 1–9; Ole Hjorth Caspersen and Anton Stahl Olafsson, 'Recreational mapping and planning for enlargement of the green structure in greater Copenhagen', *Urban Forestry & Urban Greening* 9, no. 2 (2010): 104.

7 Mind, *Ecotherapy: The green agenda for mental health executive summary* (London: Mind, 2007).

8 See, for instance, Roger S. Ulrich, 'View through a window may influence recovery from surgery', *Science* 224 (1984): 420–21.

9 HSCIC, *Health Survey for England – 2013* (London: HSCIC, 2014).

10 Magdalena van den Berg et al., 'Health benefits of green spaces in the living environment: A systematic review of epidemiological studies', *Urban Forestry & Urban Greening* (2015): 806–816.

11 Anne Ellaway, Sally Macintyre, and Xavier Bonnefoy, 'Graffiti, greenery, and obesity in adults: Secondary analysis of European cross sectional survey', *BMJ* 331, no. 611 (2005), Online only: http://dx.doi.org/10.1136/bmj.38575.664549.F7.

12 See, for instance, Health Scotland, *Health impact assessment of greenspace: A guide* (Stirling: Greenspace Scotland, 2009), 23.

13 T. S. Nielsen and K. B. Hansen, 'Do green areas affect health? Results from a Danish survey on the use of green areas and health indicators', *Health Place* 13, no. 4 (2007): 842–43; Matsuoka and Kaplan, 'People needs in the urban landscape: Analysis of landscape and urban planning contributions'.

14 Grahn and Stigsdotter, 'Landscape planning and stress', 11.

15 Paul H. Gobster, 'Perception and use of a metropolitan greenway system for recreation', *Landscape and Urban Planning* 33 (1995): 401–13.

16 WHO, *Mental health and older adults facsheet n.381* ed. WHO (2013).

17 Foresight Mental Capital and Wellbeing Project, *Mental capital and wellbeing: Making the most of ourselves in the 21st century – State-of-science review: SR-DR2.The effect of the physical environment on mental wellbeing* (London, 2008), 219.

18 Sjerp de Vries et al., 'Natural environments – Healthy environments? An exploratory analysis of the relationship between greenspace and health', *Environment and Planning A* 35(2003): 1717–31; Richard Mitchell and Frank Popham, 'Effect of exposure to natural environment on health inequalities: An observational population study', 372, no. 9650 (2008): 1655–60.

19 CABE, *Summary – Future health: Sustainable places for health and well-being* (London: CABE, 2009), 4.

20 Mathew P. White, Ian Alcock, Benedict W. Wheeler and Michael H. Depledge, 'Would you be happier living in a greener urban area? A fixed-effects analysis of panel data', *Psychological Science* 24, no. 6 (2013): 920–28.

21 WHO, *Burden of disease from Ambient Air Pollution for 2012* (Geneva: World Health Organization, 2014).

22 European Commission, 'Cleaner air for all: Why is it important and what should we do?', ed. Environment (2013), http://ec.europa.eu/environment/pubs/pdf/factsheets/air/en.pdf.

23 B. A. Maher, I. A. Ahmed, B. Davison, V. Karloukovski and R. Clarke, 'Impact of roadside tree lines on indoor concentrations of traffic-derived particulate matter', *Environmental Science & Technology* 47, no. 23 (2013): 13737–44.

24 D. J. Nowak, D. E. Crane and J. C. Stevens, 'Air pollution removal by urban trees and shrubs in the United States', *Urban Forestry & Urban Greening* 4, no. 3 (2006): 115–23; M. Tallis, G. Taylor, D. Sinnett and P. Freer-Smith, 'Estimating the removal of atmospheric particulate pollution by the urban tree canopy of London, under current and future environments', *Landscape and Urban Planning* 103, no. 2 (2011): 129–38.

25 M. J. Tallis, J. H. Amorim, C. Calfapietra, P. Freer-Smith, S. Grimmond, S. Kotthaus, F. L. de Oliveira, A. I. Miranda and P. Toscano, 'The impacts of green infrastructure on air quality and temperature', in *Handbook on green infrastructure planning, design and implementation*, ed. Danielle Sinnett, Nicholas Smith and Sarah Burgess (Cheltenham: Edward Elgar Publishing, 2015).

26 I. McHarg, *Design with nature* (New York: Natural History Press, 1969), 56.

27 Ibid., 57.

28 Lewis Mumford, 'Landscape and townscape (1960–61)', in *The urban prospect*, ed. Lewis Mumford (London: Secker & Warburg, 1968), 91.

29 Christopher Alexander, Sara Ishikawa and Murray Silverstein, *A pattern language: Towns, buildings, construction*, Center for Environmental Structure series (New York: Oxford University Press, 1977), 23.

30 Ibid., 25.

31 Kevin Lynch, *A theory of good city form* (Cambridge, MA; London: MIT Press,1981), appendix D.

32 Cliff Moughtin, *Urban design: Green dimensions* (Oxford: Butterworth Architecture, 1996).

33 Ulf G. Sandström, Per Angelstam and Abdul Khakee, 'Urban comprehensive planning – Identifying barriers for the maintenance of functional habitat networks', *Landscape and Urban Planning* 75, no. 1–2 (2006): 43–57.

34 European Union, *Building a green infrastructure for Europe* (Luxembourg: European Commission, 2013), 7.

35 See, for instance, UK National Ecosystem assessment, 'Ecosystem services', http://uknea.unep-wcmc.org/EcosystemAssessmentConcepts/ EcosystemServices/tabid/103/Default.aspx (accessed 21 January 2016).

36 Henrik Ernstson et al., 'Scale-crossing brokers and network governance of urban ecosystem services: The case of Stockholm', *Ecology & Society* 15, no. 4 (2010): 1–25.

37 See, for instance, CABE *Green space strategies: A good practice guide* (London: CABE, 2004); Mark A. Benedict and Edward McMahon, *Green infrastructure: Linking landscapes and communities* (Washington, DC: Island Press, 2006); Natural England, *Green infrastructure guidance* (Natural England, 2009).

38 European Commission, *The EU biodiversity strategy to 2020* (Luxembourg: Publications Office of the European Union, 2011).

39 See, for instance, CCRA, *UK climate risk assessment: Government report* (London, 2012); UN-HABITAT, *Climate change strategy 2014–2019* (Nairobi, 2015); IPCC, *Climate change 2014: Synthesis report* (Geneva 2015).

40 KfC, *Climate proof cities 2010–2014: Final report* (2014).

41 For example, in the UK, it is worth noting the cases of Liverpool, the New Forest District, Doncaster, Chelmsford, Harrogate, Leicester, Harrow, Peterborough, York and many others. See: The Mersey Forest, '*Liverpool green infrastructure strategy: Action plan* (Liverpool, 2010); Harlow City Council, *Harlow local development plan: Green wedge review* (Harlow: Harlow City Council, 2014); Leicestershire County Council et al., 'Green spaces in Leicester and Leicestershire'.

42 Richard T. T. Forman and Michel Godron, *Landscape ecology* (New York: Wiley, 1986), 83–189.

43 Ibid., 144–45.

44 Ibid., 177.

45 Charles Waldheim, *The landscape urbanism reader* (New York: Princeton Architectural Press, 2006), 11.

46 WWF, *Living planet report 2010: Biodiversity, biocapacity and development* (Gland: WWF, 2010).

47 Brundtland Report, '*Our common future* (UN World Commission on Environment and Development, 1987).

48 Marcial H. Echenique et al., 'Growing cities sustainably: Does urban form really matter?', *Journal of the American Planning Association* 78, no. 2 (2012): 123–24.

49 Richard Rogers, *Towards an urban renaissance: Final report of the Urban Task Force* (London: Department for the Environment, Transport and the Regions, 1999); M. Jenks and Rod Burgess, *Compact cities: Sustainable urban forms for developing countries* (London: E. & F. N. Spon, 2000).

50 Echenique et al., 'Growing cities sustainably: Does urban form really matter?', 123–24.

51 For instance, M. Jenks and Nicola Dempsey, *Future forms and design for sustainable cities* (Oxford: Architectural Press, 2005); Susan Roaf, David Crichton and F. Nicol, *Adapting buildings and cities for climate change: A 21st century survival guide* (Oxford: Elselvier Architectural, 2009); Timothy Beatley, *Green urbanism learning from European cities* (Washington, DC: Island Press, 2000).

52 Fabiano Lemes de Oliveira, 'Ecocities: The role of networks of green and blue spaces', in *Cities for smart environmental and energy futures*, ed. Stamatina Rassia and Panos Pardalos (Berlin: Springer, 2013); Elizabeth Rapoport, 'Utopian visions and real estate dreams: The eco-city past, present and future', *Geography Compass* 8, no. 2 (2014): 137–49; Bogachan Bayulken and Donald Huisingh, 'Are lessons from eco-towns helping planners make more effective progress in transforming cities into sustainable urban systems: A literature review (part 2 of 2)', *Journal of Cleaner Production* (2015): 1–14.

53 Petter Naes, 'Urban planning and sustainable development', *European Planning Studies* 9, no. 4 (2009): 506.

54 Yosef Jabareen, 'Planning the resilient city: Concepts and strategies for coping with climate change and environmental risk', *Cities* 31, no. April (2013): 220–29; Christine Wamsler, Ebba Brink and Claudia Rivera, 'Planning for climate change in urban areas: From theory to practice', *Journal of Cleaner Production* 50, no. July (2013): 68–81.

55 Carl Folke, 'Resilience: The emergence of a perspective for social-ecological systems analyses', *Global Environmental Change* 16 (2006): 253–67.

56 B. H. Walker et al., 'Resilience, adaptability and transformability in social–ecological systems', *Ecology & Society* 9, no. 2 (2004): 5; B. Smit and J. Wandel, 'Adaptation, adaptive capacity and vulnerability', *Global Environmental Change* 16, no. 3 (2006): 282–92.

57 Carl Folke et al., 'Resilience and sustainable development: Building adaptive capacity in a world of transformations', *Ambio* 31, no. 5 (2002): 437–44.

58 Aleksandra Kazmierczak and Jeremy Carter, *Adaptation to climate change using green and blue infrastructure: A database of case studies* (Manchester: University of Machester, 2010).

59 H. Erixon, S. Borgström and E. Andersson, 'Challenging dichotomies – Exploring resilience as an integrative and operative conceptual framework for large-scale urban green structures', *Planning Theory & Practice* 14, no. 3 (2013): 367.

60 Ibid., 352; Folke, 'Resilience: The emergence of a perspective for social-ecological systems analyses'.

61 Janne Bengtsson et al., 'Reserves, resilience and dynamic landscapes', *Ambio* 32, no. 6 (2003): 389–96.

Chapter 6

1 COMMIN, 'Planning system of Sweden', in *BSR interreg III B project: Promoting spatial development by creating COMmon MINdscapes* (2007), 4–5.

2 Stockholm County Council, *Regional development plan for the Stockholm region – RUFS 2010* (Stockholm: Stockholm County Council, 2010), 11.

3 The Office of Regional Planning, 'Dense and green: The Stockholm region's ten wedges – As they will be preserved, improved and made more accessible', in *Stockholmsregionen* (Stockholm: The Office of Regional Planning, 2010), 3.

4 Bette Malmros, Interview by author. Personal Interview. 12 September 2014.

5 Stockholm County Council, *Regional development plan for the Stockholm region – RUFS 2010*, 157.

6 Ibid., 147.

7 Malmros, Interview by author. 12 September 2014.

8 Ulrika Egerö, Interview by author. Personal Interview. 15 September 2014.

9 Malmros, Interview by author. 12 September 2014.

10 Egerö, Interview by author. 15 September 2014.

11 E. Andersson et al., 'Reconnecting cities to the biosphere: Stewardship of green infrastructure and urban ecosystem services', *Ambio* 43, no. 4 (2014): 450.

12 The Office of Regional Planning and Urban Transportation, *Social values in urban green areas – The green wedges of the Stockholm region* (Stockholm: The Office of Regional Planning and Urban Transportation, 2005).

13 Stockholms läns landsting, *När, vad och hur? Svaga samband i Stockholmsregionens gröna kilar* (Stockholm: Stockholms läns landsting, 2012).

14 It contains approximately 35,000 people living and working in the area. A key goal was to halve the total environmental impact in comparison with a standard development built in the early 1990s. See GlashusEtt, *Hammarby Sjöstad: A unique environmental project in Stockholm* (Stockholm, 2007), 8.

15 Ibid., 15.

16 Stockholm city counts with over fourteen islands and is surrounded by Lake Mälaren and its basin. RTK, *Upplevelsevärden i ABC-stråket – en studie av gröna och blå värdens attraktivitet* (Stockholm: Regionplane- och trafikkontoret, 2007).

17 Stockholm County Council, *Regional development plan for the Stockholm region – RUFS 2010*, 217.

18 The City Planning Administration, *The walkable city – Stockholm city plan* (Stockholm: The City Planning Administration, 2010).

19 Ibid., 40.

20 See Erixon, Borgström and Andersson, 'Challenging dichotomies – Exploring resilience as an integrative and operative conceptual framework for large-scale urban green structures'.

21 Jan Gehl, *Cities for people* (Washington, DC: Island Press, 2010).

22 Egerö, Interview by author. 15 September 2014.

23 City of Stockholm, *Vision Järva 2030: Visions and proposals for the Järva area* (Stockholm: City of Stockholm).

24 Erixon, Borgström and Andersson, 'Challenging dichotomies – Exploring resilience as an integrative and operative conceptual framework for large-scale urban green structures', 355.

25 Luyao Kong, 'Break the green belt? The differences between green belt and its alternative green wedge: A comparative study of London and Stockholm' (2012), 42.

26 The City Planning Administration, *The walkable city – Stockholm city plan*, 64–5.

27 Miljøministeriet, *Forslag til Fingerplan 2007 – Landsplandirektiv for hovedstadsområdets planlægning* (Copenhagen: Miljøministeriet, 2007), 5.

28 The jury of the European Green Capital singled out Copenhagen as a model in terms of urban planning and design, awarding it first prize in 2014. See European Commission, 'European Green Capital: 2014 – Copenhagen, Green cities fit for life', http://ec.europa.eu/environment/europeangreencapital/winning-cities/2014-copenhagen/ (accessed 19 August 2015).

29 The Regional Plan 1989 was published just before the dismantlement of the Greater Copenhagen Council, which had been responsible for planning matters since 1974.

30 Miljøministeriet, *Forslag til Fingerplan 2007 – Landsplandirektiv for hovedstadsområdets planlægning*, 10.

31 Danish Ministry of the Environment, *Spatial planning in Denmark* (Copenhagen: Danish Ministry of the Environment, 2007).

32 *The Planning Act in Denmark* (Copenhagen: Ministry of the Environment, 2007), 9.

33 Matsuoka and Kaplan, 'People needs in the urban landscape: Analysis of landscape and urban planning contributions'; Nielsen and Hansen, 'Do green areas affect health? Results from a Danish survey on the use of green areas and health indicators'; Kaplan, *The experience of nature: A psychological perspective*.

34 Caspersen, Konijnendijk and Olafsson, 'Green space planning and land use: An assessment of urban regional and green structure planning in Greater Copenhagen', 18.

35 The City of Copenhagen, *CPH 2025 climate plan: A green, smart and carbon neutral city* (Copenhagen, 2012), 29.

36 Mijominsteriet Naturstyrelsen, *Fingerplan 2013 – Hovedbudskaber* (Copenhagen, 2013), 3.

37 Caspersen and Olafsson, 'Recreational mapping and planning for enlargement of the green structure in greater Copenhagen', 109–10.

38 Ibid., 104–6.

39 Københavns Kommune, *københavns Grønne Cykelruter* (Copenhagen: Københavns Kommune, 2015).

40 O. Fryd et al., 'Water sensitive urban design retrofits in Copenhagen – 40% to the sewer, 60% to the city', *Water Science & Technology* 67, no. 9 (2013): 1950.

41 Tobias Grindsted and Sara Berg, Interview by author. Personal Interview. Copenhagen, 15 September 2014. Vallensbæk Kommune, *Tillæg nr 1. Kommuneplan 2013–2025* (Vallensbæk: Vallensbæk Komunne, 2014), 18.

42 The Ringby Light Rail Partnership, *Ring 3 Light Rail* (Copenhagen, 2013).

43 Brøndby Kommune, *Bevægelse i alle planer* (Brøndby: Brøndby Kommune, 2012); 'Byrum og grønne områder – vi indretter byen til det gode liv', Brøndby Kommune, http://brondby.viewer.dkplan.niras.dk/DKplan/dkplan .aspx?pageId=523 (accessed 8 February 2016).

44 Matti O. Hannikainen, *Classification of green spaces in Helsinki and Vantaa* (Helsinki: University of Helsinki, 2013), 4.

45 City of Helsinki, *Helsinki city planning 2012:3 – Detailed planning in Helsinki* (Helsinki: Helsinki City Planning Department, 2012).

46 Helsinki City Planning Department, *Green areas system in Helsinki* (Helsinki: Environmental Office), 7–10.

47 City of Helsinki, *Helsinki city plan: Vision 2050 – Urban plan – The new Helsinki city plan* (Helsinki: Helsinki City Planning Department, 2013), 52.

48 Liisa Tyrväinen, Kirsi Mäkinen and Jasper Schipperijn, 'Tools for mapping social values of urban woodlands and other green areas', *Landscape and Urban Planning* 79, no. 1 (2007): 9.

49 Rikhard Manninen, Interview by author. Personal Interview. Helsinki, 22 August 2014.

50 By the time of the completion of the writing of this book, this proposal was under consideration by the City of Helsinki City Planning Committee and undergoing public consultation.

51 City of Helsinki, 'Proposal for the Helsinki city plan submitted to decision-making process', http://www.yleiskaava.fi/en/2015/proposal-for-the-helsinki-city-plan-submitted-to-decision-making-process/ (accessed 19 January 2015); *Urban Plan – Helsinki city plan draft – Helsinki plans 2015:1* (Helsinki: Helsinki City Planning Department, 2015).

52 Frans M. Dieleman, Martin J. Dijst and Tejo Spit, 'Planning the compact city: The randstad Holland experience', *European Planning Studies* 7, no. 5 (1999): 609.

53 For instance, Zonneveld, 'A sea of houses: Preserving open space in an urbanised country', 672; Manfred Kühn, 'Greenbelt and green heart: Separating and integrating landscapes in European city regions', *Landscape and Urban Planning* 64, no. 1–2 (2003): 25.

54 OECD, 'Randstad Holland, Netherlands', in *Territorial Reviews* (Paris: OECD, 2007), 18.

55 Planning and Environment Dutch Ministry of Housing, *Randstad 2040: Summary of the structural vision* (Ministry of Housing, Planning and Environment, 2008), 20.

56 Arjen J. van der Burg and Bart L. Vink, 'Randstad Holland towards 2040 – Perspectives from national government', in *44th ISOCARP Congress* (Dalian, 2008), 9.

57 Alexandra Tisma et al., 'Metropolitan landscape characterization: A typo-morphological approach', in *The production of place 2012* (London: University of East London, 2012); Thomas Sieverts, *Cities without cities: An interpretation of the Zwischenstadt: Between place and world, space and time, town and country* (London: Routledge, 2003).

58 H+N+S Landschapsarchitecten, *Gebiedsvisie Deltapoort 2025* (Amersfoort: Deltapoort, 2012).

59 Government of South Australia, *The 30-year plan for greater Adelaide* (Adelaide: Department of Planning and Local Government, 2010), 26; NSW Government, *A plan for growing Sydney* (Sydney: NSW Government, 2014), 11; Act Planning and Land Authority, *The Canberra spatial plan* (Canberra: Act Planning and Land Authority, 2004), 12.

60 Chhetri Prem et al., 'Mapping urban residential density patterns: Compact city model in Melbourne, Australia', *City, Culture and Society* 4 (2013): 77.

61 State of Victoria, *Melbourne 2030: A planning update – Melbourne @ 5 million* (Melbourne: Department of Planning and Community Development, 2008).

62 *Melbourne 2030: Planning for sustainable growth* (Melbourne: Department of Infrastructure, 2002), ii.

63 Ibid., 66.

64 Ibid., 9.

65 Planisphere, *Kingston green wedge plan* (Kingston: City of Kingston, 2012).

66 Cardinia and City of Casey, *Westernport green wedge management plan – Draft* (Cardinia and City of Casey, 2014), 15.

67 Yarra Ranges Council, *Yarra Ranges green wedge management plan* (Yarra Ranges, 2010), 32.

68 Brimbank City Council, *Brimbank green wedge management plan* (Brimbank: Brimbank City Council, 2010), 16.

69 Yarra Ranges Council, *Yarra Ranges green wedge management plan*, 33.

70 Ibid., 23.

71 State of Victoria, *Know your plan Melbourne* (Melbourne, 2014), 2.

72 Ibid., 18.

73 The State of Victoria, Department of Transport, Planning and Local Infrastructure, *Plan Melbourne* (Melbourne: Impact Digital, 2014), 161.

74 Ibid., 139.

75 Jan Scheurer and Peter Newman, 'Vauban: A European model bridging the green and brown agendas', in *Case study prepared for Revisiting Urban Planning: Global Report on Human Settlements* (UN-Habitat, 2009), 3.

76 Stadt Freiburg I. Br., *Freiburg i. Br. Landschaftsplan 2020* (Freiburg: Stadt Freiburg I. Br., 2006), 80.

77 365° freiraum + umwelt, *Freiraumkonzept 2020+* (Freiburg: Stadt Freiburg im Breisgau, 2005), 11.

78 Badische Zeitung, *10 Prognosen: So entwickelt sich der Freiburger Wohnungsmarkt* (Freiburg: Badische Zeitung, 2015).

79 City of Freiburg im Breisgau, *Green City Freiburg: Approaches to sustainability* (Freiburg: FWTM, 2014).

80 Ibid., 15.

81 Stadt Freiburg I. Br., *Freiburg i. Br. Landschaftsplan 2020*, 80.

82 Ibid., 359.

83 City of Freiburg im Breisgau, *Environmental policy in Freiburg* (Freiburg: City of Freiburg im Breisgau, 2011), 8.

84 Helmut Mayer, 'KLIMES – A joint research project on human thermal comfort in cities', in *Berichte des Meteorologischen Instituts der Albert-Ludwigs Universität Freiburg N.17*, ed. Helmut Mayer (Freiburg: Universität Freiburg, 2008).

85 Christopher O'Malley et al., 'Urban Heat Island (UHI) mitigating strategies: A case-based comparative analysis', *Sustainable Cities and Society* (2015).

86 Gunter Baumbach and Ulrich Vogt, 'Experimental determination of the effect of mountain-valley breeze circulation on air pollution in the vicinity of Freiburg', *Atmospheric Environment* 33 (1999): 4020–1.

87 N. Kalthoff et al., 'Influence of valley winds on transport and dispersion of airborne pollutants in the Freiburg-Schauinsland area', *Journal of Geophysical Research* 105, no. D1 (2000): 1585.

Chapter 7

1 European Commission, *Hamburg winner 2011 – European Green Capital* (Luxembourg: Publications Office of the European Commission, 2011).

2 Britta Kellermann, 'Die Entwicklung des Freiraumverbundsystems für Hamburg: Von Schumachers Achsenkonzept zum Grünen Netz Hamburg' (2003).

3 Behörde für Stadtentwicklung und Umwelt – Hamburg, *GrünesNetzHamburg – The Landscape Programme Hamburg* (Hamburg: Behörde für Stadtentwicklung und Umwelt – Hamburg).

4 Giovanni Sala, Interview by author. Personal Interview. Milan, 13 February 2015.

5 Andreas Kipar and Valeria Pagliaro, 'Green rays in Milan', *Topos: European Landscape Magazine* no. 77 (2011): 53.

6 AIM and Milano Urban Center, 'I Raggi Verdi', http://www.raggiverdi.it/raggi _verdi.htm (accessed 5 September 2015).

7 Lucy Bullivant, *Masterplanning futures* (London and New York: Routledge, 2012), 193.

8 Andreas Kipar, 'Milano: New landscape territories in urban design', Paper presented at the Urban Groth ithout Sprawl: A way towards sustainable urbanization (Porto, 2009), 104.

9 Comune di Milano, *PGT – Piano del Servizi: Relazione Generale e Catalogo della Ricognizione dell'Offerta dei Servizi* (Milan: Comune di Milano, 2012), 82.

10 *PGT – Piano di Governo del Territorio* (Milan: Comune di Milano, 2014).

11 Sasaki, 'Songzhuang Arts and Agriculture City', http://www.sasaki. com/project/265/songzhuang-arts-and-agriculture-city/ (accessed 12 September 2016).

12 Dennis Pieprz and Michael Grove, 'Songzhuang creative clusters', *Topos*, no. 84 (2013).

13 City of Helsinki, *Viikki: Science park and Latorkantano guide* (Helsinki: Helsinki City Planning Department, 2010), 25.

14 *Eco-Viikki: Aims, implementation and results* (Vantaa: Ministry of the Environment, 2005), 10.

15 Ibid., 15.

16 Ibid., 29.

17 Ibid., 33.

18 Stadt Freiburg I. Br., *The new district of Freiburg-Rieselfeld: A case study of successful, sustainable urban development* (Freiburg: Riesefeld Project Group, 2009).

19 'Ein neuer Stadtteil gegen die Wohnungsnot', Stadt Freiburg I. Br., http://www.freiburg.de/pb/,Lde/495838.html (accessed 12 August 2015).

20 City of Freiburg im Breisgau, *Green City Freiburg: Approaches to sustainability*, 11.

21 Stadt Freiburg I. Br., *Freiburg im Breisgau: Quartier Vauban Historie – History* (Freiburg: Stadt Freiburg I. Br., 2008).

22 Horst Franz, 'Natur in der Stadt', in *Nachhaltige Stadtentwicklung beginnt im Quartier*, ed. Carsten Sperling (Freiburg: Forum Vauban, 1999), 198.

23 Pollard Thomas Edwards, 'Dunsfold Park', http://pollardthomasedwards.co.uk/ project/dunsfold-park/ (accessed 22 December 2015); The Rutland Group, 'Dunsfold Park: A new Surrey Village', http://www.dunsfoldparkmasterplan .com/masterplan/landscape-open-space (accessed 22 December 2015).

24 European Commission, *The EU biodiversity strategy to 2020*.

25 Ajuntament de Barcelona, *Plan del Verde y de la Biodiversidad de Barcelona 2020* (Barcelona: Ajuntament de Barcelona, 2013), 65.

26 See West 8, 'Sagrera linear park', http://www.west8.nl/projects/selected _projects/sagrera_linear_park/pdf/ (accessed 20 December 2015); Barcelona Sagrera alta velocitat, *Barcelona Sagrera alta velocitat* (Barcelona, 2015).

Green Wedge Urbanism: Past, Present and Future

1   Vejre et al., *The Copenhagen Finger Plan: Keeping a green space structure by a simple planning metaphor*, 325.

2   Yvonne Rydin et al., *Five radical ideas for a better planning system* (London: UCL, 2015).

3   Erixon, Borgström and Andersson, *Challenging dichotomies – Exploring resilience as an integrative and operative conceptual framework for large-scale urban green structures.*

4   See, for instance, European Commission, *Towards an EU Research and innovation policy agenda for Nature-Based Solutions & Re-Naturing Cities – Final report of the Horizon 2020 expert group on 'Nature-Based Solutions and Re-Naturing Cities'* (Luxembourg, 2015); Timothy Beatley, *Biophilic cities: Integrating nature into urban design and planning* (Washington, DC: Island Press, 2011); Andersson et al., *Reconnecting cities to the biosphere: Stewardship of green infrastructure and urban ecosystem services*; and TCPA and The Wildlife Trusts, *Planning for a healthy environment – Good practice guidance for green infrastructure and biodiversity* (Oldham, 2012).

Bibliography

365° freiraum + umwelt. 'Freiraumkonzept 2020+'. Freiburg: Stadt Freiburg im Breisgau, 2005.

Abercrombie, Patrick. 'Town planning schemes in America: Chicago'. *Town Planning Review*, no. 1 (April 1910): 54–65.

Abercrombie, Patrick. 'Washington and the proposals for its improvement'. *Town Planning Review* 1, no. 2 (1910): 137–47.

Abercrombie, Patrick. 'Town planning in Greater London: The need for co-operation'. *Town Planning Review* 2, no. 4 (1912): 261–80.

Abercrombie, Patrick. *Town and country planning*. London: Oxford University Press, 1933.

Abercrombie, Patrick. *Greater London plan, 1944: A report prepared on behalf of the Standing Conference on London Regional Planning*. London: HMSO, 1945.

Abercrombie, Patrick, and J. Forshaw. *County of London plan prepared for the LCC, 1943*. London: Macmillan, 1943.

Act Planning and Land Authority. *The Canberra spatial plan*. Canberra: Act Planning and Land Authority, 2004.

Adams, Thomas. *The building of the city*. New York: Regional plan of New York and its environs, 1931.

Agache, Alfred. *A Cidade do Rio de Janeiro: Extensão, Remodelação e Embelezamento*. Paris: Foyer Brésilien editor, 1930.

AIM, and Milano Urban Center. 'I Raggi Verdi'. http://www.raggiverdi.it/raggi _verdi.htm (accessed 5 September 2015).

Ajuntament de Barcelona. *Plan del Verde y de la Biodiversidad de Barcelona 2020*. Barcelona: Ajuntament de Barcelona, 2013.

Alexander, Christopher, Sara Ishikawa, and Murray Silverstein. *A pattern language: Towns, buildings, construction*. Center for Environmental Structure series. New York: Oxford University Press, 1977.

Andersen, Hans Thor, and John Jorgensen. 'City profile: Copenhagen'. *Cities* 12, no. 1 (1995): 13–22.

Andersson, E., S. Barthel, S. Borgstrom, J. Colding, T. Elmqvist, C. Folke, and A. Gren. 'Reconnecting cities to the biosphere: Stewardship of green infrastructure and urban ecosystem services'. *Ambio* 43, no. 4 (May 2014): 445–53.

Aran-glikson, A. 'The approach to planning in Israel'. *Journal of the American Institute of Planners* 17, no. 1 (1951): 38–42.

Archer, R. W. 'New towns to metro towns and regional cities 1'. *The American Journal of Economics and Sociology* 28, no. 3 (1969): 257–69.

Ashworth, William. *The genesis of modern British town planning*. London: Routledge & Kegan Paul, 1954.

Badische, Zeitung. '10 Prognosen: So entwickelt sich der Freiburger Wohnungsmarkt'. *Badische Zeitung*, 2015.

Baker, F. S. 'Discussion – Cities of the present'. In *Town planning conference, London, 10–15 October 1910. Transactions*, edited by RIBA, 242. London: RIBA, 1911.

Barcelona Sagrera alta velocitat. *Barcelona Sagrera alta velocitat.* Barcelona, 2015.

Barker, Kate. *Barker review of land use planning: Final report – Recommendations.* Norwich: HMSO, 2006.

Baumbach, Gunter, and Ulrich Vogt. 'Experimental determination of the effect of mountain-valley breeze circulation on air pollution in the vicinity of Freiburg'. *Atmospheric Environment* 33 (1999): 4019–27.

Bayulken, Bogachan, and Donald Huisingh. 'Are lessons from eco-towns helping planners make more effective progress in transforming cities into sustainable urban systems: A literature review (part 2 of 2)'. *Journal of Cleaner Production* (2015): 1–14.

Beatley, Timothy. *Biophilic cities: Integrating nature into urban design and planning.* Washington, DC: Island Press, 2011.

Beatley, Timothy. *Green urbanism learning from European cities.* Washington, DC: Island Press, 2000.

Behörde für Stadtentwicklung und Umwelt – Hamburg. *GrünesNetzHamburg – The Landscape Programme Hamburg.* Hamburg: Behörde für Stadtentwicklung und Umwelt – Hamburg.

Benedict, Mark A., and Edward McMahon. *Green infrastructure: Linking landscapes and communities.* Washington, DC: Island Press, 2006.

Benevolo, Leonardo. *The origins of modern town planning.* London: Routledge and Kegan Paul, 1967.

Bengtsson, Janne, Per Angelstam, Thomas Elmqvist, Urban Emanuelsson, Carl Folke, Margareta Ihse, Fredrik Moberg, and Magnus Nystrom. 'Reserves, resilience and dynamic landscapes'. *Ambio* 32, no. 6 (2003): 389–96.

Berg, Magdalena van den, Wanda Wendel-Vos, Mireille van Poppel, Han Kemper, Willem van Mechelen, and Jolanda Maa. 'Health benefits of green spaces in the living environment: A systematic review of epidemiological studies'. *Urban Forestry & Urban Greening* (2015): 806–16.

Bliznakov, Milka. 'The realization of Utopia: Western technology and soviet avant-garde architecture'. In *Reshaping Russian architecture: Western technology, utopian dreams*, edited by William C. Brumfield, 145–75. Cambridge: Cambridge University Press, 1990.

Bloch, Marc. 'Comparaison'. *Bulletin du Centre International de Synthèse*, no. 9 (June 1930).

Blumenfeld, Hans. 'On the growth of metropolitan areas'. *Social Forces* 28, no. 1 (October 1949): 59–64.

Blumenfeld, Hans. 'Theory of city form, past and present'. *Journal of the Society of Architectural Historians* 8, no. 3–4 (1949): 7–16.

Blumenfeld, Hans. 'Hans blumenfeld'. http://www.transatlanticperspectives.org/entry.php?rec=12 (accessed 18 December 2015).

Bosma, Koos. 'New socialist cities: Foreign architects in the USSR 1920–1940'. *Planning Perspectives* 29, no. 3 (2014): 301–28.

Bredsdorff, Peter, and Steen Eiler Rasmussen. *Copenhagen regional plan: A summary of the preliminary proposal 1948–49.* Copenhagen: Tutein & Koch, 1949.

Brimbank City Council. *Brimbank Green Wedge Management Plan.* Brimbank: Brimbank City Council, 2010.

Brodie, John. 'Discussion'. In *Town planning conference, London, 10– 15 October 1910. Transactions*, edited by RIBA, 238. London: RIBA, 1911.

Brøndby Kommune. *Bevægelse i alle planer.* Brøndby: Brøndby Kommune, 2012.

Brøndby Kommune. 'Byrum og grønne områder – vi indretter byen til det gode liv'. Brøndby Kommune. http://brondby.viewer.dkplan.niras.dk/DKplan/dkplan .aspx?pageId=523 (accessed 8 February 2016).

Brown, A. J., H. M. Sherrard, and J. H. Shaw. *An introduction to town and country planning.* Melbourne: Angus and Robertson, 1969.

Brüggemeier, Franz-Josef. 'Normal pollution: Industrialization, emissions and the concept of zoning in Germany, 1800–1970'. In *Towards an urban nation: Germany since 1780*, 107–26. Oxford: Berg, 2002.

Brundtland Report. 'Our common future'. UN World Commission on Environment and Development, 1987.

Buck-Morss, Susan. *Dreamworld and catastrophe: The passing of mass utopia in East and West.* Cambridge: MIT Press, 2000.

Bullivant, Lucy. *Masterplanning futures.* London; New York: Routledge, 2012.

Bullock, Nicholas. *Building the Post-War World: Modern architecture and reconstruction in Britain.* London: Routledge, 2002.

Burke, Gerald. *Greenheart metropolis: Planning the Western Netherlands.* London: MacMillan, 1966.

Burnett, F. T. 'Open space in new towns'. *Journal of the Town Planning Institute* (June 1969): 256–62.

Burnham, Daniel, and Edward Bennett. *Plan of Chicago.* Chicago: The Commercial Club, 1909.

Burtenshaw, D., M. Bateman, and G. J. Ashworth. *The city in West Europe.* Chichester: John Wiley & Sons, 1981.

Buxton, Michael, and Robin Goodman. 'Protecting Melbourne's green wedges – Fate of a public policy'. In *Urban green belts in the twenty-first century*, edited by M. Amati, Dorchester: Ashgate, 2008 61–82.

CABE. *Green space strategies: A good practice guide.* London: CABE, 2004.

CABE. *Summary – Future health: Sustainable places for health and well-being.* London: CABE, 2009.

Cardinia, and City of Casey. *Westernport green wedge management plan – Draft.* Cardinia and City of Casey, 2014.

Carrus, Giuseppe, Raffaele Lafortezza, Giuseppe Colangelo, Ivana Dentamaro, Massimiliano Scopelliti, and Giovanni Sanesi. 'Relations between naturalness and perceived restorativeness of different urban green spaces'. *Psyecology* 4, no. 3 (2013): 227–44.

Carter, E. J., and Erno Goldfinger. *The county of London Plan explained by E. J. Carter and Erno Goldfinger.* London: Penguin Books, 1945.

Caspersen, Ole Hjorth, and Anton Stahl Olafsson. Recreational mapping and planning for enlargement of the green structure in greater Copenhagen. *Urban Forestry & Urban Greening* 9, no. 2 (2010): 101–12.

Caspersen, Ole, Cecil Konijnendijk, and Anton Olafsson. Green space planning and land use: An assessment of urban regional and green structure planning in Greater Copenhagen. *Geografisk Tidsskrift-Danish Journal of Geography* 106, no. 2 (2006): 7–20.

CCRA. *UK climate risk assessment: Government report.* London, 2012.

Chadwick, George Fletcher. *The park and the town: Public landscape in the 19th and 20th centuries.* London: Architectural Press, 1966.

Cherry, Gordon E. *The evolution of British town planning: A history of town planning in the United Kingdom during the 20th century and of the Royal Town Planning Institute, 1914–74.* Leighton Buzzard: L. Hill, 1974.

Cherry, Gordon E. *Environmental planning, 1939–1969. Vol. 2, National Parks and recreation in the countryside* (Peacetime history). London: HMSO, 1975.

Cherry, Gordon E. *Pioneers in British planning.* London: Architectural Press, 1981.

Cherry, Gordon E. *Cities and plans: The shaping of urban Britain in the nineteenth and twentieth centuries.* London: Edward Arnold, 1988.

Chicago Daily News. 'An end to urban sprawl: 3 plans for Chicago's future'. *Chicago Daily News,* 10 December 1966.

Chiesura, Anna. 'The role of urban parks for the sustainable city'. *Landscape and Urban Planning* 68, no. 1 (2004): 129–38.

Choay, Françoise. *L'urbanisme, utopies et réalités: une anthologie.* Paris: Seuil, 1965.

Choay, Françoise, and Denise Bratton. *The rule and the model: On the theory of architecture and urbanism.* Cambridge, MA: MIT Press, 1997.

City of Freiburg im Breisgau. *Environmental policy in Freiburg.* Freiburg: City of Freiburg im Breisgau, 2011.

City of Freiburg im Breisgau. *Green City Freiburg: Approaches to sustainability.* Freiburg: FWTM, 2014.

City of Helsinki. *Eco-Viikki: Aims, implementation and results.* Vantaa: Ministry of the Environment, 2005.

City of Helsinki. *Viikki: Science Park and Latorkantano Guide.* Helsinki: Helsinki City Planning Department, 2010.

City of Helsinki. *Helsinki city planning 2012:3 – Detailed planning in Helsinki.* Helsinki: Helsinki City Planning Department, 2012.

City of Helsinki. *Helsinki city plan: Vision 2050 – Urban plan – The new Helsinki city plan.* Helsinki: Helsinki City Planning Department, 2013.

City of Helsinki. 'Proposal for the Helsinki city plan submitted to decision-making process'. http://www.yleiskaava.fi/en/2015/proposal-for-the-helsinki-city-plan -submitted-to-decision-making-process/ (accessed 19 January 2015).

City of Helsinki. *Urban Plan – Helsinki city plan draft – Helsinki plans 2015:1.* Helsinki: Helsinki City Planning Department, 2015.

City of Stockholm. *Vision Järva 2030: Visions and proposals for the Järva area.* Stockholm: City of Stockholm.

Colin Buchanan and Partners. *South Hampshire study.* London: HMSO, 1966.

Collins, Christiane Crasemann. 'Urban interchange in the southern cone: Le Corbusier (1919) and Werner Hegemann (1931) in Argentina'. *The Journal of the Society of Architectural Historians* 54, no. 2 (June 1995): 208–27.

Colton, Timothy. *Moscow: Governing the socialist metropolis.* Cambridge: Harvard University Press, 1995.

COMMIN. 'Planning system of Sweden'. In *BSR Interreg III B Project: Promoting spatial development by creating COMmon MINdscapes*, 2007.

Comune di Milano. *PGT – Piano del Servizi: Relazione Generale e Catalogo della Ricognizione dell'Offerta dei Servizi*. Milan: Comune di Milano, 2012.

Comune di Milano. *PGT – Piano di Governo del Territorio*. Milan: Comune di Milano, 2014.

Cracknell, M. 'County of London Plan … a statement by the executive of the Town & Country Planning Association'. *Town and Country Planning* 11 (1943): 118–27.

Crow, Arthur. 'Town planning in relation to old and congested areas, with special reference to London'. In *Town planning conference, London, 10–15 October 1910. Transactions*, edited by RIBA, 407–25. London: RIBA, 1911.

Dal Co, Francesco. 'From parks to the region'. In *The American city: From the civil war to the new deal*, edited by Giorgio Ciucci, F. Dal Co, M. Manieri-Elia, and M. Tafuri, 143–291. London: Granada, 1980.

Danish Ministry of the Environment. *The Planning Act in Denmark*. Copenhagen: Ministry of the Environment, 2007.

Danish Ministry of the Environment. *Spatial planning in Denmark*. Copenhagen: Danish Ministry of the Environment, 2007.

DCLG. *Local planning authority green belt: England 2013/14*, edited by Communities and Local Government. London: DCLG, 2014.

Derek, Diamond. 'New towns in their regional context'. In *New towns: The British experience*, edited by H. Evans. London: C. Knight, 1972.

Diefendorf, Jeffry M. 'From Germany to America: Walter Gropius and Martin Wagner on skyscrapers and the planning of healthy cities'. *GHI Bulletin Supplement* 2 (2005): 29–50.

Diefendorf, Jeffry M. *In the wake of war: The reconstruction of German cities after World War II*. Oxford: Oxford University Press, 1993.

Diefendorf, Jeffry M. 'Konstanty Gutschow and the reconstruction of Hamburg'. In *Symposium: Continuity and change in Germany after 1945*, 143–69. Madison: Brill Academic, 2001.

Dieleman, Frans M., Martin J. Dijst, and Tejo Spit. 'Planning the compact city: The Randstad Holland experience'. *European Planning Studies* 7, no. 5 (1999): 605–21.

Duff, A. C. *Britain's new towns: An experiment in living*. London: Pall Mall Press, 1961.

Dümpelmann, Sonja. 'The Park International: Park system planning as an international phenomenon at the beginning of the twentieth century'. *GHI Bulletin*, no. 37 (2005): 75–86.

Dümpelmann, Sonja. 'Creating order with nature: Transatlantic transfer of ideas in park system planning in twentieth century Washington D.C., Chicago, Berlin and Rome'. *Planning Perspectives* 24, no. 2 (2009): 143–73.

Dutch Ministry of Housing, Planning and Environment. *Randstad 2040: Summary of the structural vision*. Ministry of Housing, Planning and Environment, 2008.

Eberstadt, Rudolf. 'Town planning in Germany: The Greater Berlin competition'. In *Town planning conference, London, 10–15 October 1910. Transactions*, edited by RIBA, 313–33. London: RIBA, 1911.

Echenique, Marcial H., Anthony J. Hargreaves, Gordon Mitchell, and Anil Namdeo. 'Growing cities sustainably: Does urban form really matter?'. *Journal of the American Planning Association* 78, no. 2 (2012): 121–37.

Egerö, Ulrika. Interview by author. Personal Interview. 15 September 2014.

Egnsplankontoret. *Skitseforslag til egnsplan for Storkøbenhavn.* Copenhagen: Egnsplankontoret, 1948.

Ellaway, Anne, Sally Macintyre, and Xavier Bonnefoy. 'Graffiti, greenery, and obesity in adults: Secondary analysis of European cross-sectional survey'. *BMJ* 331, no. 611 (2005). http://dx.doi.org/10.1136/bmj.38575.664549.F7.

Engels, Friedrich. *Die Lage der arbeitenden Klasse in England [The Condition of the Working Class in England].* Leipzig: Otto Wigand, 1845.

Erixon, H., S. Borgström, and E. Andersson. 'Challenging dichotomies – Exploring resilience as an integrative and operative conceptual framework for large-scale urban green structures'. *Planning Theory & Practice* 14, no. 3 (2013): 349–72.

Ernstson, Henrik, Stephan Barthel, Erik Andersson, and Sara T. Borgström. 'Scale-crossing brokers and network governance of urban ecosystem services: The case of Stockholm'. *Ecology & Society* 15, no. 4 (2010): 1–25.

Esher, Lionel Brett. *Interview, national life story collection: Architects' lives.* London: British Library, 1997–07. Interview.

Essex, Stephen, and Mark Brayshay. 'Boldness diminished? The post-war battle to replan a bomb-damaged provincial city'. *Urban History* 35, no. 03 (2008): 437–61.

European Commission. *Hamburg winner 2011 – European green capital.* Luxembourg: European Commission, 2011.

European Commission. *The EU biodiversity strategy to 2020.* Luxembourg: Publications Office of the European Union, 2011.

European Commission. 'Cleaner air for all: Why is it important and what should we do?' edited by Environment, 2013. http://ec.europa.eu/environment/pubs/pdf/factsheets/air/en.pdf. Accessed 15 October 2016.

European Commission. 'European green capital: 2014 – Copenhagen, green cities fit for life'. http://ec.europa.eu/environment/europeangreencapital/winning-cities/2014-copenhagen/ (accessed 19 August 2015).

European Commission. 'Towards an EU Research and Innovation policy agenda for Nature-Based Solutions & Re-Naturing Cities – Final Report of the Horizon 2020 Expert Group on "Nature Based Solutions and Re-Naturing Cities"'. Luxembourg, 2015.

European Union. *Building a green infrastructure for Europe.* Luxembourg: European Commission, 2013.

Fehl, Gerhard. 'The Nazi garden city'. In *The garden city: Past, present and future,* edited by Stephen Ward, 88–106. London: Spon Press, 1992.

Folke, Carl. 'Resilience: The emergence of a perspective for social-ecological systems analyses'. *Global Environmental Change* 16 (2006): 253–67.

Folke, Carl, Steve Carpenter, Thomas Elmqvist, Lance Gunderson, C. S. Holling, and Brian Walker. 'Resilience and sustainable development: Building adaptive capacity in a world of transformations'. *Ambio* 31, no. 5 (2002): 437–44.

Foresight Mental Capital and Wellbeing Project. *Mental capital and well-being: Making the most of ourselves in the 21st century – State-of-science review: SR-DR2. The effect of the physical environment on mental wellbeing.* London, 2008.

Forestier, J. C. N. *Grandes villes et systèmes de parcs.* Paris: Hachette, 1906.

Forman, Richard T. T., and Michel Godron. *Landscape Ecology.* New York: Wiley, 1986.

Forshaw, J. 'Town planning and health. Mr Forshaw's Chadwick Trust Lecture'. *The Builder* November–December (1943): 14–15.

Franz, Horst. 'Natur in der Stadt'. Chap. 4 In *Nachhaltige Stadtentwicklung beginnt im Quartier*, edited by Carsten Sperling, 161–200. Freiburg: Forum Vauban, 1999.

Freestone, Robert. 'Exporting the garden city: Metropolitan images in Australia, 1900–1930'. *Planning Perspectives* 1, no. 1 (1986): 61–84.

Fryd, O., A. Backhaus, H. Birch, C. F. Fratini, S. T. Ingvertsen, J. Jeppesen, T. E. Panduro, M. Roldin, and M. B. Jensen. 'Water sensitive urban design retrofits in Copenhagen – 40% to the sewer, 60% to the city'. *Water Science & Technology* 67, no. 9 (2013): 1945–52.

Geddes, Patrick. *Cities in evolution*. Revised ed. London: Williams & Norgate, 1915.

Gehl, Jan. *Cities for people*. Washington, DC: Island Press, 2010.

Gibberd, Frederick. *Harlow new town: A plan prepared for the Harlow Development Corporation*. London: HMSO, 1947.

Gibberd, Frederick. 'Landscaping the new town: Town-planning article with special reference to Harlow'. *The Architectural Review* March (1948): 85–90.

Gibberd, Frederick. 'The master design; landscape; housing; the town centres'. In *New towns: The British experience*, edited by H. Evans, 88–101. London: C. Knight, 1972.

Gibson, D. E. 'Problems of building reconstruction'. *The Builder* (1940): 159, 579.

Giedion, Siegfried. 'Chapter 3: City planning in the nineteenth century'. Chap. 3 In *Space, time and architecture: The growth of a new tradition*, 609–79. New York: Harvard University Press, 1942.

Giedion, Siegfried. *Space, time and architecture: The growth of a new tradition*. New York: Harvard University Press, 1942.

GlashusEtt. *Hammarby Sjöstad: A unique environmental project in Stockholm*. Stockholm, 2007.

GLRPC. *First report of the Greater London regional planning committee*. London: Greater London Regional Planning Committee, 1929.

GLRPC. *Second report of the Greater London regional planning committee*. London: Greater London Regional Planning Committee, 1933.

Gobster, Paul H. 'Perception and use of a metropolitan greenway system for recreation'. *Landscape and Urban Planning* 33 (1995): 401–13.

Gold, John R. '"Commoditie, firmenes and delight": Modernism, the mars group's "new architecture" exhibition (1938) and imagery of the urban future'. *Planning Perspectives* 8, no. 4 (1993): 357–76.

Gold, John R. 'The MARS plans for London, 1933–1942'. *Town Planning Review* 66, no. 3 (1995): 243–67.

Government of South Australia. *The 30-year plan for Greater Adelaide*. Adelaide: Department of Planning and Local Government, 2010.

Grahn, Patrik, and Ulrika A. Stigsdotter. 'Landscape planning and stress'. *Urban Forestry & Urban Greening* 2, no. 1 (2003): 1–18.

Grew, Raymond. 'The case for comparing Histories'. *The American Historical Review* 85, no. 4 (1980): 763–78.

Grindsted, Tobias, and Sara Berg. Interview by author. Personal Interview. Copenhagen, 15 September 2014.

H+N+S Landschapsarchitecten. *Gebiedsvisie Deltapoort 2025.* Amersfoort: Deltapoort, 2012.

Habermas, Jürgen. 'Modernity: An unfinished project'. In *Critical theory, the essential readings,* edited by David Ingram and Julia Simon Ingram, 158–69. New York: Paragon House, 1991.

Hall, Peter. *London 2000.* London: Faber and Faber, 1971.

Hall, Peter. *Cities of tomorrow: An intellectual history of urban planning and design in the twentieth century.* Oxford: Blackwell, 1996.

Hall, Peter, and Mark Tewdwr-Jones. *Urban and regional planning.* 5th ed. London: Routledge, 2011.

Hall, Thomas, ed. *Planning and urban growth in the Nordic countries, studies in history, planning and the environment.* London: E & FN Spon, 1991.

Hall, Thomas, ed. 'Urban planning in Sweden'. In *Planning and urban growth in the Nordic countries,* edited by Thomas Hall, 167–246. London: E & FN Spon, 1991.

Hannikainen, Matti O. *Classification of green spaces in Helsinki and Vantaa.* Helsinki: University of Helsinki, 2013.

Harlow City Council. *Harlow local development plan: Green wedge review.* Harlow: Harlow City Council, 2014.

Hasegawa, Junichi. *Replanning the blitzed city centre: A comparative study of Bristol, Coventry and Southampton 1941–1950.* Buckingham: Open University Press, 1992.

Hasegawa, Junichi. 'The rise and fall of British reconstruction in 1940s Britain'. *Twentieth Century British History* 10, no. 2 (1999): 137–61.

Healey, Patsy. *Urban complexity and spatial strategies: Towards a relational planning for our times.* The RTPI Library Series. London: Routledge, 2007.

Health Scotland. *Health Impact Assessment of greenspace: A Guide.* Stirling: Greenspace Scotland, 2009.

Hegemann, Werner. 'Discussion'. In *Town planning conference, London, 10–15 October 1910. Transactions,* edited by RIBA, 239. London: RIBA, 1911.

'Heiz- Kraftwerk Wettiner Platz (Westkraftwerk) – Funktional- sachliche Industriearchitektur'. http://www.das-neue-dresden.de/heizkraftwerk-dresden-mitte.html (accessed 3 February 2016).

Helsinki City Planning Department. *Green areas system in Helsinki.* Helsinki: Environmental Office.

Hénard, Eugène. *Études sur les transformations de Paris,* edited by Jean-Louis Cohen Paris: Editions L'Equerre, 1902 (1982).

Hewitt, Lucy. 'Towards a greater urban geography: Regional planning and associational networks in London during the early twentieth century'. *Planning Perspectives* 26 (2011): 551–68.

Hilberseimer, Ludwig. *The nature of cities: Origin, growth, and decline pattern and form planning problems.* Chicago: Paul Theobald, 1955.

Home, Robert. *Of planting a planning: The making of British Colonial Cities.* London: Routledge, 2013.

Homer, Andrew. 'Creating new communities: The role of the neighbourhood unit in post-war British planning'. *Contemporary British History* 14, no. 1 (2000): 63–80.

Howard, Ebenezer. *Garden cities of tomorrow.* London: Faber, 1902.

HSCIC. *Health survey for England – 2013.* London: HSCIC, 2014.

IPCC. *Climate change 2014: Synthesis report*. Geneva, 2015.

J47485. *A hundred new towns for Britain: A scheme for national reconstruction*. London: Simpkin Marshall, 1934.

Jabareen, Yosef. 'Planning the resilient city: Concepts and strategies for coping with climate change and environmental risk'. *Cities* 31, no. April (2013): 220–29.

Jackisch, Barry A. 'The nature of Berlin: Green space and visions of a new German capital, 1900–45'. *Central European History* 47, no. 2 (2014): 307–33.

Jankowski, Jósef. 'Plany regulacyjne'. *Dom, Osiedle, Mieszkanie*, no. 6 (1930): 14–25.

Jankowski, Stanislaw. 'Warsaw: Destruction, secret town planning, 1939–44, and postwar reconstruction'. In *Rebuilding Europe's bombed cities*, edited by Jeffry M. Diefendorf, 77–93. Basingstoke: Macmillan, 1990.

Jefferies, Julie. 'The UK population: Past, present and future'. In *Focus on people and migration*, edited by Roma Chappell, 1–18. Norwich: Palgrave Macmillan, 2005.

Jenks, M., and Nicola Dempsey. *Future forms and design for sustainable cities*. Oxford: Architectural Press, 2005.

Jenks, M., and Rod Burgess. *Compact cities: Sustainable urban forms for developing countries*. London: E. & F.N. Spon, 2000.

Johnson, D. A. *Planning the great metropolis: The 1929 regional plan of New York and its environs*. London: Spon, 1996.

Kalthoff, N., V. Horlacher, U. Cotsmeier, et al. 'Influence of valley winds on transport and dispersion of airborne pollutants in the Freiburg-Schauinsland area'. *Journal of Geophysical Research* 105, no. D1 (2000): 1585–97.

Kaplan, Rachel, and Stephen Kaplan. *The experience of nature: A psychological perspective*. Cambridge: Cambridge University Press, 1989.

Kaupungin, Helsingin. *Helsingin yleiskaavaehdotus: Laadittu asemakaavaosastolla 1953–1960*. Helsinki: Tilgmann, 1960.

Kazmierczak, Aleksandra, and Jeremy Carter. *Adaptation to climate change using green and blue infrastructure: A database of case studies*. Manchester: University of Machester, 2010.

Kellermann, Britta. 'Die Entwicklung des Freiraumverbundsystems für Hamburg: Von Schumachers Achsenkonzept zum Grünen Netz Hamburg'. 2003.

KfC. 'Climate proof cities 2010–2014: Final report'. Amsterdam: Climate Proof Cities consortium, 2014.

Kipar, Andreas. 'Milano: New landscape territories in urban design'. Paper presented at the Urban Growth without Sprawl: A way towards Sustainable Urbanization, Porto, 2009.

Kipar, Andreas, and Valeria Pagliaro. 'Green rays in Milan'. *Topos: European Landscape Magazine*, 2011, 50–54.

Kommune, Københavns. *københavns Grønne Cykelruter*. Copenhagen: Københavns Kommune, 2015.

Kodym-Kozaczko, Grażyna, and Mieczysław Kozaczko. 'Master plan for Poznań (1931–1939) as compared with European theory and practice of city development'. In *Modernism in Europe, modernism in Gdynia: Architecture of 1920s and 1930s and its protection*, edited by Robert Hirsch, Maria Jolanta Sołtysik, and Waldemar J. Affelt. Poznań University of Technology, 105–14. Gdynia: The City of Gdynia, 2009.

Koeppen, Walter. *Die Freiflächen der Stadtgemeinde Berlin-Denkschrift des Amtes für Stadtplanung*. Vol. 2, Berlin: Amt für Stadtplanung der Stadt Berlin, 1929.

Kong, Luyao. *Break the green belt? The differences between green belt and its alternative green wedge: A comparative study of London and Stockholm*. Karlskrona: blekinge tekniska högskola, 2012.

Kopp, Anatole. *Town and revolution: Soviet architecture and city planning, 1917–1935*. London: Thames & Hudson, 1970.

Korn, Arthur, and Felix Samuely. 'A master plan for London: Based on research carried out by the town planning committee of the M.A.R.S. Group'. *Architectural Review*, no. 91 (1942): 143–50.

Kühn, Manfred. 'Greenbelt and green heart: Separating and integrating landscapes in European city regions'. *Landscape and Urban Planning* 64, no. 1–2 (2003): 19–27.

Kühn, Manfred, and Ludger Gailing. 'From green belts to regional parks: History and challenges of suburban landscape planning in Berlin'. Chap. 10 In *Urban green belts in the twenty-first century*, edited by M. Amati, 185–202: Ashgate, 2012.

Ladd, Brian. *Urban planning and civic order in Germany, 1860–1914*. Cambridge, MA; London: Harvard University Press, 1990.

Lanchester, Henry Vaughan. 'Park systems for great cities'. *The Builder*, no. 95 (October 1908): 343–48.

Lanchester, Henry Vaughan. 'Cause and effect in the modern city'. In *Town planning conference, London, 10–15 October 1910. Transactions*, edited by RIBA. London: RIBA, 1911.

Lanchester, Henry Vaughan. 'Informal meetings: Exhibition of lantern slides'. In *Town planning conference, London, 10–15 October 1910. Transactions*, edited by RIBA, 269. London: RIBA, 1911.

Lanchester, Henry Vaughan. 'An architect's view of reconstruction: The large city'. *The Builder* 161 (1941): 569–70.

Langen, Gustav. *Stadtplan und Wohnungsplan vom hygienischen Stadtpunkte*. Leipzig: Verlag von S. Hirzel, 1927.

Larkham, P. J. *The London Regional Reconstruction Committee: Architects, exhibitions, and post-war visions for replanning*. Birmingham: Birmingham City University, 2013.

Larkham, P. J., and K. D. Lilley. *Planning the 'City of Tomorrow'. British reconstruction planning, 1939–1952: An annotated bibliography*. Pickering: Inch's books, 2001.

Latham, C. 'The planning problems of London: Lord Latham's survey'. *The Builder* 162, no. 421–3 (1942).

Laugier, Marc-Antoine. *Essay on architecture*. T. Osborne and Shipton: London, 1755.

LCC. *Interview with comptroller and Mr Miles, December 1940*. CL/TP/1/33. London: London Metropolitan Archives, 1940.

LCC. *London County Council. Memorandum by the architect, 6th December 1940*. CL/TP/1/33. London: London Metropolitan Archives, 1940.

LCC. *London County Council. Memorandum on replanning and reconstruction of London, first draft*. CL/TP/1/33. London: London Metropolitan Archives, 1940.

LCC. *London County Council. Post-war reconstruction of London, notes of a conference held on 7th October 1940.* CL/TP/1/33. London: London Metropolitan Archives, 1940.

LCC. *London County Council. Letter, 8th April 1941.* CL/TP/1/34. London: London Metropolitan Archives, 1941.

LCC. *London County Council. 'Exhibition of the County of London Plan', 1943.* LMA/4062/06/040. London: London Metropolitan Archives, 1943.

LCC. *London County Council. County of London Plan. Parks Committee. Report (31.05.43) by Comptroller of the Council.* CL/TP/1/34. London: London Metropolitan Archives, 1943.

LCC. *London County Council. County of London Plan. Report (04.06.43) by chief officer of the Parks Department.* CL/TP/1/34. London: London Metropolitan Archives, 1943.

LCC. *London County Council. Town Planning Committee. Report by valuer (24.05.43).* CL/TP/1/37. London: London Metropolitan Archives, 1943.

LCC. *London County Council. County of London Plan – Housing density. Housing and Public Health Committee. Joint report by architect, chief assistant, valuer and comptroller of the council.* CL/TP/1/34. London: London Metropolitan Archives, 1944.

LCC. *London County Council. County of London Plan. Observations by government departments, Metropolitan Borough councils and other bodies – Open space proposals. Town Planning Committee. Report (12.10.44) by Architect (N.4).* CL/TP/1/37. London: London Metropolitan Archives, 1944.

LCC. *London County Council. County of London Plan. Observations by government departments, Metropolitan Borough councils and other bodies – Open space proposals. Town Planning Committee. Report (4.1.45) by comptroller of the council, A. R. Wood.* CL/TP/1/34. London: London Metropolitan Archives, 1945.

LCC. *London County Council. County of London Plan. Town Planning Committee. Draft report of the Town Planning Committee, 11th June 1945. Eric Salmon, clerk of the council.* CL/TP/1/37. London: London Metropolitan Archives, 1945.

Ledoux, Claude-Nicolas. *L'Architecture considerée sous le rapport de l'art, des moers et de la législation.* 1804.

Lefevre, Henrique. 'Planejamento e problemas de São Paulo'. *Revista de Engenharia* 11, no. 126 (1953): 139–47.

Leicestershire County Council, Leicester City Council, Oadby and Wigston Borotuh Council, North West Leicestershire District Council, Charnwood, Blaby District Council, and District of Harborough. 'Green Spaces in Leicester and Leicestershire'.

Lemes de Oliveira, Fabiano. *Modelos Urbanísticos Modernos e Parques Urbanos: as Relações entre Urbanismo e Paisagismo em São Paulo na Primeira Metade do Século XX.* Polytechnic School of Catalonia, 2008.

Lemes de Oliveira, Fabiano. 'Ecocities: The role of networks of green and blue spaces'. Chap. 9 In *Cities for smart environmental and energy futures*, edited by Stamatina Rassia and Panos Pardalos, 163–76. Berlin: Springer, 2013.

Lemes de Oliveira, Fabiano. 'Green wedges: Origins and development in Britain'. *Planning Perspectives* 29, no. 3 (2014): 357–79.

Lemes de Oliveira, Fabiano. 'Abercrombie's green-wedge vision for London: The County of London Plan 1943 and the Greater London Plan 1944'. *Town Planning Review* 86, no. 5 (2015): 495–518.

Lenger, Friedrich. 'Building and perceiving the city: Germany around 1900'. In *Towards an urban nation: Germany since 1780*, edited by Friedrich Lenger, 87–106. Oxford: Berg, 2002.

Lenger, Friedrich. *Towards an urban nation: Germany since 1780*. Oxford: Berg, 2002.

Lepetit, Bernard. 'Propositions pour une pratique restreinte de l'interdisciplinarité'. *Revue de Synthèse* 4, no. 3 (July–September 1990): 331–38.

Lewis, Nelson Peter. *Planning of the modern city: A review of principles governing city planning*. New York: John Wiley & Sons, 1916.

Lissitzky, El. *Russia: An architecture for world revolution*. Cambridge: MIT Press, 1970.

Lodi, Carlos. 'O Plano Diretor de São Paulo'. *Revista de Engenharia Municipal*, no. 8 (1957): 17–22.

London Society. *Minutes of the London Society Committee*. London: London Society Archives, 1914.

Loudon, John Claudius. 'Hints for breathing places for the metropolis, and for country towns and villages, on fixed principles'. *The Gardener Magazine* v (1829): 686–90.

LRRC. *Greater London: Towards a master plan: The second interim report of the LRRC of the RIBA*. London: London Regional Reconstruction Committee, 1943.

Luque, José Valdivia. *Constructores de la ciudad contemporánea: aproximación disciplinar a través de los textos*. Madrid: Cie Inversiones Editoriales, 2004.

Lynch, Kevin. *A theory of good city form*. Cambridge, MA; London: MIT Press,1981.

Maher, B. A., I. A. M. Ahmed, B. Davison, V. Karloukovski, and R. Clarke. 'Impact of roadside tree lines on indoor concentrations of traffic-derived particulate matter'. *Environmental Science & Technology* 47, no. 23 (2013): 13737–44.

Maia, Francisco Prestes. *Estudo de um Plano de Avenidas para a Cidade de São Paulo*. São Paulo: PMSP, 1930.

Malisz, Bolesław. 'Urban planning theory: Methods and results'. In *City and regional planning in Poland*, edited by Jack C. Fischer, 57–84. Ithaca, NY: Cornell University Press, 1966.

Malmros, Bette. Interview by author. Personal Interview. 12 September 2014.

Manieri-Elia, Mario. 'Toward an "Imperial City": Daniel H. Burnham and the city beautiful movement'. In *The American city: From the civil war to the new deal*, edited by Giorgio Ciucci, F. Dal Co, M. Manieri-Elia, M. Tafuri. London: Granada, 1980.

Manninen, Rikhard. Interview by author. Personal Interview. Helsinki, 22 August 2014.

Marmaras, Emmanuel, and Anthony Sutcliffe. 'Planning for post-war London: The three independent plans, 1942–3'. *Planning Perspectives* 9, no. 4 (1994): 431–53.

Marx, Karl, and Frederick Engels. *Manifest of the Communist Party*. Moscow: Progress Publishers, 1848.

Matsuoka, Rodney H., and Rachel Kaplan. 'People needs in the urban landscape: Analysis of landscape and urban planning contributions'. *Landscape and Urban Planning* 84, no. 1 (2008): 7–19.

Mattocks, Robert. 'The park system'. *Town Planning Review* 17, no. 3 (1937): 161–83.

Mawson, Thomas. *Bolton as it is and as it might be.* Bolton: Tillotson and Son, 1915.

Mawson, Thomas. 'Public parks and gardens: Their design and equipment'. In *Town planning conference, London, 10–15 October 1910. Transactions*, edited by RIBA, 434–50. London: RIBA, 1911.

Mayer, Helmut. 'KLIMES – A joint research project on human thermal comfort in cities'. In *Berichte des Meteorologischen Instituts der Albert-Ludwigs Universität Freiburg N.17*, edited by Helmut Mayer, 101–17, Freiburg: Universität Freiburg, 2008.

McElligott, Anthony. *The German urban experience, 1900–1945: Modernity and crisis.* London: Routledge, 2001.

McHarg, I. *Design with nature.* New York: Natural History Press, 1969.

McLoughlin, J. Brian. *Shaping Melbourne's future? Town planning, the state and civil society.* Melbourne: Cambridge University Press, 1992.

Meller, Helen. *Patrick Geddes: Social evolutionist and city planner.* London: Routledge, 1990.

Metropolitan Town Planning Commission. *Plan of general development of Melbourne: Report of the Metropolitan Town Planning Commission.* Melbourne: Metropolitan Town Planning Commission, 1929.

MHLG. *The South East Study 1961–1981*, edited by Ministry of Housing and Local Government. London: HMSO, 1964.

Mijoministeriet Naturstyrelsen. *Fingerplan 2013 – Hovedbudskaber.* Copenhagen, 2013.

Miliutin, Nikolai. *Sotsgorod: The problem of building socialist cities.* Cambridge: MIT Press, 1974.

Miljøministeriet. *Forslag til Fingerplan 2007 – Landsplandirektiv for hovedstadsområdets planlægning.* Copenhagen: Miljøministeriet, 2007.

Miller, Mervyn. 'The elusive green background: Raymond Unwin and the greater London regional plan'. *Planning Perspectives* 4, no. 1 (1989): 15–44.

Mind. *Ecotherapy: The green agenda for mental health executive summary.* London: Mind, 2007.

Ministry of Town and Country Planning. *Advisory committee for London regional planning. Open spaces sub-committee, 20th March 1946.* MCC/MIN.65/006. London: London Metropolitan Archives, 1946.

Ministry of Town and Country Planning. *Greater London Plan – Open spaces and recreation areas. Memorandum prepared for interdepartmental committee by the Ministry of Town and Country Planning, 8th April 1946.* MCC/MIN.65/006. London: London Metropolitan Archives, 1946.

Ministry of Town and Country Planning. *Greater London Plan, memorandum by the Ministry of Town and Country Planning on the report of the Advisory Committee for London Regional Planning.* AR/TP/5/9. London: London Metropolitan Archives, 1947.

Mitchell, Richard, and Frank Popham. 'Effect of exposure to natural environment on health inequalities: An observational population study'. 372, no. 9650 (2008): 1655–60.

Morrison, Nicky. 'A green belt under pressure: The case of Cambridge, England'. *Planning Practice & Research* 25, no. 2 (2010): 157–81.

Moughtin, Cliff. *Urban design: Green dimensions*. Oxford: Butterworth Architecture, 1996.

Mumford, Eric. 'CIAM urbanism after the Athens charter'. *Planning Perspectives* 7, no. 4 (1992): 391–417.

Mumford, Eric. *The Ciam discourse on urbanism, 1928–1960*. Cambridge: MIT Press, 2000.

Mumford, Lewis. *The city in history: Its origins, its transformations, and its prospects*. London: Secker & Warburg, 1961.

Mumford, Lewis. 'Landscape and townscape (1960–61)'. In *The Urban prospect*, edited by Lewis Mumford. London: Secker & Warburg, 1968.

Myhre, Erik Lorange, and Jan Eivind. 'Urban planning in Norway'. In *Planning and urban growth in the Nordic countries*, edited by Thomas Hall, 117–66. London: E & FN Spon, 1991.

Naes, Petter. 'Urban planning and sustainable development'. *European Planning Studies* 9, no. 4 (2009): 503–24.

NAI. 'Chaos and order (1920–1927)'. NAI, http://schatkamer.nai.nl/en/projects/chaos-en-orde (accessed 13 April 2015).

National Museum in Norway. *Forms of Freedom – African Independence and Nordic Models. The Nordic Pavilion exhibition at the Biennale Architettura di Venezia*. Venice: La Biennale di Venezia, 2014.

Natural England. *Green infrastructure guidance*. Natural England, 2009.

New Towns Committee. 'Final report of the new towns committee (Command Paper 6876)'. 1946.

Nicholas, R. *City of Manchester Plan, prepared for the City Council*. Norwich and London: Jarrold & Sons, 1945.

Nielsen, T. S., and K. B. Hansen. 'Do green areas affect health? Results from a Danish survey on the use of green areas and health indicators'. *Health Place* 13, no. 4 (December 2007): 839–50.

Nowak, D. J., D. E. Crane, and J. C. Stevens. 'Air pollution removal by urban trees and shrubs in the United States'. *Urban Forestry & Urban Greening* 4, no. 3 (2006): 115–23.

NSW Government. *A plan for growing Sydney*. Sydney: NSW Government, 2014.

O'Malley, Christopher, Poorang Piroozfar, Eric Farr, and Francesco Pomponi. 'Urban Heat Island (UHI) mitigating strategies: A case-based comparative analysis'. *Sustainable Cities and Society* (2015): 1–14.

OECD. 'Randstad Holland, Netherlands'. In *Territorial Reviews*. Paris: OECD, 2007.

Olmsted, Frederick Law. 'Public parks and the enlargement of towns'. In *American Social Science Association*, 1870. https://catalog.hathitrust.org/Record/008726621.

Osborn, Frederic James. *New towns after the war*. London: J. M. Dent and Sons Ltd, 1942. First Pub. 1918.

Panzini, Franco. *Per i piaceri del popolo: l'evoluzione del giardino publico in Europa dalle origini al XX secolo*. Bologna: Zanichelli Editore, 1993.

Pepler, G. L. 'Greater London'. In *Town planning conference, London, 10–15 October 1910. Transactions*, edited by RIBA, 611–20. London: RIBA, 1911.

Pepler, G. L. 'Open spaces'. *Town Planning Review* 10, no. 1 (1923): 11–24.

Peterson, Jon A. 'The birth of organized city planning in the United States, 1909–1910'. *Journal of the American Planning Association* 75, no. 2 (2009): 123–33.

Petz, Ursula Von. 'Robert Schmidt and the public park policy in the Ruhr district, 1900–1930'. *Planning Perspectives* 14, no. 2 (1999): 163–82.

Phillips, Richard. *A morning walk from London to Kew*. London: J. Adlard, 1817.

Piccinato, G. *La construzione del l'urbanística Germania 1871–1914*. Roma: Officina, 1974.

Pieprz, Dennis, and Michael Grove. 'Songzhuang creative clusters'. *Topos*, no. 84 (2013): 44–50.

Planisphere. *Kingston green wedge plan*. Kingston: City of Kingston, 2012.

Plunkett, G. T. 'Open spaces and running waters'. In *Town planning conference, London, 10–15 October 1910. Transactions*, edited by RIBA, 465–75. London: RIBA, 1911.

Pollard Thomas Edwards. 'Dunsfold park'. http://pollardthomasedwards.co.uk/ project/dunsfold-park/ (accessed 22 December 2015).

Prem, Chhetri, Han Jung Hoon, Chandra Shobhit, and Corcoran Jonathan. 'Mapping urban residential density patterns: Compact city model in Melbourne, Australia'. *City, Culture and Society* 4 (2013): 77–85.

Proudfoot, Malcom J. 'New city patterns: The analysis of and a technique for urban reintegration'. *Geographical Review* 37, no. 2 (April 1947): 349–50.

Rapoport, Elizabeth. 'Utopian visions and real estate dreams: The eco-city past, present and future'. *Geography Compass* 8, no. 2 (2014): 137–49.

Reichow, Hans Bernhard. *Organische Stadtbaukunst: von der Groflstadt zur Stadtlandschaft*. Braunschweig: Westermann, 1948.

Reiss, R. L. The London Plan and satellite town. Address to town and country planning association'. *The Builder*, no. 254 (September 1943).

RIBA. *Minutes of the RIBA development of towns and suburbs subcommittee*. 312–3. London: RIBA Archives, 1907.

Roaf, Susan, David Crichton, and F. Nicol. *Adapting buildings and cities for climate change: A 21st century survival guide*. Oxford: Elsevier Architectural, 2009.

Robinson, C. M. 'Cities of the present as representative of a transition period in urban development – The evidence of standardised streets'. In *Town planning conference, London, 10–15 October 1910. Transactions*, edited by RIBA, 201–2. London: RIBA, 1911.

Rogers, Richard. *Towards an urban renaissance: Final report of the Urban Task Force*. London: Department for the Environment, Transport and the Regions, 1999.

Rosenau, Helen. *The ideal city: Its architectural evolution*. 2nd ed. London: Studio Vista, 1974.

Różański, Stanisław, Stanisław Filipkowski, and Maria Buckiewiczówna. 'Plan ogólny Wielkiej Warszawy'. *Architektura i Budownictwo* (1928): 410–38.

RTK. *Upplevelsevärden i ABC-stråket – en studie av gröna och blå värdens attraktivitet*. Stockholm: Regionplane- och trafikkontoret, 2007.

Rubenstein, James M. *The French new towns*. Baltimore: The John Hopkins University Press, 1978.

Rydin, Yvonne, Yeasminah Beebeejaun, Marco Bianconi, Juliana Martins, Ben Clifford, Claire Colomb, Harry Dimitriou, et al. *Five radical ideas for a better planning system*. London: UCL, 2015.

Sala, Giovanni. Interview by author. Personal Interview. Milan, 13 February 2015.

Sanders S. E., and A. J. Rabuck. *New city patterns: The analysis of and a technique for urban reintegration*. New York: Reinhold Publishing Corporation, 1946.

Sandström, Ulf G., Per Angelstam, and Abdul Khakee. 'Urban comprehensive planning – Identifying barriers for the maintenance of functional habitat networks'. *Landscape and Urban Planning* 75, no. 1–2 (2006): 43–57.

Schaffer, Frank. 'The new town movement'. In *New Towns: the British Experience*, edited by H. Evans, 11–21. London: C. Knight, 1972.

Scheurer, Jan, and Peter Newman. 'Vauban: A European model bridging the green and brown agendas'. In *Case study prepared for revisiting urban planning: Global report on human settlements*: UN-Habitat, 2009.

Schmidt, Robert. *Denkschrift betreffend Grundsätze zur Aufstellung eines General-Siedelungsplanes für den Regierungsbezirk Düsseldorf (rechtsrheinisch)*. Essen: Fredebeul & Koenen, 1912.

Schneider, Jerry B. *Transit and the polycentric city.* Washington, DC: University of Washington, 1981.

Schubert, Dirk. 'Theodor Fritsch and the German (völkische) version of the Garden City: The Garden City invented two years before Ebenezer Howard'. *Planning Perspectives* 19, no. 1 (2004): 3–25.

Schulmann, Ulrich Maximilian. 'The hidden roots of the garden city idea: From John Sinclair to John Claudius Loudon'. *Journal of Planning History* 2, no. 4 (2003): 291–310.

Semper, Gottfried. *The four elements of architecture and other writings.* Cambridge: Cambridge University Press, 1989.

Sert, Jose Luis. *Can our cities survive?: An A.B.C. of urban problems, their analysis, their solutions, based on the proposals formulated by the Congrès Internationaux d'Architecture Moderne.* Cambridge: Harvard University Press, 1942.

Shestakov, Sergei. *Bol'shaia Moskva [Large Moscow].* Moskva, 1925.

Sica, Paolo. *Historia del Urbanismo. Siglo XIX.* Madrid: IEAL, 1980.

Sieverts, Thomas. *Cities without cities: An interpretation of the Zwischenstadt: Between place and world, space and time, town and country.* London: Routledge, 2003.

Silkin, L. 'London replanned: Decentralization of industry and population'. *The Times*, 13 July 1943, 5.

Smit, B., and J. Wandel. 'Adaptation, adaptive capacity and vulnerability'. *Global Environmental Change* 16, no. 3 (2006): 282–92.

Sohn, Elke. 'Hans Bernhard Reichow and the concept of Stadtlandschaft in German planning'. *Planning Perspectives* 18, no. 2 (2003): 119–46.

Sohn, Elke. 'Organicist concepts of city landscape in German planning after the Second World War'. *Landscape Research* 32, no. 4 (2007): 499–523.

South East Economic Planning Council. *A strategy for the South East: A first report by the South East Economic Planning Council*, edited by Department of Economic Affairs. London: HMSO, 1967.

Special Park Commission. *Report of the Special Park Commission to the City Council of Chicago on the subject of a metropolitan park system.* Chicago: Chicago Special Park Commission, 1905.

Stadt Freiburg I. Br. *Freiburg i. Br. Landschaftsplan 2020.* Freiburg: Stadt Freiburg I. Br., 2006.

Stadt Freiburg I. Br. *Freiburg im Breisgau: Quartier Vauban Historie – History.* Freiburg: Stadt Freiburg I. Br, 2008.

Stadt Freiburg I. Br. *The new district of Freiburg-Rieselfeld: A case study of successful, sustainable urban development.* Freiburg: Rieselfeld Project Group, 2009.

Stadt Freiburg I. Br. 'Ein neuer Stadtteil gegen die Wohnungsnot'. Stadt Freiburg I. Br., http://www.freiburg.de/pb/,Lde/495838.html (accessed 12 August 2015).

Stasse, E, and H. de Bruyne. 'Bruxelles Aux Champs'. In *Town planning conference, London, 10–15 October 1910.* Transactions, edited by RIBA, 636–53. London: RIBA, 1911.

State of Victoria, Department of Transport, Planning and Local Infrastructure. *Melbourne 2030: Planning for Sustainable Growth.* Melbourne: Department of Infrastructure, 2002.

State of Victoria. *Melbourne 2030: A planning update – Melbourne @ 5 million.* Melbourne: Department of Planning and Community Development, 2008.

State of Victoria. *Know Your Plan Melbourne.* Melbourne, 2014.

State of Victoria. *Plan Melbourne.* Melbourne: Impact Digital, 2014.

Stites, Richard. *Revolutionary Dreams: Utopian vision and experimental life in the Russian revolution.* Oxford: Oxford University Press, 1989.

Stockholm County Council. *Regional development plan for the Stockholm region – RUFS 2010.* Sentenza media. Stockholm: Stockholm County Council, 2010.

Stockholms läns landsting. *När, vad och hur? Svaga samband i Stockholmsregionens gröna kilar.* Stockholm: Stockholms läns landsting, 2012.

Stockholms stad. *Generalplan för Stockholm.* Stockholm,1952.

Stübben, Joseph. *Der Städtebau. Handbuch der Architektur.* Braunschweig: Vieweg, 1890.

Sutcliffe, Anthony. *British town planning: The formative years.* Leicester: Leicester University Press, 1981.

Sutcliffe, Anthony. *Towards the planned city: Germany, Britain, the United States and France 1780–1914.* Oxford: Basil Blackwell, 1981.

Szulczewska, Barbara, and Kaliszuk, Ewa. 'Problems of green structure planning and management in Warsaw'. In *Report of COST Action C11 – Green structure and urban planning: Final report,* edited by Ann Caroll Werquin, Bernard Duhem, Gunilla Lindholm, Bettina Oppermann, Stephan Pauleit, and Sybrand Tjallingii, 90–102. Luxembourg: Office for Official Publications of the European Communities, 2005.

Tallis, M., G. Taylor, D. Sinnett, and P. H. Freer-Smith. 'Estimating the removal of atmospheric particulate pollution by the urban tree canopy of London, under current and future environments'. *Landscape and Urban Planning* 103, no. 2 (2011): 129–38.

Tallis M., J. Amorim, C. Calfapietra, P. Freer-Smith, C. Grimmond, S. Kotthaus, F. Lemes de Oliveira, A. Miranda, and P. Toscano. 'The impacts of green infrastructure on air quality and temperature'. Chap. 2 In *Handbook on green infrastructure planning, design and implementation,* edited by Danielle Sinnett, Nicholas Smith, and Sarah Burgess, 30–49. Cheltenham: Edward Elgar Publishing, 2015.

Taut, Bruno. *Die Stadtkrone.* Jena: Eugen Diederichs, 1919.

TCPA, and The Wildlife Trusts. *Planning for a healthy environment – Good practice guidance for green infrastructure and biodiversity.* Oldham, 2012.

The Builder. 'Town and country planning'. *The Builder,* no. 162 (1942): 333.

The City of Copenhagen. *CPH 2025 Climate Plan: A green, smart and carbon neutral city.* Copenhagen, 2012.

The City Planning Administration. *The walkable city – Stockholm city plan*. Stockholm: The City Planning Administration, 2010.

The Mersey Forest. *Liverpool green infrastructure strategy: Action plan*. Liverpool, 2010.

The Office of Regional Planning. 'Dense and green: The Stockholm region's ten wedges – As they will be preserved, improved and made more accessible'. In *Stockholmsregionen*. Stockholm: The Office of Regional Planning, 2010.

The Office of Regional Planning and Urban Transportation. *Social values in urban green areas – The Green Wedges of the Stockholm region*. Stockholm: The Office of Regional Planning and Urban Transportation, 2005.

The Ringby Light Rail Partnership. *Ring 3 Light Rail*. Copenhagen, 2013.

The Rutland Group. 'Dunsfold park: A new surrey village'. http://www .dunsfoldparkmasterplan.com/masterplan/landscape-open-space (accessed 22 December 2015).

The Times. 'Mr A. Trystan Edwards'. *The Times*, 3 February 1973, 16.

The Times. 'Obituary: Mr A. Trystan Edwards: A town planning pioneer'. *The Times*, 31 January 1973, 16.

The Times. 'Town planning'. *The Times*, 19 February 1909.

Thomas, Kevin, and Steve Littlewood. 'From green belts to green infrastructure? The evolution of a new concept in the emerging soft governance of spatial strategies'. *Planning Practice and Research* 25, no. 2 (2010): 203–22.

Thomassen, Ole, and Bo Larsson. 'Urban planning in Denmark'. In *Planning and urban growth in the Nordic countries*, edited by Thomas Hall, 6–59. London: E & FN Spon, 1991.

Tichelar, M. 'The conflict over property rights during the Second World War: The Labour Party's abandonment of land nationalization'. *Twentieth Century British History* 14, no. 2 (2003): 165–88.

Tiratsoo, Nick. 'The reconstruction of blitzed British cities, 1945–55: Myths and reality'. *Contemporary British History* 14, no. 1 (2000): 27–44.

Tisma, Alexandra, Rene van der Velde, Steffen Nijhuis, and Michiel Pouderoijen. 'Metropolitan landscape characterization: A typo-morphological approach'. In *The Production of Place 2012*, 1–16. London: University of East London, 2012.

TNA. *County of London Plan 1943: Consultation with the Ministry of Works*. HLG 79/375. London: The National Archives, 1943–4.

TNA. *County of London Plan 1943: Consultation with the Ministry of Works*. HLG 79/376. London: The National Archives, 1943–6.

TNA. *Notes on a meeting between Mr Salmon, Professor Abercrombie, Mr Forshaw, Mr Pepler and HYL, 16th September 1941*. HLG 71/116. London: The National Archives, 1941.

TNA. *Greater London Plan. Individual matters for comment, etc. Open spaces, 14 January 1944*. HLC 85/17. London: The National Archives, 1944.

Tomaszewski, Leonard. 'Urbanistyka w Z.S.R.R.' *Architektura i Budownictwo*, no. 8 (1931).

Town Planning Review. 'Chronicle of passing events: St. Louis Outer Park, or public reservation district'. *Town Planning Review* 1, no. 3 (1910): 262–63.

Town Planning Review. 'Chronicle of passing events: York competition'. *Town Planning Review* 6, no. 1 (1916): 275–81.

Trystan Edwards, Arthur. 'A plan for "Greater London"'. *The Builder* (February 5 1943): 128–29.

Tubbs, Ralph. *Living in cities*. London: Penguin, 1942.

Tyrväinen, Liisa, Kirsi Mäkinen, and Jasper Schipperijn. 'Tools for mapping social values of urban woodlands and other green areas'. *Landscape and Urban Planning* 79, no. 1 (2007): 5–19.

Tyrväinen, Liisa, Ann Ojala, Kalevi Korpela, Timo Lanki, Yuko Tsunetsugu, and Takahide Kagawa. 'The influence of urban green environments on stress relief measures: A field experiment'. *Journal of Environmental Psychology* 38 (2014): 1–9.

UK National Ecosystem assessment. 'Ecosystem services'. http://uknea.unep-wcmc.org/EcosystemAssessmentConcepts/EcosystemServices/tabid/103/Default.aspx (accessed 21 January 2016).

Ulrich, Roger S. 'View through a window may influence recovery from surgery'. *Science* 224 (1984): 420–21.

UN-HABITAT. *Climate change strategy 2014–2019*. Nairobi, 2015.

Unwin, Raymond. 'The Berlin exhibition of town planning'. *The Builder* (2 July 1910): 17–19.

Uyttenhove, Pieter. 'The garden city education of Belgium planners around the First World War'. *Planning Perspectives* 5, no. 3 (1990): 271–83.

Vallensbæk Kommune. *Tillæg nr 1. Kommuneplan 2013–2025*. Vallensbæk: Vallensbæk Komunne, 2014.

Vejre, Henrik, Jorgen Primdahl and Jesper Brandt. 'The Copenhagen finger plan: Keeping a green space structure by a simple planning metaphor'. Chap. 19 In *Europe's living landscapes. Essays on exploring our identity in the countryside*, edited by B. Pedroli, A. Van Doorn, G. De Blust, M. L. Paracchini, D. Wascher, and F. Bunce, 311–28, 2007. http://www.uniscape.eu/pagelmg.php p?idCont=962&idSez=20&idlink=100&lang=en.

Vink, van der Burg L. and Arjen J. Bart 'Randstad Holland towards 2040 – Perspectives from national government'. In *44th ISOCARP Congress*, 1–12. Dalian, 2008.

Vries, Sjerp de, Robert A. Verheij, Peter P. Groenewegen, and Peter Spreeuwenberg. 'Natural environments – Healthy environments? An exploratory analysis of the relationship between green space and health'. *Environment and Planning A* 35 (2003): 1717–31.

Wagner, Martin. 'Das sanitäre grün der Städte: ein Beitrag zur Freiflächentheorie'. 1915.

Waldheim, Charles. *The landscape urbanism reader*. New York: Princeton Architectural Press, 2006.

Walker, B. H., C. S. Holling, S. R. Carpenter, and A. P. Kinzig. 'Resilience, adaptability and transformability in social–ecological systems'. *Ecology and Society* 9, no. 2. (2004): 5.

Wamsler, Christine, Ebba Brink, and Claudia Rivera. 'Planning for climate change in urban areas: From theory to practice'. *Journal of Cleaner Production* 50, no. July (2013): 68–81.

Ward, Stephen. *Planning and urban change*. London: Sage, 2004.

Ward, Stephen. 'What did the Germans ever do to us? A century of British learning about and imagining modern town planning'. *Planning Perspectives* 25, no. 2 (April 2010): 117–40.

Ward, Stephen. 'Soviet communism and the British planning movement: Rational learning or Utopian imagining?' *Planning Perspectives* 27, no. 4 (2012): 499–524.

Watanabe, Takashi, Marco Amati, Kenya Endo, and Makoto Yokohari. 'The abandonment of Tokyo's green belt and the search for a new discourse of preservation in Tokyo's Suburbs'. In *Urban green belts in the twenty-first century*, edited by Marco Amati, 21–57. London: Ashgate, 2008.

Watson, J. P., and Abercrombie, P. *A plan for Plymouth*. Plymouth: Plymouth City Council, 1943.

West 8. 'Sagrera Linear Park'. http://www.west8.nl/projects/selected_projects/sagrera_linear_park/pdf/ (accessed 20 December 2015).

White, Mathew P., Ian Alcock, Benedict W. Wheeler, and Michael H. Depledge. 'Would you be happier living in a greener urban area? A fixed-effects analysis of panel data'. *Psychological Science* 24, no. 6 (2013): 920–28.

WHO. *Mental health and older adults facsheet n.381*, edited by WHO, 2013.

WHO. *Burden of disease from Ambient Air Pollution for 2012*. Geneva: World Health Organization, 2014.

Whyte, William. 'The 1910 Royal Institute of British Architects' Conference: A focus for international town planning?' *Urban History* 39, no. 1 (2012): 149–65.

Wolf, P. *Städtebau: das Formproblem der Stadt in Vergangenheit und Zukunft*. Klinkhardt & Biermann, 1919.

Works, Melbourne and Metropolitan Board of. 'Planning Policies for the Melbourne Metropolitan Region'. Melbourne, 1971.

WWF. *Living Planet Report 2010: Biodiversity, biocapacity and development*. Gland: WWF, 2010.

Yarra Ranges Council. *Yarra ranges green wedge management plan*. Yarra Ranges, 2010.

Yokohari, Makoto, Kazuhiko Takeuchi, Takashi Watanabe, and Shigehiro Yokota. 'Beyond greenbelts and zoning: A new planning concept for the environment of Asian mega-cities'. *Landscape and Urban Planning* 47, no. 3–4 (4/10/2000): 159–71.

Zonneveld, Wil. 'A sea of houses: Preserving open space in an urbanised country'. *Journal of Environmental Planning and Management* 50, no. 5 (2007): 657–75.

Index